RETHINKING SOCIAL POLICY

 in CULTURAL and MEDIA STUDIES

Series Editor: Stuart Allen

Published titles

Media, Risk and Science
Stuart Allen

News Culture
Stuart Allen

Television, Globalization and Cultural Identities
Chris Barker

Culture of Popular Music
Andy Bennett

Masculinities and Culture
John Beynon

Cinema and Cultural Modernity
Gill Branston

Violence and the Media
Cynthia Carter and C. Kay Weaver

Ethnic Minorities and the Media
Edited by Simon Cottle

Moral Panics and the Media
Chas Critcher

Culture on Display
Bella Dicks

Modernity and Postmodern Culture
Jim McGuigan

Media and Audiences
Karen Ross and Virginia Nightingale

Sport, Culture and the Media 2nd edition
David Rowe

Cities and Urban Cultures
Deborah Stevenson

Cultural Citizenship
Nick Stevenson

Compassion, Morality and the Media
Keith Tester

RETHINKING
CULTURAL POLICY

Jim McGuigan

OPEN UNIVERSITY PRESS

Open University Press
McGraw-Hill Education
McGraw-Hill House
Shoppenhangers Road
Maidenhead
Berkshire
England
SL6 2QL

email: enquiries@openup.co.uk
world wide web: www.openup.co.uk

First published 2004   **UWE, BRISTOL LIBRARY SERVICES**

Copyright © Jim McGuigan 2004

A catalogue record of this book is available from the British Library

ISBN 0 335 20701 4 (pb)   0 335 20702 2 (hb)

Library of Congress Cataloging-in-Publication Data
CIP data has been applied for

Typeset by RefineCatch Limited, Bungay, Suffolk
Printed in the UK by Bell & Bain Ltd, Glasgow

This one's for Lesley

Ya Basta! (Enough is enough)
Zapatista slogan

CONTENTS

SERIES EDITOR'S FOREWORD

Jim McGuigan's *Rethinking Cultural Policy* is an important contribution to policy-oriented cultural studies. It succeeds in illuminating a new line of enquiry into several exciting topics at the heart of current debates. In the course of elaborating a critically reflexive approach, McGuigan challenges the prevailing instrumental imperatives of much cultural policymaking, where policies are formulated and enacted for economic and social purposes that are not specifically cultural. In a sense, McGuigan argues, cultural policy is being asked to do too much. Moreover, he believes, it has become increasingly implicated in neo-liberal ideology, that is, the belief that the 'free market' is the only satisfactory means of organizing culture and society around the world.

Rethinking Cultural Policy invites a thorough reconsideration of pressing concerns that goes beyond a narrowly instrumental and reductive treatment of cultural policy. It addresses a set of critical issues that include the relations between brand culture and global exploitation, the use of cultural policies in the interests of national aggrandisement and corporate business, and the impact of neo-liberalism on poor countries with regard to developmental tourism. In so doing, McGuigan questions emergent cultural capitalism from a position that stresses the need for research in the public interest and democratic debate. This is a fascinating discussion, and as such sure to be welcomed by everyone seeking to reinvigorate the key ideas informing the field of culture and policy.

The *Issues in Cultural and Media Studies* series aims to facilitate a diverse range of critical investigations into pressing questions considered to be central to current thinking and research. In light of the remarkable speed at which the conceptual agendas of cultural and media studies are changing, the series is committed to contributing to what is an ongoing process of re-evaluation and critique. Each of the books is intended to provide a lively, innovative and comprehensive introduction to a specific topical issue from a fresh perspective. The reader is offered a thorough grounding in the most salient debates indicative of the book's subject, as well as important insights into how new modes of enquiry may be established for future explorations. Taken as a whole, then, the series is designed to cover the core components of cultural and media studies courses in an imaginatively distinctive and engaging manner.

Stuart Allan

ACKNOWLEDGEMENTS

Earlier versions of some parts of this book were published in *Cultural Studies* <–> *Critical Methodologies*, the *International Journal of Cultural Policy* and Nick Stevenson's edited book, *Culture and Citizenship*. The case study in Chapter 3 on the Millennium Dome reports the findings from my Arts and Humanities Research Board project, 'The Meanings of the New Millennium Experience'.

Various conferences, guest lectures and research seminars have given me the opportunity to try out my ideas on cultural policy. The conferences include most notably: the Teaching Culture and Cultures of Teaching Conference at the University of Sussex as long ago as March 1996; the Popular Culture strand of the Collective Identity and Symbolic Representation Conference at Science Po in Paris in July 1996; the Cultural Crossroads – Ownership, Access and Identity Conference in Sydney in November 1997; the Association of Media, Communication and Cultural Studies Conference in Sheffield in December 1997; the Nordic Tribunal on Cultural Policy at the University of Copenhagen in April 1999; the Third International Crossroads in Cultural Studies Conference in June 2000 at the University of Birmingham; the Cultural Policies – New Technologies, Arts and Politics summer school at the University of Jyvaskyla in August 2000; the Power, Aesthetics and Media Conference at Bergen in December 2000; the Second International Conference on Cultural Policy Research at Wellington in January 2002; the Intercultural Communication Conference of the International Association for Media and Communication Research at Barcelona in July 2002; and the Culture in Knowledge Society workshop hosted by the Swedish Institute for Studies of Education and Research at Stockholm in March 2003.

During this period I have also had the opportunity to speak about cultural policy at the University of London's Goldsmiths College, Leeds Metropolitan University, the University of Sheffield, Vaxjo University College, the University of Warwick, and on return visits there and at Bergen and Jyvaskyla. On my travels I have had fruitful conversations with a great many colleagues and students that have helped me develop my thinking on cultural policy. I would particularly like to thank Alison Beale, Eleonora Belfiore, Oliver Bennett, Peter Dueland, Terry Flew, Lisanne Gibson, Jostein Gripsrud, Dave Hesmondhalgh, Anita Kangas, Nabuko Kawashima, David Looseley, Per Mangset, Albert Moran, Kevin Mulcahy, Maurice Roche, Mark Schuster, Alan Stanbridge, Matts Trondmann, Geir Vesthem, Michael Volkerling and Paul Willis.

In recent years I have been very fortunate indeed to work in an excellent Department of Social Sciences at Loughborough University. I am particularly grateful for the help I have received in researching and writing this book from close colleagues: Mick Billig, Alan Bryman, Dave Deacon, John Downey, Mike Gane, Abigail Gilmore, Peter Golding, Graham Murdock, Mike Pickering, Dennis Smith and Dominic Wring. I should also like to thank Stuart Allen for his patience and thorough editorial advice.

Last but not least, I thank my family – Lesley, Christopher and Jenny – for their forbearance yet again.

Leamington, July 2003

INTRODUCTION

We live in an age dominated by **economic reason**, not just the grinding necessity of working hard and making money in order to live but the very definition of social reality itself. To rid ourselves of reality-defining economic reason, libertarian socialist Andre Gorz (1989 [1988]) has argued that reform is desirable: how wealth is produced and distributed should be changed and work for remuneration shared more equitably. Why? Would this boost growth? No, that is not the point. The point is to reduce economic servitude so that people can do things for their own sake, to express themselves and enjoy the company of others without calculation, which is one definition of cultural activity, as opposed to economic activity. Gorz's condition of post-scarcity equality, self-fulfilment and mutuality is Utopian and easily dismissed as unrealistic. Yet, its promise is glimpsed routinely in our free time when we do things just for fun.

What does it mean for cultural life when economic reason predominates? That is the key question for this book to address. It is a matter of policy. In the past, **cultural policy** has been rationalized in various ways, including the amelioration of 'market failure' for practices deemed to have a *cultural* value that is not reducible to economic value. While this rationalization persists residually, it has very largely been superseded by an exclusively economic rationale. In this sense, cultural practices are deemed worthy of public support because they are of *economic* value. Cultural policy has been rethought in such a way that it no longer requires a specifically cultural rationale. This is a manifestation of the pervasive dominance of economic reason today: to put it bluntly, naked **capitalism**.

Towards the end of his life, Pierre Bourdieu (1998a and b), the great sociologist of culture, became increasingly concerned about the dominance of economic reason in all spheres of life. He talked of how, 'in a period of neo-conservative reconstruction', an 'economic fatalism' had erected 'defining standards for all practices'. It represented 'a return to a sort of radical capitalism' that stressed 'efficiency' through 'modern forms of domination ("management") and manipulative techniques like market research, marketing and commercial advertising' (Bourdieu 1998a: 125). Bourdieu was talking about **neo-liberalism** (not 'liberal' in the American sense of Leftish politics but, rather, in the sense of a renewal of capitalist economics that comes from the Right). Bourdieu (1991) was always sensitive to the linguistic mediation of power. His definition of neo-liberalism takes its symbolic force into account: 'Neo-liberalism is a powerful economic theory *whose strictly symbolic strength, combined with the effect of theory, redoubles the force of the economic realities it is supposed to express*' (Bourdieu 1998a: 126). Against neo-liberalism, and to break its spell, Bourdieu argued for 'reasoned utopianism' in intellectual work and scholarship (1998a: 128). This relates directly to the study of cultural policy. Bourdieu (1998b: 102) believed that neo-liberalism was responsible for what he called 'the progressive disappearance of the autonomous world of cultural production'.

Neo-liberalism has become the focus of much social criticism. There is good reason for such a focus of critical attention since the major structural changes that have occurred in the world over the past thirty years can be accounted for in terms of the rise of neo-liberalism on a global scale, *neo-liberal **globalization***. The solution to the capitalist crisis of the 1970s and the collapse of Soviet Communism in the 1980s, most notably, contributed to the victory of neo-liberalism, briefly defined as a 'revival of doctrines of the free market' (Gamble 2001: 127). Neo-liberalism was, in the first instance, itself a critique, a critique of the **Keynesian** economics that had prevailed in capitalist countries since the Second World War to boost economic activity and secure wellbeing through public investment and welfare provision for all. State intervention and its costs in terms of public ownership and regulation of markets were considered by neo-liberal economists to have suppressed the free play of market forces to the detriment of the economy, resulting in uncontrollable inflation and all sorts of social ills. Massive public expenditure and poor management, not only in public administration but also in private business, were major targets for neo-liberal economists and their management theory partners.

The neo-liberal doctrine of monetarism called for cutbacks in public spending that would facilitate reductions in income tax. Consumers were to be set free to make sovereign choices and look after themselves, for instance, by insuring privately against illness and old age. In social policy, it was trumpeted, the state should no longer featherbed the lazy and feckless. And, in cultural policy, argued extremists, the state should withdraw from promoting unpopular culture, such as experimental art, and leave the stage clear for the market forces that cater so successfully to popular tastes.

Andrew Gamble (2001: 129) sums it up: 'In Britain and the United States the political interventions represented by Thatcherism and Reaganism established neo-liberalism as the new dominant common sense, the paradigm shaping all policies.' He goes on to say:

> In the 1990s the revival of the United States economy appeared to reinforce the neo-liberal message. Neo-liberalism became assimilated with globalisation and

the policies of international agencies such as the IMF and the World Bank pushing neo-liberal agendas. In this context neo-liberalism began to take on the mantle of a new hegemonic creed.

(Gamble 2001: 133)

Gamble also warns, however, against exaggerating the ideological **hegemony** of neo-liberalism across the globe and of underestimating diversity and differences of opinion concerning economic policy and other policy. Moreover, it is important not 'to reify neo-liberalism and to treat it as a phenomenon which manifests itself everywhere and in everything'. In his view, it is 'better to deconstruct neo-liberalism into the different doctrines and ideas which compose it, and relate them to particular practices and political projects' (Gamble 2001: 134). In this book, these two points are taken seriously. First, by examining the influence of neo-liberal **ideology** in its various guises on **culture** and cultural policy. Second, it looks specifically at ideological contest between neo-liberalism, on the one hand, and residual and emergent principles and practices, on the other hand, concerning cultural policy. It is vital to examine the impact of neo-liberalism on issues of culture and policy, accommodation and resistance to it. Jo Caust (2003) has questioned the effect of neo-liberalism on public cultural policy in Australia, describing how it has been captured, in effect, by economic reason and marketing. She wants to put art back into arts policy.

This book is critical of the relation between neo-liberalism and cultural policy. It aims to open up questions of culture and policy that are neglected by instrumental thought and research. **Instrumentalism** justifies cultural policy most typically on economic grounds and, to a lesser extent, social grounds as well, that is, grounds that are not specifically cultural. In contrast, the approach taken here may be called *critical and reflexive cultural policy analysis*. To clarify this approach, something needs to be said about both **criticism** and **reflexivity**. It is mistaken to equate criticism with negativity. And it certainly is not cynicism. There is a good deal more cynicism in uncritical theory and practice. Criticism is actually an indispensable dynamic in the production of knowledge and the project of human betterment. Questioning what has gone before, identifying faults in current arguments and thinking independently instead of simply accepting the nostrums of conventional wisdom – these are all features of the critical attitude of ancient philosophy and modern thought from the **Enlightenment** onwards. In a symposium on criticism and the growth of knowledge, Thomas Kuhn (1970: 6), the philosopher of science, once remarked, 'it is [. . .] the tradition of claims, counter-claims, and debates over fundamentals which, except perhaps during the Middle Ages, have characterized philosophy and much of social science'. I hope we have not entered a new Middle Ages, though sometimes I fear we have done so. It may be objected, of course, that it is all right for 'pure' theorists pushing back the frontiers of knowledge to be critical, such as Max Horkheimer (1972), but the study of cultural policy is an applied field of enquiry and, therefore, should be more pragmatic. This is a widely held view in 'the real world' of cultural policy studies and is no doubt justifiable in many respects on practical grounds. However, it is gratifying to discover that I am not the only one in the field who does not wholeheartedly subscribe to it. In their introduction to a recent edited collection of 'critical cultural policy studies' from various quarters, Justin Lewis and Toby Miller say:

> A critical approach to cultural policy is [. . .] a reformist project that necessitates both an understanding of the ways in which cultural policies have traditionally been deployed, and a disciplined imagining of alternatives. It also means making connections with progressive social and cultural movements as well as technical bureaucracies. A critical approach to cultural policy [. . .] involves both theoretical excavations and practical alternatives.
>
> (Lewis and Miller 2003: 2)

This leads into the question of reflexivity. Lewis and Miller refer to 'an understanding of the ways in which cultural policies have traditionally been deployed, and a disciplined imagining of alternatives'. The first point here refers to reflexivity in scholarly activity and practical action, awareness of how the field of study is constituted in relation to practice. This should not, however, only refer to traditional operations but also to what is going on now, which may not be traditional in the sense implied by Lewis and Miller: it may be all too modern.

Specifically with regard to sociology, Alvin Gouldner (1970) famously called for critical reflexivity in the field. This involved, first, the self-awareness and passionate engagement of the sociologist and, second, a sociology of sociology. His argument rejected false objectivism – hence, personal awareness and engagement – and called for recognition of the ideological assumptions and purposes of sociology in the effort to make it more critical. There is an obvious danger of navel-gazing in all this which does not tempt me. Pierre Bourdieu was cognizant of such danger when he also, with the aid of Loic Wacquant, spelt out his own views on reflexive social and cultural research. Talking about sociology – he could just as well have been talking about cultural policy studies – he said:

> Ordinary sociology, which bypasses the radical questioning of its own operations and of its own instruments of thinking, and which would no doubt consider such a *reflexive intention* the relic of a philosophical mentality, and thus a survival from a prescientific age, is thoroughly suffused with the object it claims to know, and which it cannot really know because it does not know itself.
>
> (Bourdieu and Wacquant 1992: 236)

The relevance here is to do with alternative directions and purposes for cultural studies in its policy-oriented mode, which I have written about previously (McGuigan 1996). I think that cultural studies should analyse and seek, as well, to contribute towards policy. However, it must not just serve as an instrument of governmental policy. It also needs to maintain and renew its connections with progressive movements for social and cultural justice. Enough said on that, for the moment.

Cultural policy is 'adjectival policy' (Colebatch 2003: 86). It is a sub-set of policy in general, which is often called 'public policy'. This refers to governance, not only its enactment of policies from inception to implementation and evaluation, but also a contested terrain where campaigns are waged over issues, that is, the **public sphere** of rational-critical debate. Like policy in general, cultural policy can be viewed narrowly and/or broadly: narrowly, in the sense of what those in charge of it actually do and the consequences of their actions; and, broadly, in the sense of disputation over cultural issues. This book takes a broad view of cultural policy while also zooming in upon particular operations in public and private sectors of the cultural field.

In the first chapter, Cultural Analysis, Technology and Power, the very notion of culture is interrogated and a case is made for a comparatively narrow definition for cultural policy study. I happen to think the term 'culture' has become so widely used, referring to a range of such different practices, that it has, in certain respects, been drained of meaning. I am particularly perturbed about 'the cultural' standing in for 'the social', a point that is taken up again in Chapter 2. Cultural policy, from the point of view of cultural and media studies, is about culture and **power**. In Chapter 1, the relations of culture and power are discussed with regard to the impact of newer **information and communication technologies** (ICTs) and the problem of **technological determinism**; and, the 'cool' attitude of **branding** culture and its dependence on a global system of **exploitation**. This chapter also introduces the argument for a **multidimensional analysis** that is policy-oriented. It is subsequently illustrated by a number of cases throughout the book and at greatest length in my research on the New Millennium Experience recounted in Chapter 3.

In the second chapter, Discourses of Cultural Policy, three extant **discourses of cultural policy** are distinguished: **state, market** and **civil/communicative**. The transition from state to market thinking – especially in Western Europe and at its extreme perhaps in Britain – serves as particular substantiation for my general argument concerning the impact of neo-liberalism on public cultural policy in theory and practice. The civil/communicative discourse represents opposition and is exemplified with reference to campaigns that challenge prevailing cultural arrangements.

In the third chapter, Cultural Policy **Proper** and as **Display**, a distinction once made in passing by Raymond Williams is explicated and developed further in discussion of the operations of official policy and how culture is used for national aggrandizement and economic purposes. Here, the history of French cultural policy is examined and the tradition of great exhibitions and kindred events traced. The case study of London's Millennium Dome is meant to demonstrate cultural policy as display in this instance. It also illustrates the value of multidimensional analysis of culture and cultural policy.

In the fourth chapter, Rhetorics of Development, Diversity and Tourism, the cultural development and diversity **paradigm** is interrogated for its rhetorical qualities and practical effects. Variously considered, it may represent either an accommodation to neo-liberal globalization or a means of resistance to it. The role of tourism is analysed critically with respect to the cultural development and diversity paradigm.

Developmental tourism around the world, including ecological tourism, is a very important manifestation of neo-liberal globalization.

The fifth and final chapter, Culture, Capitalism and Critique, addresses questions concerning cultural value and the growing importance of culture in capitalism resulting in the emergence of **cultural capitalism**. Specific issues to do with, for instance, **'dumbing down'**, **privatization** and globalization are discussed, rounding out the general argument concerning cultural policy and neo-liberalism that runs through the book. It concludes by commenting upon alternative research agendas and stresses the need for critical and reflexive analysis.

There is a sequential narrative to the chapters. Issues are introduced and taken up in greater depth later on. However, the chapters are relatively self-contained so that they can be read out of order. The terms that appear in bold type have entries in the Glossary at the back of the book.

CULTURAL ANALYSIS, TECHNOLOGY AND POWER

1

Introduction

This opening chapter addresses two general topics at issue that are especially germane for critical and reflexive cultural policy analysis. First, there are the theoretical relations between cultural analysis and cultural policy. Second, in light of developments concerning information and communication technologies (ICTs), which include debates raging over their epochal significance, it is necessary to reconsider the problem of technological determinism and, also, remark upon the global dynamics and power relations of capitalism. Consideration of these issues should be seen as connected to the general task of making sense of change in culture and society. This relates to a host of characterizations of what has been going on lately, such as 'the postmodern condition' (Lyotard 1984 [1979]) or 'the condition of postmodernity' (Harvey 1989), titles of influential books. As well as 'postmodernization' (Crook, Pakulski and Waters 1992), characterizations include 'runaway world' (Giddens 1999), 'global risk society' (Beck 1999), 'network society' and 'the information age' (Castells 1996, 1997a and 1998). And, as is suggested in this book, the age of neo-liberal globalization.

The most significant publication on recent and perhaps also epochal change that came out around the turn of the Millennium is Manuel Castells's trilogy, *The Information Age*. Although widely commented upon, Castells's thesis has not been much discussed with regard to the principles of cultural analysis and problems of cultural policy in what is deemed to be a dramatically transformed socio-economic condition. There are, then, theoretical, practical and empirical issues to do with the objects of cultural analysis, the role of public policy, technological forces and global relations which are considered here.

In what follows I identify some problems associated with the policy turn in cultural studies. Since its inception, cultural studies has been concerned with emancipation.

The claims made for its political impact by proponents and detractors, however, have arguably been greatly exaggerated. So, instead of remaining critically disengaged in an ivory tower of its own making, the case was put by Tony Bennett (1992a and b) that cultural studies should become 'useful' to policy-makers and administrators. Associated with this particular argument is the shift from a Gramscian model of hegemony and struggle at the levels of everyday life and state power to a **Foucauldian** model of **governmentality** which is focused not so much upon changing macro-power relations but on adjusting micro-power relations. This agenda for 'putting policy into cultural studies' has been contested. According to the counter-position, cultural studies in general need not and should not confine itself to research in an exclusively policy framework. That objection is extremely serious if cultural policy study is to be conceived only in the narrow sense of a more or less direct relation to governmental action and were to eschew critical issues of emancipation.

In a broader sense, though, there may not be so much at stake since cultural studies has generally been represented as 'political'. After all, its subject matter is often defined as culture and power. There are more precise issues, however, to do with cultural studies' specific engagement in the policy process that cannot be subsumed by such a general notion. In direct response to Bennett's argument, Tom O'Reagan insisted that even attention to policy should not be restricted to administrative usefulness. He identified four possible and conflicting purposes for cultural policy studies: state, reformist, antagonistic and diagnostic (O'Reagan 1992: 418). For instance, cultural policy research may aid in the efficient management of public resources (state purpose) or it may challenge and critique public cultural policy (antagonistic purpose). Thus, a dividing line is drawn between those who want to aid the current administration of culture and society, on the one hand, and those who want to keep the spirit of criticism and the promise of better times alive, on the other hand. This reruns a very old tension between 'administration' and 'culture', as Theodor Adorno (1991 [1978]) noted long before the recent debates on cultural policy studies. The present chapter does not seek to resolve that old tension between culture and administration. Rather, it aims to exacerbate the tension by asking awkward questions about the concept of culture and the terms of policy engagement.

It was never wise to confine policy-oriented cultural analysis solely to the workings of the nation-state: it is even less so now in a late-modern condition in which 'global' economic and cultural determinations are said to be reshaping the world in ways that transcend nation-state politics and perhaps politics itself. Capitalism has undergone dramatic transformation, according to the likes of Castells and also, but rather differently, Jeremy Rifkin (2000), who names the new phase 'cultural capitalism', that is, a social order in which signs and symbols are of immense economic importance.

Castells has made a valuable contribution in studying the social and cultural impact of ICTs. However, Castells's thesis on the information age is susceptible to the critique of technological determinism, initiated by Raymond Williams (1974). There is no doubt that the newer technologies make a difference. But, there is continuity as well as change in the economic and political aspects of culture and society. Recent techno-logical developments have great potential for improving social and cultural conditions. At the same time, they are also implicated in the reproduction of unequal power relations across the world that are becoming more pronounced, not less so.

To illustrate what is at stake, branding culture – its material as well as ideological aspects – is examined in the concluding section of this chapter. It is necessary to take into account the sheer scale of global exploitation conducted by branding corpor-ations, the political oppression of workers who manufacture the goods and the **com-modity fetishism** of 'cool' culture among relatively affluent consumers and the not so affluent as well. Commodity fetishism in this respect refers to how a sense of identity is somehow magically associated with possession of fashionable products such as the latest generation of mobile phone. The preponderance of branding culture and resist-ance to it are exemplary features of the present condition that are not, however, pecu-liarly technological as such. Alissa Quart (2003), in her study of 'the buying and selling of teenagers', has looked, for instance, at both the lengths to which marketers are prepared to go in capturing the desires of the young and how some young people refuse entrapment by the brands. Such resistance to the brands – Nike and the rest – may seem irrelevant and even tedious to affluent youth just wanting to have fun. Yet, it remains a sad fact that currently stylish consumption at affordable prices for the comparatively wealthy by global standards is connected to exploitative and oppressive working condi-tions among the poor of the Earth.

As it happens, then, Karl Marx's critical inspiration may still be relevant for making sense of the world in spite of the collapse of international communism and the techno-logical reconstruction of capitalism (Wheen 1999). From this point of view, **political economy** is essential to cultural analysis that is policy-oriented, critical and reflexive.

Analysing

Use of the term 'culture' has proliferated to such an extent that it has become virtually meaningless. Everything is culture, so we are told. Here, we are not just talking about the arts and leisure but, literally, everything. Apparently, there is such a phenomenon as 'management culture' and there is 'culture change' in business (Anthony 1994). There are cultures of everything: 'body culture', 'consumer culture', 'work culture', 'depend-ency culture', 'black culture', 'white culture', 'Western culture' and so on.

It has even been declared that we live in 'the culture society'. What does this mean? In the early 1990s, Hermann Schwengell (1991) compared the 'enterprise culture' pro-moted by late-Thatcherism in Britain with West Germany's *Kulturgesellschaft*. Both responded to changing economic conditions, the shift from a **Fordist** industrial econ-omy to a **post-Fordist** informational economy in which making things was giving way to making meanings. While manual work, actually making the stuff, was being shuffled off to cheap labour markets in poor parts of the world, rich countries, with their voracious consumerism and great metropolitan centres, were the coordinating nodes for distribution and valorization on a global scale. Research, development, design and marketing were also becoming increasingly prominent features of economic activity in the affluent world.

Thatcherism had sought to overthrow British social democracy in order to create a thoroughly Americanized culture and society driven by free-market imperatives: the objective and, indeed, subjective reality of 'enterprise culture'. At the same time, European continental states like the Federal Republic of Germany were still seeking a 'middle way'. In some sense, *Kulturgesellschaft* was supposed to ameliorate the harsh realities of a rapidly changing economy, providing cultural comfort in the face of social turbulence. In contrast, 'enterprise culture' was supposed to intensify those harsh realities, making everyone a risk-taking capitalist, sovereign consumer and flexible subject.

Angela McRobbie (1999) adopted the concept of *Kulturgesellschaft* to name the social reality of Britain a few years later. The meaning of 'the culture society', however, is somewhat obscure. It is perhaps closer to *Kunstgesellschaft* than *Kulturgesellschaft* or, in Mike Featherstone's (1991: 65) phrase, 'the aestheticization of everyday life', which he says is to do with 'the effacement of the boundary between art and everyday life'. In this formulation, life itself has become art, not just for Oscar Wilde but for everyone. We're all dandies now, so that line of reasoning goes. 'The aestheticization of everyday life' depicts the semiosis of consumption whereby commodities are said to be sought more for their sign value, in a Baudrillardian sense, than for their use value, which conveniently neglects the question of exchange value, that is, paying for the symbolically loaded goods.

It is not entirely clear why McRobbie chose the term 'culture society'. It seems to have something to do with cultural work, its growth and the policy problems arising due to a shift from state subsidy to market survival in the cultural field. McRobbie is troubled by the increasingly dire material circumstances of many cultural workers. While this is reasonable enough, there has to be a necessary scepticism, however, about the novelty of such trends. Problems of making and sustaining creative careers under conditions of intense competition, exploitation and public indifference are not new. McRobbie's foray into cultural policy, then, manifests a kind of postmodernist amnesia. Anything longer than short-term memory is collapsed into the present and elided in mainstream political discourse and policy discussion about 'modernization', with little recognition of its significance in a timescale greater than that of a particular governmental regime. McRobbie was arguing with the New Labour Government in Britain that was elected in 1997 and re-elected in 2001. Governments are always 'modernizing', and cultural analysts who wish to be relevant are forever caught in the slipstream of day-to-day politics. Cultural workers in general, however, have never had it easy. Even under conditions of the modern state's patronage at its height, only the select few benefited substantially from public largesse (for a further discussion, see McGuigan 1981).

As McRobbie says, 'There has to be some way of being an artist and making a living' (1999: 8). This is her apology for the marketing ploys of 'young British art' – the loose grouping of young British artists such as Damien Hirst and Tracey Emin that emerged in the 1990s – much of which she otherwise finds deplorable. McRobbie's comments on this artistic 'movement' are fierce. To quote her: 'cynical, apolitical individualism, as well as the weary, not to say, tawdry, disengagement'; 'casual, promiscuous, populist art, which wishes to be repositioned inside the chat show world of celebrity culture, alongside sponsorship deals, in the restaurants and at the very heart of consumer culture' (McRobbie 1999: 6). That generation of artists, tutored in Marxism and feminism, cocked a snook at their Leftist elders and took the advertising executive Charles Saatchi's money to concoct the exhibition 'Sensation' just for the hell of it, or, more precisely, the money of it (Hatton and Walker 2000; Stallabrass 1999). McRobbie asks wryly, 'Given the "Nikeification" of culture, are the artists [. . .] literally "Just doing it"?' (1999: 8). She implies there is nothing else to do. On the other hand, the *demimonde* of black dance music, drum'n'base, and DJing, a subversive aesthetic in McRobbie's estimation, compares favourably with degenerate high art. But, like young British fashion designers trained in aesthetics rather than cutting and sewing, yet feeding mostly off street culture for inspiration, 'the economies underpinning their activities are more apparent, indeed virtual, than real' (1999: 19). The last Conservative government's start-up schemes for small businesses were more useful to all these currents of cultural production than any judgemental arts policy or waffle about 'rebranding' Britain (Leonard 1997), according to McRobbie. Get real, get an MBA, seems to be the message for seriously ambitious cultural workers.

Albeit stated with a remnant of critical distance, McRobbie's viewpoint is not so very different from the economic realism of Demos, the New Labour think tank. It recommended 'governing by cultures' (Perri 6 1995), 'the new enterprise culture' (Mulgan and Perri 6 1996), and 'the creative age' (Seltzer and Bentley 1999); and applauded 'Britain's new cultural entrepreneurs' (Leadbeater and Oakley 1999). McRobbie herself, likewise, is concerned with the coalescence of art and business, the connections between culture and economy, which is a curious switch of attention for such an epitome of anti-economistic cultural studies. McRobbie does not comment, however, upon the proliferating use of 'culture' to obliterate distinctions between quite different practices. To be caught up in the empty abstraction of 'the culture society' might have something to do with the impact of cultural studies itself. Or, perhaps, the academic *enfant terrible* of cultural studies is not so radically alternative to mainstream thought as is usually made out.

Earlier cultural studies challenged the exclusivity of Culture with a capital C. It was a spectacularly successful populist move in the academic/political game (McGuigan 1992 and 1997a). This critical intervention became muted, however, as belief in the possibility of socialism diminished and as the micro-politics of mundane consumption, resistance and identity rose to the ascendancy. Stuart Hall, the guru of neo-Gramscian hegemony theory, went down the identity route, still, however, with a critical edge (Hall and du Gay 1996). Others, most notably Tony Bennett (1992a and b), went down the route of managerial usefulness.

Earlier cultural studies had also sought to relate expressive culture in general to culture in the anthropological sense, the customs and routines of everyday life. Raymond Williams (1971 [1958]) established the holistic perspective of cultural analysis as 'the study of relations in a whole way of life'. Recent commentators, such as Nick Couldry (2000), however, have identified holism as the problem rather than the solution. We are supposed, instead, to study flows of meaning and interaction, differentiating and intersecting *cultures* in any space, not *culture* as a unitary whole in one space.

There is a danger here of forgetting some of the original questions that connected expressive form to everyday life: for instance, what would analysing television flow and watching television tell us about the social world we live in? Williams's (1974: 26) answer focused upon **mobile privatization**, 'an at once mobile and home-centred way of living'. The ordinary person is simultaneously cut off physically from the outside world, turned inwards, while transported outwards to other worlds through screened images. This 'unique modern condition' formed much of the texture of everyday life in older industrial states and has become increasingly global. It reached its nadir in the United States, where the automobile, the emblematic companion to the television set – and, now, the on-line computer and mobile phone as well – protects its passengers from terrifying public space (McGuigan 1993). As Williams later remarked:

> What it [mobile privatization] means is that at most active social levels people are increasingly living as private small-family units, or, disrupting even that, as private and deliberately self-enclosed individuals, while at the same time there is a quite unprecedented mobility of such restricted privacies.
>
> (1985 [1983]: 188)

Now and again a stock-taking of cultural studies occurs (Ferguson and Golding 1997, for example). This happened yet again at the turn of the Millennium when cultural studies returned nostalgically to its ostensible place of origin, the University of Birmingham in the English Midlands, for the third international Crossroads Conference, just two years before the department there was, in effect, closed down. There was also a flood of actuarial books (such as Tudor 1999; Couldry 2000; Eagleton 2000; Garnham 2000a; Mulhern 2000; Wilson 2001). One of the most interesting of these is Terry Eagleton's *The Idea of Culture*. Eagleton is possibly Williams's most illustrious student in the field.

Retracing Williams's steps and going a little further, Eagleton explores the history of discourses around 'culture', particularly stressing the critical response of **Romanticism** to capitalist 'civilization'. There are traces of cultural romanticism in **postmodernism**. Like Eagleton, Nicholas Garnham (2000a) believes that postmodernists are rerunning a series of counter-Enlightenment themes, familiar from the work of Nietzsche and other descendants of Romanticism. Eagleton does not offer an unqualified defence of the Enlightenment legacy or its Romantic complement (see McGuigan 1999). 'Capital C' Culture and Civilization are challenged quite rightly by lower-case cultures and, indeed, civilizations. This is especially so when it comes to the Rest's revenge on the West. Postcolonialism, identity politics and various movements of opposition all make perfectly legitimate claims to challenge the Reason and Romance of Modernity.

Most incisively, Eagleton questions the ubiquity of cultural discourse: 'The primary problems which we confront in the new millennium – war, famine, poverty, disease, debt, drugs, environmental pollution, the displacement of peoples – are not especially cultural at all' (2000: 130). According to Eagleton, 'culture' needs to be 'put back in its place' (2000: 131). The difficulty is that the term 'culture' is, on the one hand, too broad and, on the other hand, too narrow. For reining in culture, Eagleton rejects Williams's mature solution to the problem. Williams had moved from 'the analysis of culture' as 'the study of relations in a whole way of life' of *The Long Revolution* (Williams 1961) – which is really a general sociology – to the more precisely focused study of culture as 'signifying practice'. He gave a communicational definition of the concept in his book of 1981, *Culture*. Eagleton describes this solution as 'a semiotic definition of culture which was ephemerally popular in the 1970s' (2000: 33). In Eagleton's opinion, it merely restates 'the traditional aesthetic/utility dichotomy' (2000: 34). While simple dichotomies and binary thinking in general are to be avoided, Eagleton's own normative view of culture as in some sense transcendent and not utilitarian rather contradicts his objection to defining culture as 'signifying practice'.

Nicholas Garnham (2000a and b) also objects to this definition of culture as 'signifying practice' but on slightly different grounds from Eagleton. First, for Garnham, it is associated with the 'linguistic turn' brought about by French structuralism and poststructuralism, reiterated in Hall's (1997) irreducible meaningfulness of all social practices. The trouble is that in this theoretical framework there is a tendency for everything to become language or discourse with no material outside of signification. Second, Garnham (2000b) has argued that it is impossible to distinguish between manifestly signifying practices and practices that may not be so much about signification if every practice is treated as of equally symbolic weight and, therefore, cultural.

There is, however, a solution to the problem implicit in Williams's formulation of culture as a 'realized signifying system' (1981a: 207). Some systems are not first and foremost about signification and symbolic exchange or dialogue, for instance, economic and social systems. As Williams observes, 'This distinction is not made to separate and disjoin these areas, but to make room for analysis of their interrelations' (1981a: 207): exactly. It is analytically useful to be able to distinguish between that which is primarily cultural, in the sense of signifying practice, from that which is not. For example, 'business culture' is not cultural in the precise and restricted sense of signifying practice as its *raison d'être*. 'Business culture' is not first and foremost about processes of symbolization, dialogue, pleasure and identity. It is principally about the exchange of commodities and services. A feature film may be a commodity and the cinematic institution provides a service in the cultural marketplace but, nevertheless, it is principally about communication, pleasure and identification. In this sense, 'cinematic culture' is different from 'business culture', however meaningful that may be, and should, therefore, be distinguished from it on analytical grounds, and probably ontological grounds as well.

It makes sense to focus upon those practices, forms and products that are primarily about symbolic communication, dialogic relations, pleasurable experience and meaningful social identity as the special objects of cultural analysis. Yet, it would be mistaken to isolate them from their actual and material conditions of social production and circulation (Williams 1981b). Cultural analysis should draw upon a range of perspectives in order to open up the multidimensionality and sociality of culture. Douglas Kellner (1997: 34) identifies three dimensions of cultural analysis: '(1) the production and political economy of culture; (2) textual analysis and critique of its artefacts; (3) study of audience reception and the use of media and cultural products.' Kellner's model begins from production and is critical in intent. It has affinities with the **circuit of culture** model, which adds, however, two further dimensions – **identity** and **regulation** – to **production**, **representation** and **consumption** (du Gay et al. 1997). Although questionably disposed to begin with consumption rather than production, the circuit of culture model usefully connects cultural analysis to cultural policy by inserting issues of identity and regulation into the circuit.

A cultural circuit model of analysis in some form is the most satisfactory means of framing research on practices that are first and foremost about signification. While the general framework needs to be kept in mind, this does not mean that particular studies should always and necessarily complete the circuit. In many and perhaps most cases this analytical protocol would be far too demanding. None the less, commitment to the study of culture in circulation, on ontological and methodological grounds, is a vital check on various kinds of partiality.

The analytical issues are to do with methodological scope and self-imposed limitation. The position outlined here makes sense but there is no way of enforcing it. Cultural analysts are by no means obliged to confine their studies to practices that are first and foremost about signification, symbolic exchange, pleasure and identity. In fact, the field of cultural studies has been characterized by what might be considered profligacy in this respect. It should, arguably, have been yet more profligate and have looked closely, for instance, at the cultural aspects of business if it were really serious about the relations between culture and power. Paul du Gay's (1996) work in this area is a notable exception, though curiously uncritical in its approach to the 'making up' of workers. Its use of 'culture' is closer to a managerial paradigm than critical cultural analysis.

There is absolutely no point, however, in trying to prohibit, by definitional fiat, use of the term 'culture' to refer to the significatory features of any practice, including practices that are not principally about making meanings, like making money. Still, the term 'culture' is over-used, possibly to the point of meaninglessness, and this raises all sorts of problems, not only methodological but also political.

Governing

The problem of the scope and limitation of cultural discourse is particularly manifest in the project of 'putting policy into cultural studies' (T. Bennett 1992a). It is generally agreed that a focal concern of cultural studies – perhaps even its defining feature – is the interrelation of culture and power. Tony Bennett was right, however, to suggest that cultural studies, as normally practised, was largely detached from the real world of politics, in the sense of policy-making and administration. For a field of study that prides itself on being 'political', this was a damning indictment. Bennett went on to argue, somewhat more controversially, that education and research in cultural studies should aim to turn out 'technicians' who engage with what actually happens on the field of play instead of detached 'critics' shouting or muttering from the sidelines. This argument was justified according to a particular reading of Michel Foucault's (1991 [1978]) notion of governmentality and supplemented by that theorist's interest in 'technologies of the self' (Foucault 2000 [1982]); so that cultural policy studies was focused upon the regulation of social conduct and the formation of self-identity.

Foucault's concept of governmentality, it should be noted, refers very generally to the administrative apparatus of modernity, the emergence of the modern state and its powers of social regulation. This opens up a much larger space of power than the modern state's role in cultural policy, that is, if 'culture' is restricted to practices that are first and foremost about signification. The state's economic and penal policies may be meaningful but they are not first and foremost about signification; they are about wealth creation and incarceration. The twentieth-century idea of 'cultural policy' was focused upon a comparatively narrow conception of culture – referring to practices that are principally about communication, meaningful exchange and pleasure. States intervened in the cultural field to subsidize 'the arts' and so forth for various purposes: nationalistic, propagandistic, redistributive; in general, therefore, regulating the production and circulation of symbolic forms.

The Foucauldian-Bennett position has many virtues, particularly to do with its attention to the discursive mediation of social practices and the nexus of knowledge and power. Language in context forms conceptions of the world and self-identity, and it articulates power relations. The analytical applications are virtually endless: hence, the use of Foucault's ideas in many fields of research. From the point of view of cultural analysis, specifically, it makes sense to examine how aesthetic practices and policies are constructed discursively and enacted. However, Foucauldian cultural policy studies has also been criticized for its instrumentalism, excessive pragmatism, managerialism and lack of critical responsibility (McGuigan 1996). In addition to these criticisms, there are two further issue clusters to consider regarding cultural policy studies. The first cluster of issues is historical and conceptual: the second, sociological and empirical.

Foucault's notion of governmentality obscures historical distinctions between state and market, politics and economics. This derives from a theoreticism that treats the empirical phenomenon of actual government, state rule, as a naive object. Moreover, government and capitalism – which is hardly mentioned as such – are treated as undifferentiated elements of disciplinary power. From this perspective, disciplinary power is the driving force of modernity, a view which is as reductive in its own way as an economistic Marxism that would reduce everything to capital accumulation and the logic of capital so that actual differences of government are rendered irrelevant. For the Foucauldian, it is the imposition of disciplinary power and resistance to it that matters, subjective enslavement and micro-political manoeuvres. Such a position makes it very difficult to grasp some of the nuances of the historical record of actual governance. For instance, the broad political difference made by social democracy to the capital/labour struggle and distribution of rights and rewards during the twentieth century (Sassoon 1997 [1996]; Lipset and Marks 2000), not to mention its specific impact on cultural policy as such, become obscure. Which is not to say there is no disputation within the Foucauldian church itself: you can have Left or Right Foucauldianism. Left Foucauldianism, broadly defined, suggests anarchistic resistance to the system in general, which was the late Foucault's own position in supporting the politics of resistance on the margins of mainstream society. Were he still alive, Foucault may even have been sympathetic to the 'anti-capitalist' movement of recent years. Right Foucauldianism, on the other hand, involves accommodation to the prevailing powers of social management in order to make technical adjustments, as proposed by Bennett's argument concerning cultural policy studies.

Although Foucauldianism tends to play down the politics of actual government, it is, nevertheless, in practice, curiously constrained by the nation-state framework of governmentality, which becomes particularly problematic for addressing globalization. In effect, the Foucauldian approach to cultural policy tends to repeat the elementary sociological fallacy of treating society as a nation-state. This is not unrelated to the conflation of state and capital in 'governmentality'. It is symptomatic of such a theoretical position, in terms of apparently innocent research, that Tony Bennett himself, the leading exponent of Foucauldian cultural policy studies, has engaged mainly with nationalistic agendas concerning culture and cultural policy. He did so as Director of the Key Centre for Cultural and Media Policy's work in connection with the Australian Labour Government's 'Creative Nation' agenda in the 1990s. More recently, in the British Open University's 'National Everyday Cultures' programme, Bennett's research agenda was yet again framed by nation-state priorities.

While privileging important issues from a nation-state perspective, such a theoretical position provides little, if any, conceptual grounds for formulating and addressing empirical questions of culture and power internationally, except that is under the auspices of formal inter-state collaboration, as in the European Union and Council of Europe. It has nothing really to say about culture and capitalism. Capital operates, indeed, in alliance with nation-states and inter-state arrangements, such as represented by the **International Monetary Fund (IMF)**, the **World Bank** and the **World Trade**

Organization (WTO), but it is not entirely formed by governmental alliances and arrangements. Although major corporations are based typically in particular countries, especially the USA, transnational capitalism is in an important sense stateless; so is much of cultural flow, in addition to financial flow.

The anti-economism of the Foucauldian-Bennett perspective has no in-depth account of how the late-modern world may be changing with regard to the balance of power between nation-states and economic forces in their command or beyond their control. That is exactly the kind of problem that Manuel Castells has made such strenuous efforts to explain in his thesis on 'the information age'. This connects up with a fundamental political issue of the present: how does democratically representative power – as inscribed in actual governments, not just governmentality in the abstract – promote and/or resist the powers of global capital? The problem turns on the question of regulation in general and, for our purposes here, cultural regulation in particular.

Regulating

Like so many terms in cultural discourse, 'regulation' has several different contextual meanings. To differentiate these meanings, it is useful, in the first instance, to distinguish between theoretical and empirical usage regarding issues, roughly, of control. Several versions of regulation in contemporary theory may be identified. These include the Althusserian theory of ideology and ideological state apparatuses (the ISAs); Gramscian hegemony theory, concerned with 'moral regulation', and its economistic offshoot in 'regulation theory', which makes a crucial distinction between 'regime of accumulation' (capitalism) and 'mode of regulation' (social conduct); and, Foucauldian 'discursive formation' theory (K. Thompson 1997). Such theories can be seen as radically incommensurate with each other or, alternatively, available for synthesis. The general point to make, though, is that, in one way or another, they all assume that social relations and cultural practices are regulated. Theoretical debate in this area often turns on which regulatory determination predominates – economic, political, ideological/discursive – or whether there is some multi-causal determination of the tacit rules and regulations of culture and society.

Whatever way round, social and cultural theories of regulation operate typically in a rather different discursive field from the usual public debates concerning 'regulation, de-regulation and re-regulation', in effect, at a completely different level of abstraction. For instance, cultural and media industries previously owned by the state may be privatized. It might commonly be assumed that they have thus been 'de-regulated'. It is more accurate, however, to see them as having been 're-regulated'. Most obviously, regulation has moved, in this case, from the preserve of the state to the operation of market forces, from manifestly political to economic regulation. However, state power, in the empirical sense of government, and law will still play a role in regulating the market, lightly or otherwise. This may take national and international forms. At the extreme, for governments not to set ground rules at all is effectively a regulatory policy. This is where theory and practice might just about meet. The question becomes, then, what kind of regulation, under what conditions and with what effects? As with social process in general, it is reasonable to expect a complex interplay between agency and structure, resulting in unintended as well as intended consequences, which is an elementary sociological proposition (Giddens 1984).

Much less concerned with theory than with the 'real world' of politics, Richard Collins and Christina Murroni (1996) have set out an imaginative framework for media and communications policy in Britain. This is situated in reference to, first, their dissatisfaction with both 'Old Left' and 'New Right' policies and, second, the opportunities and problems arising from technological change in the media, digitalization, convergence and so forth. According to Collins and Murroni:

> The assumptions of the new right and the old left are fundamentally opposed. The new right starts from consumer sovereignty, the old left from a desire to protect the public from itself – correcting consumer tastes, or at least the results of consumer choice. The new right's solution, competition, is the old left's problem. The new right's problem, corporatism, is the old left's solution. In these circumstances, it is not surprising that the media reform debate has resembled a dialogue of the deaf. This would have been of limited concern if one of the sides had proved its case. However, media policy on both sides has been restricted by different, but equally flawed assumptions. We need to abandon such tribalism to allow a new, radical, synthesis of these approaches.
>
> (1996: 10)

Collins and Murroni concede a great deal to the New Right by pointing to the beneficial cultural and economic effects of marketization in broadcasting (for example, the introduction of commercial television into Britain in the 1950s) and the privatization of telecommunications in the 1990s. However, they do not agree with a generalized free-market fundamentalism. In many cases, market forces must be restrained in the public interest. Inspired by the 1994 Borrie Report, Commission on Social Justice, Collins and Murroni identify four principles to be applied not only in social policy but also in media policy: security, opportunity, democracy and fairness. These principles, according to Collins and Murroni, need to be applied case by case in recognition of the variable benefits and deficiencies of both state and market regulation. For instance, in the case of the British Broadcasting Corporation (BBC), it should remain the flagship for public service broadcasting, become more accountable to producer and, most especially, consumer/citizen interests, while also competing commercially in international markets. In order to achieve these different goals successfully, argue Collins and Murroni, organizational change at the BBC is necessary, going beyond the new managerialism of the 1990s, particularly in order to stop the corporation subsidizing its commercial operation from the public interest budget. The BBC went on doing exactly that in order to develop its digital services in the late 1990s and into the twenty-first century. Even Collins and Murroni's carefully thought-out technical solutions to the problem of reconfiguring public service broadcasting in a dramatically changed media environment did not readily translate into sympathetic governmental policy. Their book, *New Media, New Policies*, like the Social Justice report, was produced under the auspices of the New Labour think tank, the Institute for Public Policy Research.

The Blair government's actual thinking on communications and media policies around the turn of the Millennium was not so much about protecting and extending 'the public interest'. It was rather more to do with regulating the market so that, ostensibly, media corporations based in Britain – including the BBC – could build upon their comparative advantages and become yet more competitive internationally. This orientation was focused particularly on bringing together the regulatory authorities for broadcasting and telecommunications into one overseeing body, the Office of Communications, Ofcom, in order to push British-based media into the vanguard of 'the information age' (J. Harding 2000). In actual fact, recent communications policy in Britain has been extremely contradictory. While on the one hand it aimed to develop British-based business, on the other hand, it opened up national commercial broadcasting to international ownership and control by the likes of News Corp and Viacom. Britain already had the second most successful system of broadcasting with regard to indigenous production and exports in the world, making it an attractive proposition for transnational operators (Petley 2003). The so-called 'de-regulation' of British broadcasting, then, was a particularly dogmatic exercise in neo-liberal globalization undertaken by a nominally social-democratic government.

Identifying problems in a realistic manner and offering practical solutions to governments and other agencies are indeed proper tasks for applied cultural and media studies. In this respect, the positions of both Bennett, from a Foucauldian perspective, and Collins and Murroni, from a political economy perspective, are strikingly similar. Such engagement is necessary and vital but, in the short term and quite possibly the longer term as well, it may frequently lead to frustration with the 'real world' of politics. Paradoxically, a critical independence in cultural policy studies is less frustrating since the imminence of enlightened government and reason is considered unlikely, albeit at the risk of practical irrelevance in the shorter term. Critical and reflexive cultural policy analysis is permitted to ask awkward questions about the conditions of culture and society in the world at large that go beyond the self-imposed limitations of management consultancy and policy-wonking (McGuigan 1995).

Determining

The title of Collins and Murroni's book, *New Media, New Policies*, reasonably implies the need for policy responses to the emergence of newer communications media. Although Collins and Murroni themselves are not technological determinists, the title of their book lends itself to such a misinterpretation of their position. Also, it has to be said, whether new media technologies are met with obstinate suspicion or inordinate enthusiasm, pessimism or optimism, it is too frequently the case that the determinate power of technology over culture and society is simply taken for granted.

Technological determinism assumes a linear process of autonomous scientific discovery that is more or less rapidly applied to technical invention, resulting in smooth diffusion and eventual social transformation. It is not just a simplistic model of socio-technical change; it is a dominant ideology, combined with faith in the magic of the market, the prevailing myth of the age. Information and communication technologies – satellites, microchips, desktop and laptop computers, the Internet, the World Wide Web, mobile phones, digitalization, convergence – are said by experts and politicians to be changing our world totally. Notable examples are MIT expert Nicholas Negroponte's (1995) 'being digital' and former US Vice-President Al Gore's declaration of the 'Information Super Highway'. The Americans were anxious about the Japanese getting ahead in these matters. The Europeans were worried that the Americans had the edge over them (Bangemann Report 1995). There is a rhetoric of 'catching up' and of not being 'left behind'. The British, for instance, typically see themselves simultaneously ahead of the game *and*, somehow, behind it, as both inventive and commercially inept. Hence, the mad rush into the Klondike of 'e.commerce' a few years ago to make amends (*New Statesman* 10 July 2000).

On technological determinism and its hype – expert, political and in common sense – there are two general questions to ask. First, how do new media technologies come about? Second, what is the relation of new technology to social and cultural change? With regard to both questions, it is worth recalling what Raymond Williams had to say.

Williams's (1974) critique of technological determinism, with reference to the invention and social use of television, is well known but the complexity of his position is not always fully appreciated. Williams contested the 'orthodox' view that the relation between technology and social organization is that of a single cause and linear development, moving unimpeded from the former to the latter. He also challenged the opposite viewpoint, that of 'symptomatic technology', which assumes that technological innovation is only the effect of deeper social change. Instead of seeing technology as the sole determinant, characteristic of 'post-industrial' theory and politics, or as merely symptomatic of, say, the processes of capital accumulation, Williams insisted on *intentionality*. Scientific discovery occurs in determinate social and cultural conditions and is applied quite deliberately to produce technical solutions to problems that are identified and selected in an active process of transformation.

Television derives technologically from the combination of inventive developments in electricity, telegraphy, photography, cinematography and radio from the late nineteenth century. It became part of everyday life from the 1930s onwards as the result of specific economic and political decisions that varied from one nation to another. In Britain, there was centralized transmission by a public corporation for domestic reception; in the USA, a federalized system based on advertising revenue; in Germany, at first, reception in public rather than private spaces. There was nothing inevitable about the advent of television, nor need there be anything strictly inevitable about its future. The technological possibilities associated with cable and satellite transmission, video-cassette recording, large-screen receivers and the rest, already on the agenda when Williams was writing about television in the early 1970s, are open to differential deployment according to alternative ideologies and investment strategies.

The argument about television connects up with Williams's general position on **determination**, enunciated against both economic and technological *determinism*: 'the reality of determination is the setting of limits and the exertion of pressures, within which variable social practices are profoundly affected but never necessarily controlled' (Williams 1974: 130). New media technologies might trigger further democratic cultural expansion, according to Williams, but that would depend upon the prevailing balance of forces, particularly resistance to the limits and pressures exerted by capital. Williams concluded *Television – Technology and Cultural Form* on a prophetic note:

> Over a wide range from general television through commercial advertising to centralised information and date-processing systems, the technology that is now or is becoming available can be used to affect, to alter, and in some cases to control our whole social process. And it is ironic that the uses offer such extreme social choices. We could have inexpensive, locally based yet internationally extended television systems, making possible communication and information-sharing on a scale that not long ago would have seemed utopian. These are the contemporary tools of the long revolution towards an educated and participatory democracy, and of the recovery of effective communication in complex urban and industrial societies. But they are also tools of what would be, in context, a short and successful counter-revolution, in which under the cover of talk about choice and competition, a few para-national corporations, with their attendant states and agencies, could reach farther into our lives, at every level from news to psycho-drama, until individual and collective response in many different kinds of experience and problem became almost limited to choice between their pro-grammed possibilities.
>
> (1974: 151)

Leaving aside the epochal question for the moment, Brian Winston (1995 [1990] and 1996) has refined Williams's basic ideas concerning the development of television into a sophisticated model of 'how media are born'. Winston (1996: 3) follows 'Williams's fundamental insight as to the primacy of the social sphere'. Also, following Fernand Braudel, he identifies the dialectic of 'accelerators' and 'brakes' in the application of scientific knowledge to technological development and diffusion. With evidence from detailed case studies, Winston demonstrates the historical contingencies of 'new media' emergence. He discusses the advent of cinema, the racism of colour film chemistry, the marginalization of 16 mm as 'amateur' until its eventual deployment in television news, the dead end of analogue high-definition television and the limbo status of holography.

There always has to be a 'supervening social necessity' behind the emergence of a new medium of communication. In the case of cinema, the formation of a mass entertainment market and the sociality of theatre in an urban-industrial society were at least as important determinants, if not more so, than the inventiveness of 'great men', the myth of orthodox cinematic history. As well as supervening social necessities, accelerating the development of a medium at a particular moment in time, there is the brake on development, what Winston calls 'the "law" of the suppression of radical potential' (1996: 9). In the case of the denigration of 16 mm film, its use thereby confined for decades to 'amateurs' and 'subversives', classic Hollywood's expensive 'standard' of 35 mm was a means of controlling entry to the industry.

The answer, then, to the first question – how do new media technologies come about? – it is through a complex interaction of largely social factors with deliberate technical innovation in specific historical circumstances. The production of scientific knowledge, it is important to stress, is itself socially conditioned in terms of resource facilitation and institutional context. There is, however, no guarantee that new knowledge will automatically be applied to technological development, certainly not in the short term. Technological development often deploys knowledge that has been around for a while but hitherto not used to create a new product or medium of communication. There are cultural, economic and political brakes on technological development. The acceleration of technological development, on the other hand, usually occurs when there are social forces in play, typically offering the prospect of economic gain, that make such development compelling.

We can now address the second question – what is the relation of new technology to social and cultural change? Like the narrower question of how new media are born, the broader question concerning epochal change can only be answered by general propositions supported by the evidence of historical research. This may be an aid to forecasting, though not necessarily so. Most likely historical knowledge of past delusions will call into question some of the wilder forecasts being made at present. The record of mistaken predictions – when the expected did not happen and when the unexpected did happen – should make us doubt excessive claims concerning what the future holds.

It is said that we are currently entering a new epoch, 'the information age', which is connected to rapid technological developments. The greatest account of this epochal transformation is Manuel Castells's three-volume study, *The Information Age* (see Castells 1997b and McGuigan 1999, ch. 5, for detailed summaries of the thesis). Castells is much less concerned with explaining the historical causes of this transformation than with identifying its contours, at the centre of which is networking, facilitated by ICTs but of more general significance for social relations and symbolic exchange throughout the whole wide world. Nevertheless, Castells is still obliged to provide a sketch of the emergence of 'network society' before describing its characteristics. In the opening pages of *The Rise of the Network Society*, Castells says:

Toward the end of the second millennium of the Christian Era several events of historical significance have transformed the social landscape of human life. A technological revolution, centered around information technologies, is reshaping, at accelerated pace, the material basis of society. Economies throughout the world have become globally interdependent, introducing a new form of relationship between economy, state, and society, in a system of variable geometry. The collapse of Soviet statism, and the subsequent demise of the international communist movement, has undermined for the time being the historical challenge to capitalism, rescued the political left (and Marxian theory) from the fatal attraction of Marxism-Leninism, brought the Cold War to an end, reduced the risk of nuclear holocaust, and fundamentally altered global geopolitics. Capitalism itself has undergone a process of profound restructuring, characterized by greater flexibility in management; decentralization and networking of firms both internally and in their relationships to other firms; considerable empowering of capital *vis-a-vis* labor, with the concomitant decline of the labor movement; increasing individualization and diversification of working relationships; massive incorporation of women into the paid labor force, usually under discriminatory conditions; intervention of the state to deregulate markets selectively, and to undo the welfare state . . .

(1996: 1–2)

This is a big picture that sets the scene for contemporary globalization processes. They include geographical shifts in manufacturing from the old industrialism of Europe and North America to other labour markets; the rise of the Pacific Rim economy; and the integration of finance and distribution across the globe mediated by instantaneous communications. In his 'Introduction to the Information Age', Castells isolates the three 'independent processes' that have brought about epochal change:

- The Information Technology Revolution, constituted as a paradigm in the 1970s.
- The restructuring of capitalism and statism in the 1980s, aiming at superseding their contradictions, with sharply different outcomes.
- The cultural social movements of the 1960s, and their 1970s aftermath (particularly feminism and ecologism).

(1997b: 7)

It is evident that, for Castells, capitalism's defeat of communism is not entirely separate from 'the information technology revolution'. In fact, his account of the collapse of Soviet statism stresses its failure to keep up with 'the informational mode of development' (Castells 1998). The supervening social necessity here, in Winston's phrase, was the renewal of capitalist power and civilization in response to the crisis of the early 1970s. There was a shift from cumbersome Fordism to a speeded-up post- or neo-Fordist mode of operation, less labour intensive and with a reduced welfare state, thus 'solving' capitalism's economic problems, undermining social democracy and, simultaneously, contributing to the demise of communism in Europe and its decline elsewhere. Organization became 'leaner', aided by ICTs, and a new product cycle of high-tech commodities was set in motion. Worker resistance was weakened but opposition persists, however, in 'cultural social movements', inheritors of the 1960s' counterculture.

Before discussing whether or not Castells is a technological determinist, it would be appropriate to consider what he actually has to say about the specifically cultural effects of 'the revolution', that is, with regard to culture as first and foremost being about signification. According to Castells, a 'culture of real virtuality' is emerging. This is both consistent with the general transformation and has its own peculiar consequences. First, 'Shifting to the cultural realm, we see the emergence of a similar pattern [to economics and politics] of networking, flexibility, and ephemeral symbolic communication, in a culture organized around electronic media, including in this communication system the computer-mediated communication networks' (1997b: 10). Second, there is 'the culture of real virtuality', which is not just about technological experiments in 'virtual reality' and their applications. Rather, on-line mediation of culture and social relations is increasingly an everyday lived reality for large numbers of people and is no longer distinguishable from a 'real' reality of unmediated experience. Castells says, 'when our symbolic environment is, by and large, structured in this inclusive, flexible, diversified hypertext, in which we navigate every day, the virtuality of this text is in fact our reality, the symbols from which we live and communicate' (1997b: 11).

For Castells, when it comes to culture, the medium really is the message. He explicitly acknowledges the influence of Marshall McLuhan (1964). Castells goes further than McLuhan in claiming that computer-mediated communications are of greater significance than the advent and diffusion of television: 'The potential integration of text, images and sounds in the same system, interacting from multiple points, in chosen time (real or delayed) along a global network, in conditions of open and affordable access, does fundamentally change the character of communications' (1996: 328). Interactivity, picking and mixing, the potential capacity to download text from any cultural archive anywhere at any time, these are the characteristics of Castells's culture of real virtuality: it's all just there on screen. Castells's rhetoric here is much closer to the extravagant hype of new media and Internet entrepreneurs than to a cool assessment of what is going on in the cultural field. That would involve taking into account determinations and processes that are not primarily derived from communications and media technologies, the mainsprings of 'the new economy'. He has little to say about long-term trends in the **commodification** of art, entertainment and information or the intensification of mobile privatization in home-based services, processes facilitated by ICTs but not exclusively engendered by them. It is not at all surprising, then, that Castells has been accused of technological determinism. However, Castells himself is astute at pre-empting such an accusation. Right at the outset of the trilogy, he declares:

Of course technology does not determine society. Neither does society script the course of technological change, since many factors, including individual inventiveness and entrepreneurialism, intervene in the process of scientific discovery, technological innovation, and social applications, so that the final outcome depends on a complex process of interaction. Indeed, the dilemma of technological determinism is probably a false problem, since technology *is* society, and society cannot be understood or represented without its technological tools.

(1996: 5)

Castells stresses the importance of the Californian context of Silicon Valley – entrepreneurial flair and freewheeling individualism inherited from the 1960s' counter-culture – and state intervention (the US federal government's funding of ICT development was for military reasons in the first instance). Unlike in the Soviet Union, it was permissible for such development to be exploited for academic, business, commercial and cultural purposes. Still, to equate society with technology – 'technology *is* society' – does rather contradict Castells's own subtle defence against the accusation of technological determinism.

One of his sternest critics, Nicholas Garnham (1998) argues that Castells's information age thesis is a sophisticated updating of Daniel Bell's (1973) post-industrial/information society thesis; and, in Garnham's opinion, just as unconvincing. As with Bell's original claims concerning a wholesale shift from manufacturing to service and knowledge work, there are doubts over the sheer novelty of the present trends identified by Castells. Networking itself, moreover, is hardly new. For instance, market capitalism has always been a complex network. Castells is not at all naive in this respect, though: he argues that the architecture of ICT networking has innovative properties, such as, for instance, decentredness and extremely unpredictable proliferation. Frank Webster (1999), however, argues similarly to Garnham that 'the information age' is not so much a fresh epoch as, in many respects, a continuation of business as usual. Such critics point to how the enduring features of capitalism have become accentuated since the collapse of European communism, the apparent eclipse of the 'socialist' alternative, and are, in effect, facilitated rather than altered by ICT development.

To clarify what is at stake, Peter Golding makes a valuable distinction between 'Technology One' and 'Technology Two':

Technology may be construed as the mechanisms by which human agency manipulates the material world. We can conceive of two forms of technological innovation. Technology One allows existing social action and process to occur more speedily, more efficiently, or conveniently (though equally possibly with negative consequences, such as pollution or risk). Technology Two enables wholly new forms of activity previously impracticable or even inconceivable. In essence many new ICTs are more obviously Technology One than Technology Two.

(2000a: 171)

As Golding observes, the invention of telephony was vastly more consequential than the invention of e-mail. E-mail may have distinctive communicational properties, as a hybrid of telephone conversation and letter writing, yet it is very much in the business of facilitating speed, efficiency and convenience instead of bringing about something completely different. The really stunning developments in technology are not occurring so much in communications media as in biology, particularly genetic engineering (for an illuminating discussion, see Rose and Rose 2000). With the capability to decode and manipulate genes, modern science has acquired enormous power over life processes. In this situation, 'sociology finds itself disconcerted by the novelty that it may be easier to change human genetics than social or cultural context' (Golding 2000a: 172).

The critique of technological determinism – which easily wins the intellectual debate if not the economic and political arguments – and scholarly questioning of its traces in Castells's information age thesis, whether in part or in total, are not inherently techno-phobic. That the succession of technologies of one kind or another, historically, enable the conduct of social life and cultural expression in general is not by any means in question. The development and use of ICTs in the recent period, with their enormous capacities for symbolic manipulation and expanded communication, are key and, in many respects, liberating features of the late-modern world. However, excessive claims for the technological determination of culture and society are reasonably called into question for their explanatory inadequacies and ideological functions.

It is only to be expected that 'new mechanisms of human association' (Slevin 2000: 90) are being explored on the Internet and that artists and designers should be creating a 'digital aesthetics' (Cubitt 1998). New media do indeed offer diverse actualities and potentialities. These are not just in the emergence of a more efficient capitalist economy and burgeoning **consumerism** – shifting market information, money and goods around at great speed – but also in facilitating identity games, democratic participation, social-movement politics, access to learning and the tools of the imagination. Still, it should be remembered, the history of communications media is not actually one of newer media completely obliterating older media. Cinema challenged but did not destroy theatre. Television threatened cinema but did not entirely replace it. Of course, digitalization and networking can – and in some ways already do – mediate all culture. Yet, the rate of book publishing continues to increase year on year. If it were just about technology, old media might cease to exist in the foreseeable future, but it is not just about technology. It is about the complex interplay of technological development with cultural, economic and political determinations in social and historical contexts.

Winston's point about the suppression of radical potential in the emergence of new media technologies is manifestly relevant to assessing the fate of the Internet since the mid-1990s when its commercial potential began to be exploited in earnest. What had been set up as a publicly funded facility by federal government in the USA for security and, subsequently, scientific purposes was rapidly privatized. For years, the Internet had largely been of use to academics in the circulation of knowledge and the counter-cultural pioneers of cyberspace concerned with its radical potential. The Net's startling growth in the late 1990s was very much spurred on by business usage and consumer services. It became another means of distributing commodities, including entertainment and consumer goods, and a vehicle for advertising. Microsoft sought controversially to seize control of access to the Net in connection with its worldwide domination of the software market. It does not follow, however, that the radical potential was lost. Protest groups have found the Net a vital means for coordinating action and an alternative to mainstream media of communication. Also, the Napster phenomenon of distributing recorded music for free on the Internet – gift exchange separate from the state and market forces – caused panic in the music industry. It was deemed necessary by the majors to smash or incorporate this form of cultural decommodification; otherwise, profits from the sale of music would plummet further.

Such battles over copyright, intellectual property and access are likely to be persistent features of culture and economy in the network society. Nevertheless, for new on-line users, in spite of various kinds of nominally free access and guerrilla use, the Net is encountered most typically through commercial gate-keeping as a medium of commodity culture and enhanced consumerism. In the year 2000, the merger of America Online and Time-Warner certainly indicated that the Net was becoming very big cultural business. The eventual fate of the Net as a medium of the public sphere is a matter of continuing debate and questioning. From a critical perspective, it is necessary to be aware of the political economy of ICT development, especially continuing struggles over commodification and decommodification. It is important, also, not to confine analysis exclusively to the properties of new media technologies in isolation from social process or to interpret the meanings of ICTs for users without regard to contextual determinations (see McChesney et al. 1998).

Although critics of techno-boosterism often stress continuity over change – such as persistent and, indeed, worsening forms of domination, exclusion and inequality in the world – it is probably wisest to assume that there is a dialectical process of continuity and change. For instance, Douglas Kellner (1999) has said that contemporary capitalism is best understood as 'technocapitalism'. Rapid technological innovation serves the accumulation of capital irrespective of the social costs. Prevailing power relations become more intensive rather than less so. However, newer media technologies are not confined exclusively to a capitalist logic in the range of use, though, to a large extent, these technologies do indeed aid in the practical operation of that logic. ICTs are also used actually and potentially for different ends, as Kellner notes, for criticism, education and resistance.

Moreover, it is vital that taken-for-granted assumptions and blatantly ideological claims about the inevitably globalizing trends and outcomes of socio-technical transformation are challenged on grounds of human agency and democratic decision-making. On urban regeneration and telecommunications, Stephen Graham (1999) insists upon the scope for local agency, very much in line with Raymond Willams's emphasis on intentionality. And, John Downey (1999), surveying debate and policy within the European Union (EU), points to Manuel Castells's own personal contribution to the High Level Group of Experts' (HLEG) critique of Martin Bangemann's (1995) report, *Europe and the Global Information Society*. The Bangemann Report displayed an all-too-familiar technological determinism, the usual bland assumption of inevitability and the catch-up anxiety at Europe's 'core'. The HLEG refused to support an uncritical business agenda and called, instead, for continental-wide policies to counter the socio-technical exclusion and marginalization of peripheral, or, in EU discourse, 'cohesion' regions and, also, within deeply divided and unequal cities at the very core of European technocapitalism.

Branding

Manuel Castells's general account of a transformed world – the arrival of 'the information age' – refers to three 'independent processes' unfolding over the past thirty to forty years: the information technology revolution; the restructuring of capitalism; and the cultural struggles of oppositional movements. ICT development is intimately connected to the restructuring of capitalism and its victory over communism, resulting in global dominance – economically, politically and culturally – on a scale and with a scope that have never previously been witnessed in history. It has even been hailed as 'the end of history' (Fukuyama 1989). That is not a view shared by Castells, who stresses human agency, struggle and perpetual change, albeit fundamentally mediated these days by ICTs, whether for dominant forces or oppositional forces. However, his accent on technology to some extent distracts attention from economic, cultural and political processes that are anterior to ICT development yet, evidently, facilitated by it. In spite of his Marxist background, Castells pays insufficient attention to the intensified business incorporation of meaning production in general and the emergence of a 'cool' culture of popular consumption in rich countries that is dependent upon extreme exploitation of factory workers in newly 'industrializing' poor countries.

In her book, *No Logo*, subtitled 'Taking Aim at the Brand Bullies', Naomi Klein (2000a) places much greater emphasis on the restructuring of capitalism, the enhanced power of transnational corporations and the ubiquity of branding culture than does Castells. She concentrates her attention particularly upon American-based corporations like The Gap, McDonald's, Microsoft and Nike, though she also considers other nationally based corporations, for instance Shell. Klein (2000b: 25) points to 'a profound shift in corporate priorities [. . .] centre[ing] on the idea of corporate branding and the quest to build the most powerful brand image'.

Nike, of course, is the epitome of the brand-led corporation and has been widely celebrated by management consultants and criticized by others as such (see Goldman and Papson 1998). Based in the USA, Nike is a marketing outfit at its core, having divested itself of responsibility for production – and, indeed, its costs – by outsourcing supplies to cheap labour markets abroad, not even bothering to own the means of production like capitalists of old. Nike concentrates on selling the goods rather than making them. Investment is pumped into advertising, marketing and product design. The swoosh logo is market leader worldwide in the construction of youthful uniformity, inscribed upon its sneakers and sweatshirts, and in defining the very meaning of sporting activity. Nike evinces an ideology of 'Just Do It', which is at the heart of the American Dream and has a transcendental resonance for fun-loving youth, individual aspiration and style consciousness across the globe.

Identifying with Nike – wearing the swoosh like a swastika, the swooshtika – is supposed to transcend the commodity itself, that is, the use value of, say, an expensively acquired pair of trainers. This is the ideological intention of the 'cool' corporation and it is realized in millions of acts of consumption every day. It is meant to be pure meaning, sign value over and above anything else. The brand is about signification first and foremost. It is culture in the comparatively narrow but not very narrow definition that was discussed earlier in this chapter. Worldwide branding culture, then, is a cardinal object of critical cultural policy analysis, though this would not necessarily be seen as a legitimate matter of cultural policy from an administrative point of view that is tied exclusively to nation-state priorities and inter-state collaboration. Yet, there could hardly be anything more significant than the ubiquitous and exploitative brands if we are interested in the ruses of culture and power.

In terms of cultural analysis, branding culture needs to be understood within its material conditions of existence as well as regarding the pleasures of consumption and ideological effects. A pair of Air Jordans retailing at, say, $150 in the USA — cheaper than in Europe – will have cost around $5 to make by sweatshop workers. Most of them are female and probably some of them children – on a dollar or two a day in so-called 'export processing zones' (EPZs) or 'free-trade zones' in what used to be dubbed 'the Third World'. Nike, in particular, is supposed to have an 'ethical' policy, prohibiting child labour, for instance, but this is difficult to monitor, to say the least. There is a problem, also, in isolating Nike as the object of complaint since they are all at it. As a BBC television documentary in the autumn of 2000 showed, child labour was being employed in a factory in Cambodia's Phnom Penh to produce both Nike and Gap apparel, a particular but exemplary case (*Panorama*, 'Gap and Nike – No Sweat', 15 October 2000). As a result of such public exposure, the children who appeared on the programme were likely to lose their jobs. The spin doctors from the two companies who showed up at the factory took different views on the implications. For the Gap spokesperson, it was enough to sack the children without compensation in order to fulfil the company's ethical responsibilities. In contrast, the slicker Nike spokesperson was prepared to countenance something more, that the company might consider funding the children's education until they were old enough to return to the factory. While the issue of child labour is particularly serious, it is important not to lose sight of the fact that pay, conditions and accommodation for all workers at the Cambodian factory – and for millions of Third World workers elsewhere – are dreadfully poor by 'Western' standards.

To place in context what is potentially at stake for cultural policy analysis, it is necessary to make a digression here concerning work and creative occupations in clothing and fashion. In her study of young British fashion designers, Angela McRobbie (1998) documents how difficult it is for them to make a career in 'the rag trade'. For McRobbie, this is an issue of cultural policy. The British government boasts about national excellence in fashion design but does little for those seeking to make it in an extremely competitive environment. This is a perfectly legitimate matter of national, educational and labour market concern.

Putting it generally, though, many feel the calling to creative and cultural work but few succeed. Unfortunately, that may be the nature of the beast in the fields of art, design, media and sport. Talented young people expend enormous amounts of energy and dedication trying to succeed. In comparison with the numbers who 'make it', however, there is always likely to be a much greater number of those who just miss out. The occasional young British fashion designer might reach the top, become a world-famous millionairess and, perhaps, a brand herself: most, however, have to settle for something less by, for instance, working in a menial role for a branding corporation or entering management in a department store.

This is a different world, however, from that of the sweatshop workers who actually make the fashionable garments on subsistence wages. The standard model of inclusion/exclusion, in effect, assumes the separation of these worlds, despite their inter-connectedness, while raising critical questions about who is allowed in and who is kept out. It veers away from the tortuous problem of making sense of the global network of exploitation which affects not only corporate profits but also has implications for the careers of struggling fashion designers.

As Castells points out, there are enclaves of extreme poverty in wealthy countries as well as in poor countries. For example, in clothing-industry sweatshops in the City of Los Angeles ethnic minorities in particular, some of them illegal immigrants, labour long hours for a pittance in order to keep the privileged of the world in fashionable attire (Gumbel 2001).

Castells himself is very much concerned about processes of inclusion and exclusion. Some are released into 'the space of flows' by access to the most advanced technologies and means of communication, while others are stuck in their places, left behind and, topographically speaking, outside the loop of 'the information age', in what he calls a 'Fourth World'. The Weberian model of inequality in Castells's work, focusing upon the market dynamics of inclusion and exclusion, is clearly relevant to understanding geopolitics, economics and culture in the world today. The excluded, no doubt, want to be included. To what extent this is possible under prevailing conditions is open to debate, to put it mildly. Perhaps the model of inclusion and exclusion describes accurately what the situation looks like on the surface, but does it explain it? Does it account satisfactorily for the underlying dynamics of the hyper-capitalist system?

There is another way of conceptualizing inequality, which is obvious and more directly relevant to considering the relation between branding culture and the manufacture of branded commodities in EPZs and in Los Angeles: this is *exploitation*, and on a grand scale. Those who actually make the branded goods are not so much excluded – they are included but in a cruelly subordinate role, paid very little for their labour power on a global scale of relative value and, also, typically denied ordinary civil and labour rights. As the evidence documented by Klein (2000a) demonstrates, the global rate of exploitation now being conducted on behalf of branding culture would probably have made a nineteenth-century capitalist seeking Calvinist election experience a severe pang of Catholic guilt.

'Affordable' style for the masses – the ubiquitous 'cool' culture – in richer parts of the world is achieved at the cost of great cruelty and misery in poorer parts of the world and enclaves in richer countries. There is, to be sure, some resistance to this global condition. Opposition forces – including trades unions, ecology groups, students and others – come together in what has been called an 'anti-capitalist' or 'anti-corporate' movement but is best named as 'the movement for social justice'. Some aspects of opposition are distinctly anarchistic and, indeed, theatrical (see St Clair 1999 and Cockburn et al. 2000 on the Seattle protest against the World Trade Organization). Acting out against big government and transnational capital is one thing; changing the power relations is another. Although Klein (2000c) herself supports the spontaneity and disorderliness of this international movement, coordinating its actions over the Internet, 'ad-busting' and 'culture-jamming', she has her reservations about its ultimate effectiveness (Klein 2000a). Court battles, like the McLibel trial (Vidal 1997), and a negotiated relationship to mainstream and governmental politics are necessary features of oppositional struggle. Forcing corporations on the defensive to produce ethical codes of practice, paper resolutions rather than genuine concessions, a typical outcome of apparently 'successful' campaigning, is not enough. Klein says: 'Political solutions – accountable to people and enforceable by their elected representatives – deserve another shot before we throw in the towel and settle for corporate codes, independent monitors and the privatization of our collective rights as citizens' (2000a: 442). In this respect, Klein's position is consistent with Jürgen Habermas's (1996 [1992]) latterday 'sluicegate' model of the public sphere in which campaigning social and cultural movements are the agents forcing issues onto governmental agendas that would not otherwise be there (McGuigan 2002).

The general position is similar to Steven Lukes's (1974) three-dimensional view of power. Political scientists were apt to study decision-making processes in isolation until it became evident that power is as much about not making decisions as making them. Both the one-dimensional view and the improved two-dimensional view, however, are behaviouristic and too limited for making sense of how power works in general. The ideological capacity to prevent potential issues from even appearing on agendas where decisions are made or not made is a greater power. That which is almost impossible to enunciate is the object of the three-dimensional view of power. The structural power of transnational corporations and branding culture fits into this more complex model, since it has become so overweening as to be safe from virtually any observable process of democratic decision-making or, for that matter, non-decision-making. Hence the desperate actions of opposition forces in order to get fundamental issues aired at all.

As Naomi Klein has shown and Raymond Williams (1974: 151) put it, the branding or 'para-national' corporations are 'reach[ing] farther into our lives [. . .] until individual and collective response in many different kinds of experience and problem became almost limited to choice between their programmed possibilities'. In addition to extreme exploitation of factory workers abroad, casualization of work and anxious consumption at home, and generalized psychic interference everywhere, the branding corporations of technocapitalism are literally privatizing public space and imposing corporate speech on every practice. Should policy-oriented cultural analysts, then, adapt themselves exclusively to a world where it is said 'there is no alternative', the TINA philosophy, or ask the kind of awkward questions that the powers-that-be prefer not to be asked?

Conclusion

In this chapter I have sought to both narrow and widen the purview of cultural policy analysis. 'Culture' has become one of the cant words of the age, referring to so many different phenomena to the point where it has, arguably, become entirely drained of meaning. That is especially so in managerial and marketing discourse. Clearly, meaning matters: for example, at work. Yet, so do pay and conditions. While privileged e.commerce workers may favour first-name management and employee relations and informal dress codes – sweatshirts and trainers, for instance – sweatshop workers who actually make the apparel might like to be able to buy it. Branding culture, it seems, is first and foremost about meaning: that's culture. It is of immense political significance. Therefore, it follows that branding culture represents, among other things, an issue of culture and politics. Critical and reflexive cultural policy analysis – that is prepared, for instance, to address such evidently acute issues as the global exploitation underlying branding culture – goes beyond immediate and routinely practical problems of policy formulation and management in the field of arts and media. That is not to deny the importance of these objects of study. As far as cultural analysis is concerned, there are innumerable problems worthy of study and various different methods that can be applied depending upon the problem under consideration. Although I criticize blind spots in the Foucauldian agenda in cultural policy studies, especially its neglect of capitalism, I have found Foucault's own insights into power/knowledge and the discursive production of 'truth' useful for analysing the discourses of cultural policy (Chapter 2 of this book). Pragmatic considerations of professional practice in the cultural field should be respected and the value of methodological pluralism appreciated. The critical perspective on issues of culture and policy goes further, however, by reflexively embracing the ethical responsibility to ask awkward questions that need to be asked from the point of view of justice, for instance about allegedly inevitable and ineluctable trends to do with globalization, capitalism and technology. As Manuel Castells has remarked, there is nothing that cannot be changed.

2 | DISCOURSES OF CULTURAL POLICY

Introduction

It is curious that as the security and rights of social citizenship were deliberately weakened in the older industrialized and de-industrializing parts of the world over recent decades, with the neo-liberal assault upon the welfare state, the issue of cultural **citizenship** rose up the agendas of public and academic debate.

In T.H. Marshall's (1992 [1950]) classic formulation, in the immediate period following the Second World War, the economic rights of trade and the political rights of democracy had to be supplemented by the material entitlements of social security. These were to cover the distresses of ill health, unemployment and old age, in order to eliminate poverty and include everyone in an egalitarian contract. The catalogue of social rights was increasingly extended under 'First World' liberal-democratic, social-democratic and welfare regimes, though variably so from country to country, with the USA being the least paternal and the Nordic countries the most paternal. 'Second World' soviet-communist countries claimed a yet more advanced social condition in terms of the state looking after all the needs of all its citizens. In none of these regimes was total equality achieved or even sought. Typically, meritocracy arrangements were made so that the talented could rise through universal secondary education and access higher education. The weak and socially disadvantaged would also be protected and treated with dignity. In Marshall's classic social-democratic agenda, the aim was specifically to reduce class inequality. As that agenda was developed subsequently, policies for removing gender discrimination and racial discrimination were also to become pronounced features of the egalitarian project. Successive questions of further entitlement were raised, not only in terms of social policy but also of cultural policy, for instance to do with access to the arts, **multiculturalism** and recognition of difference.

To some extent the growing concern with cultural citizenship and identity reflects how issues that were once considered 'social' have come increasingly to be thought of as 'cultural'. Questions of identity and a sense of belonging appear to have superseded questions of material entitlement in much social and cultural theory as well as in public policy and cultural politics. In the USA, to take the most notable example, public spending on urban programmes and welfare was slashed (M. Davis 1993a and b), thereby exacerbating the problems of the black 'underclass'. Simultaneously, the meaning of African-American identity became hotly debated among black intellectuals (Dent 1992). Anxiety over the proper nomination of identity infused the very language of the public sphere. The former President of South Africa Nelson Mandela was addressed by a witless journalist on his first ever visit to the States in the early 1990s – having just been released from a quarter century of imprisonment for his opposition to Apartheid in his own country – as 'African-American'. The status of cultural citizen of the United States was thus casually bestowed upon a statesman from another country, albeit by a slip of the tongue.

The question of cultural citizenship is extremely diffuse and reflexive, signifying perhaps how we have come to think of politics and public identity very broadly as a matter of signs. Its range vastly exceeds what has usually been instituted as *cultural policy* and the ways in which such policy has addressed social subjects. Cultural policy itself, however, is an unstable concept. It has had an uneven and often detached relationship to *communications* and *media policy*. These latter nominations have largely been thought through in the terms of political economy, signifying their industrial and economic importance and the role of the communications media in politics as narrowly conceived. In comparison, *cultural policy* is still, in spite of attempts to broaden its remit, quite closely associated with *arts policy*, the objects of which are the aesthetic, the affective, taste and symbolic value. From a practical point of view, this may be unsatisfactory: yet the emphases on representation and on the subjectivity of civic and national identity do meet up with the more diffuse idea of cultural citizenship (for an extensive discussion of such issues, see Stevenson 2001).

Another feature of cultural policy – and, to a great extent, communications and media policy as well – is its close historical association with the nation-state. In a global economy and culture, with politics increasingly shaped by transnational forces, the nation-state in general, and its cultural policies in particular, are frequently said to be redundant. So many premature obituaries have been written of the nation-state that you might be forgiven for believing – against the palpable evidence of experience – that it is indeed dead or at least in its death throes. Yet, the nation-state stubbornly persists, even under conditions of speeded-up globalization, as a major constitutive power of politics, economy and culture in the late-modern world. Specifically, it is still the key focus for the defence and extension of social citizenship and for many claims that are made for cultural citizenship. To argue thus is not to deny the importance of international and local formations. There is, for example, the role of 'Europe' in defending the social rights of citizens in Britain during the eighteen years of Conservative government that ended in 1997. There are numerous forms of cultural identity that transcend the national habitat and create localized enclaves, in many instances networked internationally, within and sometimes against the territorial command of the nation-state. In any case, the nation-state is not the same as the nation. A crucial feature of state cultural policies in multicultural countries like Malaysia, and Britain, is the object of reconciling different ethnic and national identities with one another.

In this chapter, my concern is not, however, so much with unpacking the complex relations between the nation and the state, the local and the global. It is more narrowly to do with how the modern state's cultural policies have been constructed and deconstructed, assuming that the nation-state was and continues to be important for the conditions of both social and cultural citizenship. My principal concerns in this account are to trace the rise of market reasoning within the public cultural sector during the recent period of neo-liberal hegemony, to raise critical issues concerning market reason and to explore the grounds for cultural resistance. The approach is to consider, very broadly, the discursive framing of cultural policy and to outline the role of discourse ethics in the cultural rights of citizenship.

I shall distinguish between three general **discursive formations** of cultural policy in admittedly an over-simplification, though one with a specific purpose. These formations are by no means confined solely to 'culture' and cultural policy. The three **discourses** of cultural policy – state, market and civil/communicative – all have a number of variants and are by no means internally unified. Yet, they all function in some sense to define 'the real world' of culture and to position agents and subjects, producers, consumers, citizens and mediators, within the discursive space of the cultural field.

It is necessary to digress for a moment on the matter of discourse. In a commentary on Michel Foucault's inaugural lecture at the College de France, 'The Order of Discourse', Robert Young (1981: 48) once remarked that the 'effect' of 'discursive practices' is 'to make it virtually impossible to think outside of them'. This observation is similar to the Wittgensteinian dictum that language sets the limits to our world. However, to say that it is impossible to think outside of a discourse, in Young's explication of Foucault, is to say something more. Young's observation points to the operations of power in the regulation of discourse, procedures of exclusion, reason and truth, internal policing and conditions of application (Foucault 1981).

The prevailing ideological feature of particular discourses, according to Michel Pecheux (1982: 115), is secured interdiscursively by the dominant ideological discourse of the social formation. Also, the concept of 'interdiscourse' suggests that no discourse is ever closed off entirely from other discourses or without internally disruptive elements. From these considerations, two broad observations need to be made. First, discourses of cultural policy do not exist in splendid isolation from the leading discourses of the day. Second, although discourses are indeed porous and there is interaction between them, it is difficult not to notice how some discourses 'make it virtually impossible to think outside of them'.

It is interesting, at a time when 'the **dominant ideology thesis**' (Abercrombie et al. 1980 and 1990) fell out of favour in social and cultural theory, that there should have been in strengthened existence such an outstanding candidate for designation as the dominant ideology. By which I mean the all-encompassing discourse of market reason on a global scale in alliance with technological determinism; in effect, neo-liberal globalization. I shall eventually return to this point about the spread and pervasiveness of market reasoning across many practices, after outlining selectively how the modern state has operated discursively in cultural policy, which is a necessary preliminary to examining the marketization of everything.

Stating

As well as the phenomenal rise of 'mass culture' in the marketplace, twentieth-century cultural developments were closely linked to the state. They went well beyond earlier forms of monarchical and aristocratic patronage and built upon, for instance, the public museum and library legislation of the nineteenth century, which became associated in Britain and elsewhere with Matthew Arnold's (1932 [1869 and 1875]) view of the state as society's 'better self'. The 'anarchy' of unregulated developments in culture and politics was the major stimulus to 'enlightened' state intervention. A discourse emerged in various manifestations around the idea that the modern nation-state should command the whole of society, regulate the economy and cultivate appropriate selves, an idea that was extremely widespread until quite recently. This was never exclusively a socialist or communist imaginary. It was even accepted generally within advanced capitalism as a means of containing recurrent crises by mid-century. Fordism and Keynesian economics called forth and legitimized state intervention in the multifarious workings of capitalist society. That cultural policy, moreover, might function to re-engineer the soul became a commonplace assumption of both totalitarian and, also, albeit to a much lesser extent, liberal and social-democratic thought and practice.

In the 1930s Nazism promoted the Aryan ideal in Germany, especially in its bodily form, and attacked 'degenerate art'. Adolf Hitler, himself a failed artist, hated modernism and sought to establish an eternal classicism modelled on Hellenic culture as the official art of the Third Reich (Grosshans 1983). Artists were bullied into compliance, sacked from their teaching jobs and forced into exile. The 1937 Exhibition of Degenerate Art (*Entarte Kunst*) in Munich held modernism up to ridicule. After the exhibition had toured the country, 'degenerate' pieces of art were sold off at international market prices, including major works by '*Auslanders*' like Pablo Picasso as well as German exiles such as Paul Klee.

It is particularly striking how successful the Nazis were at co-opting 'cultivated' intellectuals to enact their cultural policies and to organize and justify a massive theft of visual artworks for the greater glory of Germany. As Jonathan Petropoulis comments:

The Nazi leaders devoted an inordinate amount of time to cultural matters. Indeed, culture and propaganda may have been 'the war that Hitler won' [Herztein, 1978]. Their control of the arts was an important element of the totalitarian system. Similarly, their commitment to amassing both private and state art collections stand as a remarkable aspect of their rule.

(2000: 5)

Furthermore, of course, 'the Nazi leaders' cultural policies were inextricably bound up with their racial and geopolitical agendas' (Petropoulis 2000: 6). Curators, dealers, critics and artists themselves were in the main prepared to do the Nazis' bidding. It was not only Goebbels's media propaganda in news and documentary, denouncing Jews and others in the name of German purification, that convinced ordinary Germans of Nazism's ideological superiority. The Nazis also believed that Germany had the right to actually appropriate and possess the great European heritage of art since the Third Reich represented the pinnacle of civilization.

There is also the tragic instance of Soviet communism in which culture in the artistic sense was seen as a key device for social engineering. According to the notorious Soviet Writers' Congress of 1934, the purpose of cultural policy was to create 'socialist man', both representationally and in lived reality (Gorky et al. 1977). That was a crucial moment of ideological closure around 'socialist realism' in the Soviet Union, reacting to the controversies and clash of diverse aesthetic tendencies and *avant-garde* practices during the 1920s. For instance, the great experimental film-maker Dziga Vertov, director of *Man With a Movie Camera* (1929), in spite of that film's exemplary communist propaganda, was lucky to get away with spending the rest of his life relegated to the editing of routine newsreels. He was denied permission and resources to direct film projects of his own (Enzensberger 1977). Other 'formalists' were not so fortunate. The poet Vladimir Mayakovsky of Lef (the Left Front of Art), who was vilified as a *'petit-bourgeois* individualist and anarchist' in the late 1920s, had already committed suicide in 1930. His reinstatement as an icon of 'socialist man' in 1935 was especially ironic (Shklovsky 1974). Others died more directly at the hands of the state in the Soviet Union, as was also the case in the Third Reich.

The later operations of official cultural policy and artistic practice in the Soviet bloc were more complex and internally contradictory, however, than the image of the dictatorial and robotic culture for which it was known in 'the West' during the Cold War, from the late 1940s until the 1990s. The Hungarian writer Miklos Haraszti's (1987) *The Velvet Prison – Artists Under State Socialism* shows, in a fascinating account, how 'dissidence' had actually become by the 1980s a normative aspect of the system among officially approved and rewarded cultural workers themselves. Anne White (1990) gives a different yet equally compelling account of the actual effects of communist cultural policy in her study *De-Stalinization and the House of Culture*. White was interested in the fate of 'cultural enlightenment' as a strategy of socialist socialization after Stalin in the Soviet Union, Hungary and Poland. The houses of culture – arts centres – were established in order to inculcate humanistic and egalitarian ideals and to foster belief in human perfectability under socialism. However, by the time White was researching the practical outcomes during the period of *glasnost* in the late 1980s, she found that liberalization had occurred alongside political disillusion in general and with such cultural policy in particular among not only the people but also communist leaders. She says:

> Social changes – notably widespread disillusionment with, and rejection of, Stalinism and Stalinist cultural institutions, the spread of television and individual flat ownership, higher education levels, the emergence of organised dissent and the greater exposure of ordinary citizens to Western culture – had led to a situation by the 1980s in which the leading role of the party in determining how leisure time was spent was becoming seriously eroded.
>
> (White 1990: 4)

In a much less detached tone, Ernest Gellner made the sour yet incisive observation that:

> Far from creating a new social man, one freed from egotistic greed, commodity fetishism and competitiveness, which had been the Marxist hope, the system created isolated, amoral, cynical individualists-without-opportunity, skilled at double-talk and trimming within the system, but incapable of effective enterprise.
>
> (1996: 5)

Great and no doubt mistaken expectations were also vested in the state's cultural policies under social democracy and within the terms of liberal democracy throughout Western Europe. Although policies differed from country to country, the British experience was not altogether untypical. Nevertheless, it is always necessary to be aware of national peculiarities in cultural policy as well as identifying general trends of international significance (see McGuigan 1996). In Britain, there is a distinctive trad-ition of setting up intermediary bodies between the state, on the one hand, and civil society and the market, on the other hand. These organizations are of the state but not supposed to be directly under the sway of the current government (Williams 1979) – organizations such as the British Broadcasting Corporation (BBC), the Arts Council and English Heritage. Such bodies were modelled historically on the University Grants Committee (UGC), established in 1919, precursor to the present Higher Education Funding Council. They were all supposed to operate according to 'the arm's length principle', whereby governments controlled general allocation of resources to such organizations but were not in day-to-day operational control. This principle was meant to secure political 'neutrality' and 'impartiality' between interested parties in the spe-cific field of operation. The official aim was to achieve, for instance, 'balanced' broad-cast news and the 'fair' disbursement of grants to arts organizations according to observable criteria of judgement, thus being, in principle, accountable to 'the public'.

That the BBC should function in a similarly 'impartial' manner to the UGC, secured by the greater authority of the state over the market as well as, in theory, protecting it from the present whims of government, was an aim of political liberalism in the 1920s. It was actually brought into being by Stanley Baldwin's Conservative administration. The first Director General, John Reith, then, had his way in fashioning the BBC as the key institution of a liberal national culture, the guardian of a certain kind of communicational or cultural citizenship, and a bulwark against extremes of Left and Right. That card-carrying Liberals played leading roles in founding the welfare state in general, and 'the welfare state model' of cultural policy in particular, is itself significant historically: British social democracy to a degree realized a Liberal programme during the tenure of office of the 1945 Labour government. The central figures were William Beveridge, in the case of social welfare, and John Maynard Keynes, both as the economic guru of social democracy and architect of the Arts Council of Great Britain at the end of the Second World War as an agency for enhancing national prestige. This was a thread that became knotted in the 1960s and 1970s.

The cardinal terms to consider with regard to the forms, contradictions and tensions of social-democratic cultural policy in Britain are 'extension' and, more latterly, 'access': in the later lexicon of the European Union, 'inclusion'. The discourse was never just that of political liberalism as a state-oriented counterpoint to unrestrained economic liberalism: it was enunciated and fought over within the terms of social democracy itself. In his 1929 lectures on *Equality*, R.H. Tawney set the social-democratic agenda for appropriating 'culture' from the sole possession of a privileged elite and extending it to the masses (Tawney 1931). Tawney had already recommended the introduction of universal secondary education to the Labour Party in 1922. It is worth quoting Raymond Williams at length on the problems inherent in this Tawneyan agenda of cultural extension:

> The case for extension (the entirely appropriate word) is strong; the dangers of limitation are real and present. But to think of the problem as one of 'opening museums' or of putting the specimens in the marketplace is to capitulate to a very meagre idea of culture. Tawney's position is both normal and humane. But there is an unresolved contradiction, which phrases about broadening and enriching merely blur, between the recognition that a culture must grow and the hope that 'existing standards of excellence' may be preserved intact. It is a contradiction which, among others, the defenders of inequality will be quick to exploit. The question that has to be faced, if we may put it for a moment in one of Tawney's analogies, is whether the known gold will be more widely spread, or whether, in fact, there will be a change of currency. If the social and economic changes which Tawney recommends are in fact effected, it is the latter, the change of currency, which can reasonably be expected.
>
> (Williams 1971 [1958]: 222–3)

The 1964 to 1970 Labour governments sought to realize the Tawneyan agenda by increasing the Arts Council's annual grant-in-aid threefold as part of a general programme for raising public access to the arts and culture. A network of Regional Arts

Associations was also created. These were later renamed Regional Arts Boards in the greater devolution of funding and decision-making that occurred towards the end of the twentieth century. This included the splitting off of Arts Councils of Scotland and Wales from the Arts Council of Great Britain, leaving it the Arts Council of England (ACE).

In the 1960s, there was a drive to make secondary education more comprehensive, and there was relatively generous funding for the expansion of higher education. Such public policies, educational and cultural, were enacted in the name of 'access' to opportunities and pleasures that were previously denied to most people. But, as Williams had already noted back in the 1950s, in his discussion of Tawney, what would be disseminated more widely was bound to change with the dissemination. Trouble occurred around the meaning of 'access'. Was it confined to creating the conditions for more people down the social hierarchy and in the regions to consume established art forms? Or, did it mean popular control over the means of cultural production, redefining what counts as 'culture' and participation for groups hitherto excluded by the established structures of public patronage? – to facilitate ethnic minority arts, proletarian theatre, feminist film-making, and so on.

Much of the trouble around 'access' was concentrated upon alternative theatre and community arts. By the 1970s, the Arts Council was supporting both the National Theatre in its then newly palatial premises on the South Bank of the Thames and a range of practices throughout the country variously called 'community', 'fringe' and 'political' theatre. There was considerable variation within the field of alternative theatre but few were aiming to widen audiences for the theatrical culture of the National. Many were trying to challenge what it represented aesthetically and socially, for instance in the work of John McGrath (1981) and the 7.84 Theatre Company. Although in retrospect such opposition practices are often seen to characterize the cultural action of that period, it should be remembered just how marginal they really were. In 1978, thirty travelling theatre companies received just less than £1 million between them in Arts Council grants, while the National and the Royal Shakespeare Company shared more than £4 million (Itzin 1980). The Arts Council was also spending about £1 million a year on community arts. That same year, Su Braden provoked a bitter counter-attack against community arts when she denounced the Arts Council's support for 'bourgeois' culture in her book, *Artists and People*. The following passage in Braden's book particularly incensed the guardians of 'serious culture':

> [T]he so-called cultural *heritage* which made Europe great – the Bachs and the Beethovens, the Shakespeares and the Dantes, the Constables and the Titians – is no longer communicating anything to the vast majority of Europe's population. That the relevance of even art forms that were widely popular at the time of their creation are now only easily accessible to those already convinced that such culture is *their* heritage. It is not that these cultural forms are 'above people's heads' but that it is a *bourgeois* culture and therefore only immediately meaningful to

that group. The great artistic deception of the twentieth century has been to insist to *all* people that this was *their* culture. The Arts Council of Great Britain was established on this premise. And it is on the basis of the concept that if you educate people by constantly placing the art you wish them to 'appreciate' in front of them, that ballet, symphony orchestras, theatre and paintings have been toured around towns and villages throughout the country.

(1978: 153–4)

Braden went on to claim that the policy of cultural dissemination was based on faulty assumptions. First, it mistakenly assumed that lack of appreciation for the traditional arts is due to educational failure and could be rectified, therefore, by better education. Second, it assumed that the mass-popular culture generally appreciated by most people is inherently inferior to the traditional arts, which is an assumption that can no longer be taken for granted. Cultural democracy populists like Braden were in an embattled position. Social-democratic agents of cultural policy were running out of patience with the young Turks. In fact, by this time, grants to explicitly Leftist theatre groups were already being cut off and community arts were soon to be devolved to the Regional Arts Associations. It was eventually argued from within the cultural democracy movement (Kelly 1984) that community arts should never have become so dependent upon state subsidy. In retrospect, however, it is now quite striking how typically the cultural campaigning of the '68 Generation was couched within the terms of the social-democratic discourse of extension, access and inclusion which assumed that the state was the principal actor in the cultural field. That discourse ran contrary to the manifest powers of capital and commodity culture. To a considerable extent, then, the opposition movements were about taking such discourse seriously by redirecting resources and control to 'the people', that is, reforming rather than revolutionizing the state's mode of cultural intervention. In effect, the cultural democracy movement led unwittingly to the erosion of the social-democratic project from inside. It contributed ironically to social democracy's vulnerability to the populist assault coming from the New Right, both in general politics and in the politics of culture (for discussion of debates and developments in this period, see Baldry 1981).

Marketizing

The Senior Finance Officer at the Arts Council of Great Britain, Anthony Field, said in 1982:

It is difficult to persuade people in control of funds that the most difficult time is that involving a real expansion of activity consequent upon a growth of funds. In the period from 1970 to 1980 the Arts Council experienced such a growth and gave priority to the growth of drama groups. [. . .] The great achievement of the Arts Council subsidies is that they have made the best theatre available so widely. [. . .]

[I]n the last resort, the Arts Council has to hang on to the very best – the rest will survive (or not!) without public subsidy – the dregs of theatre, the mediocre, the work that is up-and-coming or on the way out. What needs subsidy is the forum in which the very best can develop and there are indications that it will have taken the Arts Council a decade to come to terms with how best to utilise new monies.

(1983: 89, 95)

This is the voice of an accountant and, subsequently, an educator of arts administrators at the City University in London. It was not yet the authentic voice of the British New Right in cultural policy since it was still engaged primarily in dispute over cultural value according to the elitist/populist divide, the struggle between 'the best' and 'the dregs' that was said to have flourished under social democracy. But, what Field is saying here already hints at the increasingly powerful language of money and efficiency whereby all value would be reduced to exchange value, the discourse of the market in cultural policy as in everything else.

Soon afterwards, in a position paper for the 1983 Greater London Council (GLC) conference on cultural policy, Nicholas Garnham said

while this tradition [of public cultural policy] has been rejecting the market most people's cultural needs and aspirations are being, for better or worse, supplied by the market as goods and services. If one turns one's back on an analysis of that dominant cultural process, one cannot understand the culture of our time or the challenges and opportunities which that dominant culture offers to public policy-makers.

(reprinted in Garnham 1990: 155)

When Garnham said that, the Labour-controlled GLC was, in fact, already doomed by Margaret Thatcher's 1983 General Election pledge to abolish it and thus rid Britain's capital city of socialist government. This concentrated minds at the GLC, which in its remaining years initiated an influential if only modestly realized policy of investment in 'the cultural industries'. It also showed how public-sector culture could be popular fun, with its festivals, and how exclusion could be countered, for instance in its encouragement of black film-making and positive discrimination/affirmative action in training.

Garnham was merely pointing to the glaring fact that state-subsidized and government-sponsored culture is not the means of cultural provision that captures the attention of most people most of the time, as Geoff Mulgan and Ken Worpole (1986) also later insisted in their very influential book, *Saturday Night or Sunday Morning?*, which signalled a new economic realism and managerialism on the Left of cultural policy debate in Britain. Public cultural policy was indeed small beer, and remains so, in comparison with the economic power of cultural and media businesses and the popular appeal of commodity culture. Here, two general and qualifying points need to be made, however, the second more fully than the first. First, to take a major example, that the British government permitted Rupert Murdoch to buy up a very large segment of the national press, and allowed his Sky TV to seize command over satellite broadcasting in Britain, were policy decisions with long-term consequences (Curran and Seaton 1991 [1981]; Chippindale and Franks 1991). Decisions were taken self-consciously by government in circumstances where alternative options were available. Such events in the history of what Bernard Miege (1989) has called 'the capitalization of cultural production' are not just 'trends that cannot be bucked', a favourite phrase of the 1980s. They are trends that were actively promoted in Britain and elsewhere from the 1970s onwards. Second, it is now acutely evident in Britain, and in many other countries around the world, that the apparent political hue of the party in government does not seem to matter a great deal when dealing with international operators in global *and national* media markets like Murdoch. Whether this represents an ineluctable combination of economic and technological determinism resulting in inevitable governmental capitulation to the power of transnational cultural and media corporations or a pervasive abrogation of public responsibility by national governments is open to debate.

We are plunged, then, into a discourse where it is indeed 'virtually impossible to think outside of'. It is difficult to overestimate how pervasive it became throughout politics and practice. GLC-inspired policies of public cultural investment, for instance to achieve economic regeneration and urban renewal, were pursued enthusiastically by a number of local Labour administrations from the 1980s onwards, with variable results. The point of the argument here is not to evaluate the practical outcomes of such policies in their specific contexts but, rather, to note how the language of cultural policy changed in relation to these and other practices. Simon Frith (1991: 136) posed the question, 'How have local Labour parties come to deploy terms like "market niche" and "corporate image" in their cultural arguments?' Evidently, and putting it very summarily, because of the reality-generating power of market reasoning and the new management thinking that was functioning ubiquitously across the institutions of British society and, for that matter, the world at large.

Perhaps this is 'reality' and, undoubtedly, it is wise to be 'realistic'. No reality, however, is given once and for all in social and cultural affairs. It is always a construction, the product of multiple determinations, an historical and changeable phenomenon, which is an elementary enough observation for social and cultural analysis. Yet, processes like the 'de-regulation' and 'privatization' of communicational and cultural resources are often said to be inevitable and ineluctable; and, being inevitable and ineluctable, therefore, desirable. There is a denial of agency, an abject determinism, a naturalization of contingency, in such ideological discourse. This underpins the widespread assumption that the free play of market forces and private-sector management are inherently superior, on efficiency grounds, to political deliberation and public-sector administration. It is not only a belief held in the private sector but also in the public sector. The conventional wisdom is that there is an inexorable drift of history: so it makes sense to go with the flow.

Major cultural businesses operate increasingly on an awesomely global scale and, in many respects, transcend the powers of any nation-state, with the exception of the USA. Yet, the rhetorics of 'globalization' and of 'rolling back the state', which rose to prominence in the 1980s and 1990s, should not be taken too literally at face value. In Britain, the state was not only rolled back with the official aim of returning its powers to 'the people'; it was also rolled forward and centralized (Gamble 1994a [1988]). That is why it is necessary to remark upon the colonization of the public sector by market reasoning and to identify some illustrative examples of the discourse in play.

First, there is the former chair of the British Arts Council and right-wing journalist William Rees-Mogg's at-one-time famous and dubious syllogism on the economic utility of 'investing' in the arts, delivered in his 1985 lecture, 'The Political Economy of Art' at IBM's British headquarters on the South Bank in London. It went like this: in 1984–85, the £100 million of 'taxpayer's money' spent by the Arts Council resulted in £250 million of turnover, creating 25,000 jobs. This produced £75 million of revenue for the Exchequer that was made up of National Insurance contributions and income tax paid by arts workers and VAT on box-office receipts. Some £50 million was saved in unemployment benefits. For an outlay of £100 million, then, £125 million was returned to the public coffers, a very healthy profit. The quality of Rees-Mogg's reasoning is not primarily what is at stake: it is the discourse of such reasoning itself which is of interest. The justification for public expenditure on the arts is given as making money and, moreover, 'the taxpayer', so beloved of neo-liberal discourse, is simultaneously redefined as a shareholder in Yookay PLC.

That same year (1985), the Arts Council issued its *A Great British Success Story*, subtitled 'An Invitation to the Nation to Invest in the Arts'. The significance of this particular report was not so much its substantive content as the rhetorical form. *A Great British Success Story* presented the case for continuing public expenditure on the arts in the format of a glossy and colourfully illustrated company prospectus, addressing an ideal investor who is seeking a good return on share capital. This was enunciated in the same discursive space as the selling-off of public utilities by the Thatcher governments and the much-vaunted 'spread' of share-ownership and 'popular capitalism' during the 1980s. It is hard to recall and appreciate just how novel and controversial it was, in the 1980s, for the state to deploy the techniques of business promotion in such a brash manner, because it has become so customary and normal a feature of public-sector discourse since then. It exemplifies what Andrew Wernick (1991) has called 'promotional culture'.

There are three ideal subjects of such discourse: 'the taxpayer', 'the shareholder' and 'the customer'. The taxpayer does not want his or her money wasted by government. The shareholder wants a return on investment. The customer wants choice and to be served well. His or Her Majesty the Customer, the mythical sovereign consumer, must be obeyed in market discourse. This is not only an assumption of neo-liberal economics, private enterprise and recent management theory; it is also a marked feature now of public service. So, for example, there has been an increasing use of marketing techniques in the publicly subsidized arts.

Marketing is never simply about giving the customer what he or she is said to want spontaneously but, rather, it is a means of increasing sales through a careful profiling of consumers and putting in the effort where it counts. Subscription marketing schemes in the arts (Diggle 1984), for instance, are now ubiquitous, targeted upon increasing attendance by 'attenders' and encouraging 'intenders' to actually attend, and not wasting time, effort and money on attracting 'non-attenders', as social-democratic cultural policy was supposed to do.

A good deal of time and effort is also expended on attracting business sponsorship to the arts in Britain. The situation there is rather different from the USA, which in the twentieth century developed a much greater corporate and private benefactor involvement in the arts than was so in the welfare states of Europe. Business sponsorship in the British case is often a fractional supplement to public subsidy and box-office takings. Although that fraction may be seen as vital to survival for many arts organizations, other effects also come into play. There is a strong case for arguing that the actual effects of business sponsorship in Britain, at least, have been more ideological than material. Business sponsorship exerts influence implicitly, and sometimes explicitly, over programme-planning and by giving the impression that an arts event or venue has been subsidized solely by the business corporation, which may, in fact, have contributed only marginally to its production and maintenance. In addition to functioning as an ostentatious leisure perk for managers and cheap promotional advertising, there is the further problem of rapid turnover in business sponsorship for the arts. However, much public subsidy today has been tagged to the willingness and capacity of arts and cultural organizations generally to attract private funding and to having a properly worked-out business plan.

Business sponsorship, not only in the arts but also in sport, education and broadcasting, invokes all sorts of problems concerning the relationship between the primary activity and the business motives of the sponsor (Shaw 1993). Sponsorship is never innocent or disinterested: it is done for purposes of advertising and public relations. Chin-tao Wu (1998 and 2002) studied the growth of arts sponsorship in the USA and Britain over the closing decades of the twentieth century which led to 'the unprecedented intervention of business in contemporary culture' (1998: 28). Such sponsorship is aimed at increasing sales by reaching the right kind of consumer, especially the highly educated and comparatively well-off audiences for classical music concerts and opera, who also form the majority of visitors to art museums. More diffusely, arts sponsorship is concerned with fostering an 'enlightened' corporate image for political purposes, particularly if the corporation is vulnerable to criticism. This has been especially so for tobacco manufacturers, most notably Philip Morris in the USA. Art bestows a sense of distinction upon the corporate sponsor and perhaps its products as well, even including cigarettes. Corporate involvement has affected the very ambience of public art museums in which the logos of sponsors are displayed prominently, where galleries are named after a sponsoring company and 'exclusive' events are held for executives, corporate friends, celebrities, opinion leaders and politicians. As Wu notes, 'The "PR-ization of art museums" by corporate capital is clearly articulated in the language they now speak' (1998: 43). So, the Institute for Contemporary Arts on the Mall in London acknowledges the generosity of Toshiba, and Tate Britain has a Nomura Room named after the Japanese investment bank that put up £1.5 million to refurbish it. Figures like the Tate's director, Nicholas Serota, are not just curators of the public's art but cultural entrepreneurs fusing together art and business in order to make ends meet when state funding is deemed insufficient to maintain standards and expand operations. On the opening of Tate Modern in May 2000, Serota expressed 'our deepest gratitude for supporting our vision' to 'public and private donors' (Blazwick and Wilson 2000).

In his 1993 McTaggart Lecture at the Edinburgh Television Festival, the late Dennis Potter (1994) – who in his day was Britain's leading television dramatist – attacked the 'new managerialism' at the BBC. He entitled the lecture, 'Occupying Powers'. This sense of the public sector being occupied by alien power had become intense and widespread by the early 1990s. Potter virtually spat out the following words at Marmaduke Hussey, then chair of the BBC governors, and his director general, John Birt: 'You pretend to be the commercial business that you cannot be'. Such 'pretence' was not confined to the public sector of arts and broadcasting. It is there in education, health and in the offices of national and local government. This is 'the new public management', described by Andrew Gamble (1994a [1988]: 135) as 'a set of ideas for managing all institutions in the public sector and involving devices such as internal markets, contracting out, tendering and financial incentives'. By the 1990s, such devices had become very familiar and were regarded as necessary for the effective management of everyday life in British society. The new public management was not established, however, without controversy, most particularly with regard to the National Health Service (NHS). On changes in the administration of the NHS, John Clarke and Janet Newman (1993: 428) identify 'managerialization' as an ideological discourse 'which aims to make management the driving force of a successful society'. **Managerialization** was not confined to the NHS. It spread rapidly across the public sector, including public-sector arts and media, the underlying assumption being that public agencies should function like private businesses. Clarke and Newman (1997) argue that the managerialization of the British state and public sector is not only an organizational phenomenon but also a linguistic phenomenon, an ideological discourse. It is all-encompassing yet contradictory: 'What is most striking about the processes of change around the welfare state is the pervasive importance – and elusiveness – of the language used to describe, explain and justify them' (1997: vii). For instance, 'demand' for healthcare replaced medical 'need'.

The ur-text for the managerialization of the public sector is the American book, *Reinventing Government*, by David Osborne and Ted Gaebler (1992), which British as well as American politicians, not only on the Right, took to quoting approvingly. It is said to have been hugely influential at the higher echelons of both the Democratic and Labour parties (Painter 1994). Osborne and Gaebler are disciples of the renowned management gurus Peter Drucker and Tom Peters. They claim, however, that their managerial principles are inferred primarily from the practical experiments of US city governments in response to the 'tax revolts' of the late 1970s and, more generally, derive from the structural transformations that were brought about by the transition to a 'post-industrial' society. Under tight budgetary constraints and faced with radically changed economic circumstances, governments have had to become much more 'enterprising' than they were during what Osborne and Gaebler call the 'bureaucratic-industrial' era. Their book is typical of the rhetoric of management texts. It presents a set of simple and supposedly irrefutable propositions that are driven home through didactic repetition and to each of which a chapter is devoted. The 'ten principles' that 'entrepreneurial governments' focus upon are, according to Osborne and Gaebler (1992: 19–20):

1. *Competition* between service providers;
2. *empowerment* of citizens;
3. *outputs* – not inputs;
4. *missions* – not rules and regulations;
5. *customer* choice;
6. *prevention* of problems before they emerge;
7. *earning* money;
8. *decentralization* of authority and participatory management;
9. *market* mechanisms;
10. *catalyzing* all sectors – public, private, and voluntary.

Osborne and Gaebler denied they were asking for government to be 'run like a business'. It is difficult, though, to see quite how they could justify such a denial. Their ideas were clearly formed by the practical discourses of the most dynamic business corporations in the USA: theirs is a capitalist Utopia in which the techniques of upbeat and 'postmodern' capitalism hold sway. The affinity of the American 'reinvention of government' with the **marketization** policies of successive Conservative governments in Britain during the 1980s and 1990s was plainly evident. Just as notable is the affinity with the policies of the New Labour government that came to power in 1997. The suits with their management bibles did not go away, whether at the level of elected government or anywhere else throughout the public or private sectors of British governance.

Market reasoning and public-sector marketization represent a pervasive neo-liberal ideology that frames the policies of social-democratic governments just as much as – and sometimes more than – conservative administrations. 'The myth of the market' casts a magical spell over the contemporary imagination, producing the dominant narrative and, indeed, drama of the social world. As Jeremy Seabrook notes:

Like all profound faiths, it is so widespread and unshakeable that it remains blind to all the noxious and baleful side-effects of its workings in the world: it does not see that the most basic human needs remain unanswered, and it coexists with the most grotesque excesses. Humanity continues to be ravaged, either by pitiful insufficiency or by deliberate superfluity. We have only to glance at the financial pages of the newspapers and examine the language in which the money or commodities markets are described, to see at once to what degree these have been endowed with human, even superhuman characteristics. Markets are nervous or jittery, they are capricious or fickle, or they are more settled, calm. They are sensitive, hesitant or expectant. Market sentiment is anxiously sought; its verdict awaited. Its response eagerly anticipated. Sometimes it sounds as though the language of chivalry was being deployed; at least, we are in the presence of patriarchal representations of women. We learn that the pound sterling has had a good day, the dollar is ailing, the French franc is sinking fast – bulletins issued on the state of health of a dying monarch. If the markets have taken on human attributes, this is not simply an attempt to make comprehensible what are seen as unbiddable processes, but a mode of assimilating these to a force of nature, even a reflection of the divine will on earth.

(1990: 11–12)

Seabrook alerts us to an irrational faith in the market, representing not so much the proven laws of economics, a fully rational and scientific worldview, but hopes and illusions. That is not the view, of course, of those who assert – and try to substantiate – 'the truth' of market forces.

Tyler Cowen's (1998) *In Praise of Commercial Culture* makes out a powerfully optimistic case for the positive effects of market relations and the profit motive in specifically cultural fields, and against a long line of 'cultural pessimists' from Left and Right who believe that authentic culture is undermined by commercialization. It is not only mass-popular culture that has flourished in the marketplace but also high art itself, most tellingly, according to Cowen. Capitalism is good for culture, providing markets for the products of the imagination and bringing about technological innovations that are used by creative agents. Modern state intervention and public patronage on the European model, however, have been rationalized as a means of making up for market failure. On the contrary, Cowen argues, the market has not failed culture:

Music and the arts have been moving away from government funding since the Middle Ages. The Renaissance, the Enlightenment, the nineteenth century romantic movement, and twentieth century modernism all brought art further into the market sphere. Today, most of the important work in film, music, literature, painting and sculpture is sold as a commodity. Contemporary art is capitalist art, and the history of art has been a history of struggle to establish markets. These trends will not be reversed in any foreseeable course for the current world, regardless of our opinion of government funding for the arts. Most countries in the world are not contemplating reversions to socialism.

(1998: 36)

For Cowen, it is a serious question whether or not government funding for the arts should continue at all, particularly in view of the American 'culture wars' when right-wing moralists attacked what they thought of as publicly funded obscenity. Major targets were the homo-erotic photography of Robert Mapplethorpe and the apparent blasphemy of Andres Serrano's photograph of a cheap crucifix immersed in the artist's own urine, *Piss Christ*. In fact, the money disbursed by the National Endowment for the Arts in the USA is relatively insignificant and much less consequential than tax deductions for contributing to not-for-profit cultural organizations and the effective subsidy for art and artists provided by the university system. Cowen himself is comparatively liberal in aesthetic taste – not wishing to censor – and he is neo-liberal in economics. In his view, 'The state does best in promoting the arts when it acts as simply another customer, patron, or employer, rather than as a bureaucracy with a public mandate' (1998: 37).

Such reasoning has increasingly framed public cultural policy in Europe itself, where the state has played a much greater role in arts and media provision than in the USA. In the late 1990s the French neologism, *desetatization*, was translated into English as 'privatization'. At a Circle Round Table in Amsterdam in 1997, connected to the Council of Europe, seven types of 'privatization' relevant to public-sector culture were identified:

1. *divestiture* – selling off public property;
2. *free transfer of property rights* – giving it away;
3. *change of the state organization into a more independent organization* – that is, autonomization;
4. the *agency model* of giving *internally more discrete power* to the public manager;
5. *contracting out* – tendering by private companies for parts of the work such as catering and cleaning;
6. *use of volunteers* – the deployment of free labour;
7. *private funding* – indivdual patronage and corporate sponsorship of public bodies and activities.

(McGuigan 1997b: 227)

The problem here is that not all of these forms of organizational change are, strictly speaking, 'privatization'. The first two – divestiture and free transfer of property rights – are quite definitely so, and the fifth – contracting out – is partial privatization. Arguably, the rest are not accurately described as privatization at all. Instead, in the main, they represent mechanisms for achieving greater managerial efficiency, public-private partnership, relative autonomy from the state and, perhaps, increased civic democracy and accountability. What, for instance, did the 'privatization' of

Amsterdam's Rijksmuseum in the 1990s actually mean? The state did not sell off the art collection or the building. It set up an independent foundation funded by public money. Employees were no longer classified civil servants and a new style of management influenced, no doubt, by the *modus operandi* of private business was established. A more accurate term than 'privatization' for naming such a development is 'autonomization', bringing about a constitutional arrangement similar to Britain's 'intermediary bodies' in public arts and media. The intention may well have been to make the Rijksmuseum operate more efficiently according to market principles and less inefficiently according to the tradition of state bureaucracy in the Netherlands, but it did not cease to be a public body. It could just as well be argued that organizational change at the Rijksmuseum might have brought it closer to civil society: devolving power and enabling better opportunities for public participation in the policy-making arena, rather than delivering it to the free play of market forces in the cultural field.

As Oliver Bennett (1995) has argued, there is indeed a genuine problem in justifying public cultural policy and subsidy today, particularly in face of the claims made for the beneficence of the cultural market which, in many cases, are difficult to counter. The rationale for public cultural policy has to be reconstructed, in Bennett's view. This cannot be achieved, however, by simply mimicking the market. Yet, it may just be too late, if Jeremy Rifkin's (2000) argument concerning the rise of 'cultural capitalism' is right. Following critics such as Herbert Schiller (1989), Rifkin suggests that culture has become entirely incorporated into capitalism and the cultural commons have been enclosed. It is one thing to observe how the public sector has been overcome by market reasoning: it is quite another and yet more consequential thing to note that cultural production and consumption in general are at the leading edge of 'post-industrial' capitalism, as does Rifkin.

Communicating

Inspired by Jürgen Habermas, Nicholas Garnham has remarked,

> the question of the Public Sphere now occupies a central position on the media studies agenda. In the face of the demonstrable crisis in the forms and practices of democracy in Western capitalist polities, and of attempts to reconstruct forms of democratic politics in the ex-socialist countries, it has taken over the central role previously occupied by the dominant ideology or hegemony.
>
> (1995: 376)

From this point of view, then, cultural analysis becomes less about the critique of ideological distortion and hegemonic struggle and becomes more concerned with questioning undemocratic arrangements and figuring out the conditions for democratic communications, culture and policy.

Interest in the theory and practice of the public sphere – the political space for rational-critical debate that, in principle, has consequences for policy – is closely connected to the revived notion of civil society – the social space of freedom and solidarity. They are both ideal types: the public sphere referring to the conditions of argumentation and representation; civil society, contrasted with the state but not reducible to the market, being somewhere in between. As John Keane (1998: 31) defines it, 'civil society . . . is a community of actors whose legally inscribed patterns of association are voluntary, which means that its members are equipped with the power to interpret and to transform the social and political structures within which they interact'. In fact, a great many arts and cultural organizations, even in the USA, are in this civil-society space, 'the third sector', which is neither of the state nor of the market and where goals are sought that are 'not for profit'.

On a broader front, the best hope, according to theorists of radical democracy, is the reconstruction and further development of what was a progressive bourgeois but extremely contradictory discursive formation, in the sense that it did not measure up to its own principles, dating from the eighteenth and nineteenth centuries. The public sphere, so defined, declined in the twentieth century, but there are recent signs of revival (Habermas 1992; McGuigan 2002). A revived public sphere, despite arguments to the contrary, would seem a long way from the anarchistic delight in the liberating powers of 'virtual community' on the Net (Rheingold 1995). Yet, when *Wired* put Tom Paine (1985 [1791, 1792]), the eighteenth-century theorist of human rights and democratic republicanism, on the cover of its first British edition, the connection was there to be seen. The British version of *Wired* failed because its American agenda was only thinly veiled. That does not, however, alter general claims concerning the virtualization of radical democracy, the way in which political aspirations thus engendered have been so much associated with the magical powers of computer networking and new media developments in 'the information age'.

There is a perennial issue in dispute concerning Habermas's (1989 [1962]) original account of the rise and fall of the bourgeois public sphere and its present-day manifestations: is the public sphere actual or ideal? (Calhoun 1992). For Habermas, it is both. There is evidence that the public sphere has existed in the past. Rational-critical debate among acknowledged equals – the public sphere myth – was a constitutive feature of emergent modernity in Western Europe and North America from the eighteenth century, mediating the bourgeois revolution and subsequent political emancipation – including of the working class, women and eventually colonial subjects. So, the public sphere mediated the emergence of the liberal-democratic polity of capitalism. The original public sphere of the European and American middle classes may have been undermined subsequently by increasingly manipulative communications, heavily commercialized media entertainment and news, advertising and public relations. Habermas was, however, to revise the pessimistic conclusion he reached over forty years ago in *The Structural Transformation of the Public Sphere*. From a Habermasian perspective on contemporary culture and politics, the public sphere, in one form or another, remains an actuality, albeit distorted in many respects, and may still function as a normative guide to and refreshment of democracy in the future.

Something similar can be said of Habermas's much more abstract theoretical treatment of the recursive conditions for satisfactory communication in general, which he has described as 'undistorted communication' (1970) or 'the ideal speech situation' (1979 [1976]). For Habermas (1990 [1983]), the validity claims that are made and subjected routinely to critical reflection before reaching agreement in everyday symbolic interaction demonstrate the human capacity for mutual understanding. Such claims to validity may be to do with, first, agreeing upon the *objective* nature of the world ('truth'); second, *inter-subjective* agreement may be sought between people regarding a shared state of affairs and what should be done about it ('truthfulness'); third, someone else's *subjective* feelings may need appreciation ('sincerity'). To give a simple example, in the form of a philosophical cliché: the irreparably broken and worm-ridden table is made of heavy wood (objective assessment). It will take the two of us to carry it out of the house (inter-subjective agreement). The table invokes sad memories for one of us but not necessarily so for the other (appreciation of sincere feeling). Without such reasoning, removing an old table that is no longer useful would not happen. Orientation towards mutual understanding is necessary for achieving the very simplest of cooperative tasks – like getting rid of a rotten piece of furniture – and, also, very complex acts in the social world – like electing or, indeed, getting rid of a government.

Habermas's notions of the public sphere and the orientation to mutual understanding in everyday communication are both ideal and practical. They are part of an ethical discourse which not only evinces what ought to be – a dialogic democracy – but which is sustained anyway by the routines of ordinary communicative interaction. Such a point is important to stress since Habermasian **discourse ethics** is often dismissed as 'unrealistic', as starry-eyed idealism: it is contended that people simply do not carry on in such a reasonable manner. However, it may be just as unrealistic to assume that there is no orientation to mutual understanding, that all human relationships are irredeemably conducted as power struggle, characterized by coercion and manipulation, which is a nihilistic world view of the war of all against all. To be sure, these are salient characteristics of actual life under competitive and hierarchical conditions. Quite possibly, they may never be eliminated from social interaction and structured relationships. However, the orientation towards mutual understanding, which is also a mundane feature of life, for the most practical reasons, is a perpetual challenge to oppressive and cynical ways of carrying on.

The general argument about discourse ethics connects up with Habermas's (1987 [1981]) distinction between 'life world' and 'system'. Communicative action to achieve mutual understanding in the life world is an ordinary aspect of social existence which exceeds mere instrumentality. In contrast, the systemic imperatives of the state and capital operate typically according to an instrumental rationality in strategic pursuit of predefined goals, not according to a communicative rationale for debating and agreeing goals as a prelude to action. The central problem of contemporary societies, Habermas argued in the 1980s, is 'the colonization of the life world' by instrumental reason and the resistance that is waged with the communicative resources of everyday life. It is easy to dismiss such a formulation as idealistic and romantic.

Habermas's reasoning, however, is directly relevant to discussion of cultural policy and, if nothing else, it indicates why many interested specifically in 'culture' prefer not to talk of cultural policy. To talk of cultural policy is to run the risk of potentially instrumentalizing culture, of reducing it to something other than what it is. The discourses of state and market, in effect, treat culture instrumentally, to make it, for example, a means of simply embellishing the nation-state (Williams 1984), or, as I have suggested, by reducing all value to exchange value by applying market principles to everything in a global cultural economy.

The notion of civil society is closely associated with the historical phenomenon of the bourgeois public sphere. It has been a means of checking the powers of the state while simultaneously creating the conditions for market relations to develop, which is very much how civil society was imagined in Eastern Europe in the late 1980s and early 1990s. The paradoxical problem is, however, that the civilizing force of rational-critical debate – what the public sphere is about – has contributed historically to a liberalization of the economy that may eventually threaten civil society itself as the space between state power and exclusively market relations. In our present historical conjuncture, it is again 'the market' which is the main encroachment upon the life world of civil society.

To speak of 'the public sphere', 'civil society' and 'the life world' is to speak of phenomena less immediately tangible than the powers of the nation-state or the capitalist market. Yet these remain concepts – though not necessarily named as such – that animate alternative and opposition practices. For instance, Nancy Fraser (1992) has spoken of 'the subaltern counter public' of American feminism with its communicative networks and its cultural and political impact on the system. Paul Gilroy (1993) has spoken of the public sphere Diaspora of 'the Black Atlantic'. Douglas Kellner (1995) has urged critical intellectuals to use new media and information technologies in the struggle to revivify the public sphere under late-modern conditions. Generally, social and cultural critique is dependent upon some preferred notion of a public sphere or civil discourse that is oriented towards mutual understanding as a critical measure of democratic blockage and as a practical check on systemic abuse of democracy.

In his major work of the 1990s, *Between Facts and Norms*, Habermas returned to the theme of the public sphere. There he says:

The public sphere is a social phenomenon just as elementary as action, actor, association, or collectivity . . . The public sphere cannot be conceived of as an institution and certainly not as an organization. It is not even a framework of norms . . . The public sphere can best be described as a network for communicating information and points of view (i.e. opinions expressing affirmative or negative attitudes); the streams of communication are, in process, filtered in such a way that they coalesce into bundles of topically specified *public* opinions.

(Habermas 1996 [1992]: 360)

Placing less emphasis now on the colonization thesis, although not discarding it, Habermas stresses the 'sluicegate' role of the public sphere between life-world concerns and systems of governmental administration and corporate business (see Carleheden and Gabriel 1996). Habermas talks of 'the great issues of the last decades', including the arms race, the risks of nuclear energy and scientific applications such as genetic engineering, damage to the environment, famine and global economic inequality, feminism, increased migration and multiculturalism. He says, 'Hardly any of these were *initially* brought up by exponents of the state apparatus, large organizations, or functional systems' (1996 [1992]: 381). The key players have been critical intellectuals, social movements and new subcultures.

In reviving the notion of the public sphere, Garnham (1992) has argued that it needs to be rethought on a global scale. He quite rightly points out that the public sphere originally functioned to articulate communicative and cultural rights with the rise of the modern nation-state. However, the growing power of transnational corporations, especially in communications and culture, threatening the authority of the nation-state, means that the public sphere itself must be reconstituted globally in order to check the undemocratic operations of capitalism. This argument suggests the need for a universal public sphere, not confined to the citizenship of countries but enunciated in terms of global citizenship. Garnham is surely right to argue that transnational forces undermine national public spheres and that a new internationalism is required. His argument is out of synch, though, with most recent thinking on the public sphere, which stresses its multiplication and particularization rather than unification and universality.

John Keane (1998) has usefully clarified what is at stake by distinguishing between three types of public sphere: *micro*, *meso* and *macro*. The creation of micro public spheres is a feature of social and cultural movement politics, as Fraser noted with regard to feminism. Of necessity, so-called 'single-issue campaigns', on environmental problems and so forth, involve coordinating communications and spaces of participation for deciding actions to be taken. Such practices, which are by no means novelties of the information age, are aided greatly by newer information and communication technologies. Keane also notes less formal micro public sphere developments, such as children's use of computing and playing video games as intuitive engagement and interaction with the dynamics of meaning and power.

'Meso-public spheres are those spaces of controversy about power that encompass millions of people watching, listening or reading across vast distances. They are mainly coextensive with the territorial state' (Keane 1998: 174). In this respect, Keane sees television talk and audience participation shows as an aspect of a popular public sphere, somewhat differently from the 'serious' news agenda and great public issues that concern the more solemn Habermasians. For Keane, it is mistaken to complain about the exclusion of popular voices from public discourse when forms exist that are all about letting 'the people' speak on issues of urgent concern, which are usually to do with 'private' and personal matters of relationships and everyday conduct. This is an argument that had already been put forcefully and with evidential substantiation by Sonia Livingstone and Peter Lunt (1991). It has also been applied to the charitable phenomenon of Comic Relief in which famine in Africa is the object of popular attention in Britain, mediated by entertainment (McGuigan 1998a).

Keane's category of macro public spheres has affinities with Garnham's 'one-world' view, but here also it is stated in the plural rather than in the singular. It takes in continental formations – associated with, say, the European Union – and global formations, linked to the United Nations. The 'time-space compression' (Harvey 1989) brought about by satellite communications and information technologies is not only a feature of global media, information and cultural business. It also fosters something like a global public sphere, so that atrocities like the Tiananmen Square massacre of dissident Chinese students in 1989 and various acts of war and genocide since then are instantly seen and thought about around the Earth.

The three types of public sphere are not entirely separate from one another. For instance, the identity politics of resistance, which would be located initially within Keane's category of micro public spheres, of necessity, in Manuel Castells's (1997a) analysis, must link up with macro public spheres. Such politics needs to capture the attention of the world, as classically in the Zapatistas' resistance to the North American Free Trade Agreement since the mid-1990s and, subsequently, anti-capitalist protests in London, Seattle, Prague, Genoa and elsewhere around the turn of the Millennium.

Public-sphere issues are of much broader significance, of course, than questions specifically concerning culture as signifying practice and cultural policy. However, the politics of culture is not marginal to the operations of power in general or 'the civilizing process', in Norbert Elias's (1994 [1939]) term. Art, sport and present-day media controversies occupy a similar historical space politically, says Keane:

> Music, opera, sport, painting and dancing were among the forms of communication propelling the growth of civil society and public life, and there is therefore no principled reason, aside from philosophical prejudice, why their late-twentieth century counterparts – the rambunctiousness of MTV's annual video awards, the simulated uproar of *Ricki Lake* shows or the hypertext of digital games – should not be understood as legitimate potential media of power conflicts.
>
> (1998: 185)

John Keane holds a rather sanguine view of the scope and opportunities for democratic communication in contemporary culture and media, best illustrated by his argument that talk and audience-participation shows on television, however manipulative and exploitative of ordinary people, are a public-sphere site. Others concerned with citizenship and cultural process are much less sanguine and more critical. Civil discourse on culture most typically finds something wrong with 'the culture' that needs rectifying.

For instance, Kalle Lasn's (1999) manifesto for the cultural politics of the anti-capitalist movement, *Culture Jam: The Uncooling of America*, begins by itemizing the faults of American culture, as follows:

> *America is no longer a country. It's a multitrillion-dollar brand.*
> *American culture is no longer created by the people.*
> *A free, authentic life is no longer possible in America today.*
> *Our mass media dispense a kind of Huxleyan 'soma'.*
> *American cool is a global pandemic.*
> *The Earth can no longer support the lifestyle of the cool-hunting American-style consumer.*
>
> (Lasn 1999: xii–xiv)

The remedy for the American cultural malaise, according to Lasn, is 'a rebranding strategy, a social demarketing campaign unfolding over four seasons' (xvi). In the autumn season, the question is asked: 'What does it mean when our lives and culture are no longer shaped by nature, but by an electronic mass media environment of our own creation?' (xvii). In the winter, the 'media-consumer trance' of 'our postmodern era' is criticized and a further question posed: 'Can spontaneity and authenticity be restored?' In the spring, the question is put: 'Is oppositional culture still possible?' In the summer, 'the American revolutionary impulse reignites'. All of this – theory and practice – is meant to lead to 'a *detournement* – a perspective-jarring turnabout in your everyday life'. *Culture Jam* is a book inspired by the critique of 'the society of the spectacle' and subversive tactics of French situationism (Debord 1994 [1967]). It also derives inspiration from the USA's own revolutionary tradition of independence and participatory democracy. It wishes to challenge the value and values of the most powerful culture and society in the world, in effect, the American consumerist way of life and its global reach.

Culture jamming is a form of 'semiological guerrilla warfare', in Umberto Eco's (1987a [1967]) phrase. As Eco argued in the 1960s, 'Not long ago, if you wanted to seize political power in a country, you had merely to control the army and the police. [. . .] Today a country belongs to the person who controls communications' (135). Culture jammers are unlikely, however, to take control of the communications media in the USA. Their tactics in producing 'subvertisements' that attack capitalism and in anti-media campaigning generally are those of guerrilla skirmishing in the space of signification, which is unlikely to bring the whole edifice of postmodern culture and consumerism tumbling down. The battle is conducted at the level of signification, ridiculing the dominant system of meanings in the aim of rendering 'cool' uncool. In a volatile culture, where fashion is constantly overturning itself and sudden reversals of meaning occur, counter-discourse may act like a virus entering the symbolic bloodstream of the body politic. Well, that's the theory, anyway.

More respectable, though perhaps yet more marginal in terms of policy impact, is the Cultural Environment Movement (CEM), founded in the mid-1990s and led by the distinguished media academic George Gerbner. Gerbner (1995) is well known for seeking to transcend the usual terms of the media/violence debate. It has often been argued that media representations of violence may cause impressionable young people to behave violently. The 'effects' argument is repeated loudly around horrific incidents of murder. It is claimed that the youthful perpetrators of death and mayhem have been influenced by what they have seen in films, on television or through the Internet to kill, say, their classmates. Cultural and media studies typically challenge such a reductive explanation (for instance, Barker and Petley 1997). Representations of violence in fictional forms are exactly that: fiction. Children and adolescents are perfectly well aware of the fictiveness and sheer fantasy of such representations. Media violence may have all sorts of functions that are not harmful in the sense of instigating actual violence, for instance serving as a means of releasing pent-up aggression without hurting others. Dissidents within the cultural and media studies camp, however, claim that the critique of simplistic effects has gone too far. The media must have some effect; otherwise businesses would not spend so much on advertising (Miller and Philo 1996). Also, it is mistaken to deny the genuine concerns of parents about their children's media use (Cunningham 1992).

Basing his argument on longitudinal research on American television since the 1960s, Gerbner (1995) says that the effect of media violence is not so much to cause real acts of copycat violence. Instead, with the rising body count in programmes, a 'mean world syndrome' is cultivated, creating a sense of fear and foreboding in many ordinary television viewers. This has consequences for public civility. City streets are seen on television to be places of great danger, and in the USA in particular, though not only there, racial danger. The evacuation of 'dangerous' public space, as a result, becomes a self-fulfilling prophecy. Safely holed up in the home watching images of violence, the television viewer, frightened of strangers, embraces private consumption at a distance from public citizenship.

In his manifesto for the CEM, Gerbner (1996 and 1998a) talks of a cultural environment that is constructed by overpowering corporations, the conglomerates that control the American entertainment industry and especially the electronic media. They are, in Gerbner's words, 'our private "Ministry of Culture" '. The cultural environment frames the social world for people, providing stories about how things work and are constituted. These stories are dominated by representations of excessive consumption so that the whole cycle of commodity production and circulation is kept going. It is not just about consumption, however; it is also about deeply questionable representations of life. Gerbner talks of 'distortions of the democratic process' that

> include the promotion of practices that drug, hurt, poison, and kill thousands every day; portrayals that dehumanize and stigmatize; cults of violence that desensitize, terrorize and brutalize; the growing siege mentality of our cities; the

drift toward ecological suicide; the silent crumbling of our infrastructure; widen-
ing resource gaps and the most glaring inequalities of the industrial world; the
costly neglect of vital institutions such as public education, health care and the
arts; make-believe image politicians corrupting the electoral process.

(1998a: 2)

Gerbner's catalogue of cultural incivility and social degradation may be an accurate
selection from the representations of contemporary culture and the comparative
neglect of serious issues in the mainstream media of the USA, but it is not, strictly
speaking, new. Keane (1998: 149) remarks, for instance, 'Contrary to the claims of
contemporary campaigners against violence in the media, the packaging and marketing of violence as entertainment is an old phenomenon traceable to the middle of the
eighteenth century.' He goes on to say, 'Pay-TV sexual murders, Mortal Kombat video
games, vomit-provoking splatter films' and the rest recall the 'magazine ghost stories,
horrid melodramas, newspaper sensationalism and the Gothic literature and Grave-
yard poets of the period of Enlightenment'. Modern civility is supposed to eliminate
violence from everyday life. Yet, it returns with a vengeance through popular culture.
To explain what is going on, Keane draws on Freud's concept of the uncanny, a psychic
mechanism for dealing with the inevitability of personal death, the sense of which is
suppressed yet, nevertheless, continually erupts in various forms of symbolic displacement such as the impersonal deluge of media violence. While recognizing that the
uncanny may be a universal characteristic of the human psyche, Keane also seeks to
historicize it. In modern society

there develops a dialectic of civility in which the visible reduction and practical
removal of various forms of violence from civil society coincides with the height-
ened media visibility and sensuous appreciation of simulated or virtual violence
by the citizens of that society, who get qualitatively less solace from worn-out
platitudes about salvation and the afterlife.

(1998: 151)

The CEM intervention in the 1990s may have been seeking to deal with psychic
and historical forces that are uncontrollable, quite apart from trying to negotiate
with equally uncontrollable business interests. It made an 'appeal to Hollywood' to
establish a 'voluntary code' for regaining the 'health of our culture'. This was signed
by ex-presidents Jimmy Carter and Gerald Ford; cultural conservative Michael
Medved, author of *Hollywood vs. America* (1992); radical democrat Gerbner himself; religious leaders and various campaigning organizations and individuals from
across the American political spectrum. Although he is sceptical and 'realistic', Keane
(1998: 156) does not deny the value of such efforts: 'The cultivation of *public spheres
of controversy*, in which violent exercise of power against others is resisted by
civilian-citizens' efforts to monitor it non-violently, is a basic condition for reducing
incivility.'

The Habermasian idealism of the CEM is quite extraordinary, trying to achieve media reform on a consensual basis among very different interests and tendencies without advocating censorship. Its six aims are as follows:

1. Building a new coalition and constituency;
2. opposing domination;
3. cooperating with groups in other countries that work for the integrity and independence of their cultural decision-making;
4. joining forces with creative workers in the media;
5. promoting media literacy, awareness, critical viewing and reading, and other media education efforts;
6. placing cultural policy issues on the social-political agenda.

(Gerbner 1998a: 2–3)

Unrealistic though such a cultural policy discourse may seem, none the less, it enables the articulation of widespread discontent with the dominant forces in contemporary culture. From a democratic point of view, vital questions of communications, culture and policy cannot be left solely to the decision-making of unaccountable corporations and the free play of 'market forces'. Civil-society movements and campaigning organizations are the sources of rational-critical debate in late-modern societies. They may tilt at windmills by asking Hollywood, for instance, to clean up its act. Gerbner (1998b) himself has no delusions, however: he believes that cultural diversity and the civilizing process must be mediated through democratic government. Living in the USA, he probably has too rosy a perception of the European tradition of public-sector arts and media. However, legitimate government operating with popular authority is necessary for both the regulation of cultural capitalism and the preservation of the progressive impulses of civil society.

Conclusion

In this chapter, I have identified three general discourses of cultural policy – state, market and civil/communicative – and traced their historical variants and developments. The crucial development in the recent period has been the ideological de-legitimization of state intervention and public-sector arts and media. They persist but with an uncertain and poorly defended rationale. Even where they persist, however, their operations are reconfigured increasingly by market reasoning so that publicly funded organizations must behave like private businesses, thereby further undercutting their own legitimacy. Neo-liberalism has been in the ascendancy, the assumption being that market mechanisms are the superior means for allocating resources, producing and circulating cultural products, giving the customer what he or she is said to want. However, customers are also citizens, some of whom may not be entirely satisfied with the prevailing state of affairs. Civil-society movements and campaigning organizations arise from such dissatisfaction. These forces, spanning a range of politics and ideology, put issues on governmental agendas that would not otherwise be there. In the field of culture and cultural policy, civil society and the public sphere of rational-critical debate represent the possibilities of challenge and resistance to corporations that are only accountable to their shareholders and governments that submit too readily to corporate interests. Culture jamming and the Cultural Environment Movement are examples of civilizing discourse – revolutionary and reformist – which, against great odds, seeks to counter governmental abrogation of responsibility and unrestrained cultural capitalism. The fact is that all three discourses and the forces they represent – state, market and civil/communicative – remain in play, albeit with differently ordered powers at their respective disposal.

3

CULTURAL POLICY PROPER AND AS DISPLAY

Introduction

Raymond Williams once made a distinction in passing between cultural policy 'proper' and cultural policy as display. He began by noting that cultural policy as display – though, by definition, highly visible – normally goes unnoticed as a matter specifically of public policy in the cultural arena.

> There is one aspect of the State in relation to culture which is almost always forgotten because we absorb it so very early that we can hardly recognize it at all. It is worth remembering that the State has always had this double sense: it is not only the central organ of power, but of *display* – indeed often specifically the public pomp of a particular social order. You don't have to look far in any particular society to see a culture which is not recognized as a cultural policy or an arts policy specifically, but which is culturally concerned with display.
>
> (1984: 3)

This was the Victorian commentator on Britain's unwritten constitution, Walter Bagehot's 'theatrical element of the constitution'. In the British case, much of the state's ritual display is to do with representing the mutually reinforcing relation between the monarchy and parliamentary democracy.

Commenting upon the Coronation of Queen Elizabeth II in 1953, Edward Shils and Michael Young (1953) had given a Durkheimian analysis of the symbolic importance of such stately occasions for articulating social order in the nation and maintaining political stability. Shils and Young's argument was subjected to a devastating critique for its conservative complacency. Norman Birnbaum (1955) emphasized instead the role of the British monarchy in masking over tensions, inequality and conflict within the territory of a supposedly unified nation-state. A further comment on the 1953

Coronation, going beyond the terms of the original debate occasioned by Birnbaum's critique of Shils and Young, needs to be made: it was a televisual event. The Coronation actually inaugurated popular television in Britain. Many people bought their first television set in order to watch the Coronation and those without a set crowded into the homes of those who did have one (McGuigan 2003a). Subsequently, the sale of televisions shot up dramatically.

In a curious way the funeral of Diana, Princess of Wales, in September 1997 recalled the Coronation. The recently elected New Labour government gave her a 'national funeral'. Diana was not allowed a state funeral because of her divorce from the Royal Family. Nevertheless, the funeral became a kind of postmodern re-run of the Coronation, viewed with great enthusiasm on television around the world. Even though she was dead, Diana was the perfect icon for New Labour's 'cool' yet 'caring' Britannia, since she was so much more 'modern' – or, should we say, 'postmodern' – and popular than the Royals themselves (McGuigan 2000).

Such events, then, represent 'the public pomp of a particular social order', in Williams's words. British ceremonies may be peculiarly arch, even when given a postmodern and populist gloss as in the case of the funeral, but all countries do it in one form or another to construct the 'imagined community' of the nation-state (Anderson, 1991 [1983]), including the most modern, the USA. This sense of cultural policy as display – the ritual symbolization of nationhood and state power – goes further by also encroaching upon the terrain of something like cultural policy proper. Around 'heritage', Williams remarked (1984: 3), 'the preferred orthodox idea of the nation is extended to areas of genuine artistic practice'. In Britain this is manifest in nomenclature, for instance by the *Royal* Shakespeare Company and the *Royal* National Theatre, with the 'Royal' only recently added in the latter case.

Williams makes a very interesting observation by noting 'how often in arguments about public funding of the arts people mention tourism rather early'. The cultural heritage is on display for tourists, then, with obvious pecuniary considerations. In this sense, however, the arts are not only about earning tourist revenue. As Williams remarks further:

> Indeed not only in the extension to the arts as tourism, but very specifically now, the arts as business entertainment: this is a very conscious policy in the greater metropolitan institutions. And it's a significant overlap with some versions of sponsorship of the arts by the larger private companies. Indeed, in this sense an arts policy of a certain kind turns out when examined to be not a policy for the arts but a policy for embellishing, representing, making more effective a particular social order or certain preferred features of it.
>
> (1984: 3)

So, the general purpose of cultural policy as display is to embellish the prevailing social order, which is hardly surprising. Yet more significantly, Williams identifies two sub-categories of cultural policy as display. First, there is *national aggrandizement*, symbolized, as we have seen, by pomp and ceremony. Second, there is *economic reductionism*, represented in business propositions of one kind or another which, as we shall see, are increasingly pronounced in rationalizing public cultural investment, including 'leverage' for economic growth and promoting the interests of corporations.

Neither of these does Williams regard as cultural policy 'proper'. They distort rather than enhance the proper – or ideal – role of the state in the cultural arena, which should be to aid the democratic practices of art, culture and media. Having identified two senses of cultural policy as display, the second perhaps unexpectedly material rather than symbolic, Williams goes on to identify three senses of cultural policy 'proper' in the state/culture relation.

The first sense of cultural policy 'proper' is characterized by the system of *public patronage of the arts* set up in Britain towards the end of the Second World War at the instigation of John Maynard Keynes and embodied in the newly founded Arts Council of Great Britain. Similar countries established ministries of culture. This did not happen in Britain until the 1990s. Operating at 'arm's length' from government, the early Arts Council favoured 'the fine arts exclusively'. The definition of what counted as art was broadened in the 1960s and became a major point of contention in the 1970s. It was no longer possible to exclude 'popular culture' in its various manifestations from 'the arts'. Still, there was a sharp distinction to do with the role of the market, not so much necessarily to do with value and quality. The whole point of public arts patronage had been to subsidize and protect the fine arts, including classical and experimental theatre, from market failure. These are the arts, it was assumed, that might not be commercially viable in the cultural marketplace, the most obvious examples in Britain being grand opera and Shakespearean theatre. Some versions of 'popular culture' may also not have been commercial, such as working-class writing and publishing (Morley and Worpole 1982), but that was not true of mass-popular culture in general. Mass-popular culture does not ordinarily need protection from market forces; that is where it flourishes. However, there are policy issues regarding the mass-mediation of popular culture too; in effect, the problem of media regulation (K. Thompson 1997). The tradition of public service broadcasting, the viability of a national film industry, ownership and control of the press, censorship and so forth, all feature within this fourth sense of the state/culture relation, that of *media regulation*.

Williams identifies a fifth sense of the state/culture relation and a third sense of cultural policy 'proper', one which is both implicated in and transcends the nation-state:

[I]n some ways the nation-state, for all sorts of purposes, is both too large and too small. It is too small, particularly in the world of the media as they are now developing, to be able to sustain genuine national cultural policies . . . At the same time it is too big to be able to promote the diversity of cultural policy which ought to occur even within a relatively homogeneous culture like the British.

(Williams, 1984: 5)

Williams (1985 [1983]) wrote at length on globalization and localization. He was also sensitive to what Roland Robertson (1992) later named 'glocalization'. Concerned with his own identity, Williams called himself a 'Welsh European'. In considering cultural policy beyond the nation-state and its implications for identity, Williams insisted on the civic tradition, particularly strong in great European cities, and the common European dimension. Thus, as a fifth state/culture relation, Williams highlighted a complex and *negotiated construction of cultural identity*. In his formulation, this renders problematic the dominant form of nationalism in a multinational state and stresses not only subordinate nationality but also the civic, continental and global aspects of identity politics and cultural policy.

To summarize: Williams identified five state/culture relations, two with respect to cultural policy as display and three with respect to what he regarded as cultural policy 'proper'.

Williams's five state/culture relations

CULTURAL POLICY AS DISPLAY
1. national aggrandizement
2. economic reductionism

CULTURAL POLICY 'PROPER'
3. public patronage of the arts
4. media regulation
5. negotiated construction of cultural identity

This chapter looks particularly at cultural policy as display in both of Williams's senses: national aggrandizement and economic reductionism. The manifest disjunction and latent connections between cultural policy as display and the troubled variants of cultural policy 'proper' will also be considered. By definition, policy always comes with a rationale. Reasons are given for doing this rather than that, or for doing anything at all. Cultural policy 'proper' is rationalized explicitly, whereas the rationale for cultural policy as display is most likely to be implicit instead of explicit.

Rationalizing

Williams's distinction between cultural policy 'proper' and as display may be related to different research orientations on matters of culture and policy. Research is often used in the political rationalization of cultural policy 'proper', as with all official policy, in terms of justification and evaluation. Focusing upon cultural policy 'proper' (arts patronage, media regulation and cultural identity) usually occurs within administrative frameworks representing governmental agendas. The focus upon cultural policy as display (national aggrandizement and economic reductionism), on the other hand, more typically occurs within a critical and independent framework. In such a framework, matters of culture and policy are seen less as constituting a narrowly delimited and specialist field of administration than as indicative of broader economic, ideological and political issues. One of the general aims of critical research is to bring out – that is, to explicate – what would otherwise remain implicit and, not uncommonly, masked over by ideological distortion in the interests of dominant power. This book is very much directed towards the second of these two orientations. One of its objects of attention, however, is cultural policy 'proper', how it is constructed and studied in accord with the prevailing balance of power in society.

Cultural policy 'proper' is normally studied from a nation-state point of view that is increasingly supplemented by local/regional and international considerations. This is particularly so in research on cultural policy among the members of the European Union. So, while any member country will normally have an administrative apparatus for rationalizing and researching both the justification and effectiveness of its own cultural policies nationally, locally and regionally, it will also participate in inter-state enquiry according to a common Europeanness. A typical genre of such enquiry is the mapping document. The Council of Europe sends out international groups of experts to map and evaluate the cultural policies of member states. Here, for illustrative purposes, one might refer to any one or all of a series of national reports on cultural policy conducted under the auspices of the Council of Europe in the 1990s, such as *Cultural Policy in the Netherlands – Report of a Group of Experts* (Myerscough 1994). The one on Finland (Renard 1994) is not untypical. It tells the history of the Ministry of Education's responsibility for cultural policy, the role of the Finnish Arts Council and its sectoral councils, how much public money is spent and on what, including 'cultural industries'. Such reports are regularly updated.

Members of the European Union all have, at least residually, some form of welfare-state model of cultural policy unlike, most notably, the USA where explicit public policies for arts patronage, media regulation and cultural identity are marginalized by the free-market imperative. Since the welfare state – and particularly social-democratic – model of anything has been so undermined over recent decades by neo-liberal ideology and global capitalism, there is endemic uncertainty about the value of cultural policy 'proper' everywhere. Hence, much effort is put into mapping its contours and, also, in evaluating its usefulness to interested parties. This in itself is frequently an exercise in cultural policy as display, demonstrating symbolically that something worthwhile is actually happening.

As Michael Volkerling (2000) has pointed out, the mapping exercise was a notable feature of the New Labour regime in Britain from 1997. There, a shift occurred from 'cultural industries' rhetoric to 'creative industries' rhetoric in a reductively economic perspective. A government task force – made up of departmental representatives from several ministries, including Trade and Industry as well as Culture, and leading cultural entrepreneurs – issued the *Creative Industries – Mapping Document* the year after New Labour was elected (Department of Culture, Media and Sport 1998). The Policy Studies Institute later produced a mammoth tome, collating updated statistics on every conceivable section of the cultural field in Britain, *The UK Cultural Sector – Profile and Policy Issues* (Selwood 2001). All of this 'measurement' activity is useful from a governmental perspective that requires reliable information for administering and, perhaps, altering policy. However, mapping the territory – a symbolic act – is one thing; actually reconstructing the terrain – a material act – is something else. When the action in the **cultural and creative industries** is largely dictated by market forces, the power of corporations and the heroics of small businesses wishing to grow, there is a pervasive sense that governments have little really to do whatever their rhetoric. As Volkerling (2000) observed of British cultural policy in the late 1990s, there was much mapping but not much action. On the surface of cultural policy 'proper' that was evidently so but not necessarily with regard to the more obscure features of cultural policy as display – national aggrandizement and economic reductionism – as manifested in the case of the Millennium Dome, which is examined later in this chapter.

When it comes to cultural policy 'proper' and as display according to the ups and downs of a welfare-state model, the exemplary country is, of course, France. It has been the boldest European nation-state in this respect and the most studied for that reason, not only from instrumental but also from critical perspectives. French cultural policy has attracted a good deal of British scholarship (such as Looseley 1995 and 2000; Eling 1999; Ahearne 2002) and, indeed, from American sympathizers as well (for instance, Wachtel 1987). The politics of culture in France generally, and Socialist government policies from the 1980s in particular, have provoked intense debate among French intellectuals (most famously, Finkielkraut 1988 [1987]; and Fumaroli 1991). As David Looseley (2000: 117) remarks, 'What makes France such a fascinating and exemplary case is that, unlike the UK, it has always taken culture seriously – too seriously, some might say.' Less wryly, Claude Patriat (1998: 65) says, 'out of all democratic countries, the French nation has taken furthest the assertion of an active political presence in the cultural field' (translation, Ahearne 2002: 1).

'Few countries display more self assurance than France' (Klau 2002: 36). There is a national myth that France is peculiarly cultural, having led the way historically in art, philosophy and civilized living. The myth valorizes a belief in French intellectual and still, to a residual extent, linguistic superiority. Such assumptions remain active in spite and perhaps because of anglophone cultural hegemony throughout much of the world, established by Britain's greater imperial dominion in the past and carried on now by the USA's global power.

Over a century before the French Revolution, a monarchical tradition of cultural policy in France was initiated. Under Louis XIII, the *Académie française* was founded to police 'official' art in 1635. Under Louis XIV, the *Comédie française* was founded as the 'official' theatre in 1680. A combined system of censorship and patronage was thus inaugurated (Eling 1999). Whereas the 'Sun King' enlisted the arts to absolutism, the revolutionaries of the late eighteenth century turned the Louvre palace into a public museum as a mark of republicanism.

France was also in the vanguard of popularizing and democratizing art and high culture during the period of Popular Front government in the 1930s and decentralization of theatre in the years immediately following the Second World War. It was not, however, until 1959 that a Ministry of Cultural Affairs was established with a modest budget by President de Gaulle and led by the formerly Marxist novelist André Malraux. Although Malraux had moved to the Right, his main plank of policy as Minister for Culture was crypto-Stalinist, the building of houses of culture (*maisons de la culture*) around the country. Malraux believed that only great culture could make up for loss of faith in God; so everyone should have access to it. By the late 1960s, however, these houses of culture were providing shelter for red bases, for *animateurs* dedicated to overthrowing a failed cultural elitism in its disseminationist mode. Fierce ideological contest dragged on for several years beyond May 1968 and Malraux's departure from the ministry.

It had become evident that simply making great works of art, traditional and modern, available to a wider public did not work. Even when entrance is free, there are social and educational barriers to the consumption and appreciation of art (Bourdieu and Darbel 1991 [1969]). Pierre Bourdieu's work on the unequal distribution of cultural capital was a significant sociological contribution to debates on cultural policy in France and elsewhere. One inference from this was compensatory education, to inculcate in working-class children the tasteful cultural competencies that are more readily acquired and used by the children of the middle and upper classes. More radical and consequential, however, was the calling into question of taken-for-granted assumptions concerning the hierarchy of cultural values (Bourdieu 1984 [1979]), a populist move which has had a huge impact on modern cultural policy, in effect subverting its original *raison d'être*. The turn away from Malrauxian paternalism by revaluing the popular arts and culture is at the heart of much latter-day controversy over the aims, objectives and effects of cultural policy in general.

Within the French ministry, head of research Augustin Girard went even further by turning attention from publicly subsidized art towards the commercial realm of the 'cultural industries'. He argued, 'the progress of *democratization* and decentralization is currently being brought about much more comprehensively by industrial products available on the market than by the "products" subsidized by public authorities' (1978: 102). What might be the role of public cultural policy in this regard? Was there any role to perform? Yes, according to Girard, 'to sensitize elected politicians, administrators, professionals and cultural activists to the poorly understood phenomenon constituted by a certain democratization via the play of the market' (106). Actually, the operations of cultural industries and the much greater popular appeal of their products than publicly subsidized art was not at all poorly understood, except, that is, by those employed to offer an alternative.

The election of a Socialist government in 1981 brought 'culture' yet further into the foreground of politics in France, arguably to the detriment of ameliorative social policy. Two charismatic figures – President François Mitterrand and Culture Minister Jack

Lang – promoted *le culturel* as the means of modernizing France. The culture budget was immediately doubled. It rose to over 10 billion francs a year during the second phase of the Socialists' cultural project in the early 1990s. Lang initiated a wide range of policies for developing and preserving culture in France while breaking down old barriers between the 'Culture' of arts and heritage (*la patrimonie*) and the everyday consuming life of '*le culturel*'. Although Lang was criticized for an allegedly indiscriminate populism that embraced comic strips and Rap, in actual fact, his cultural policies broadened the range of legitimate public engagement with symbolic practice rather than replacing the old with the new.

Lang delivered an extremely important speech at a UNESCO conference in Mexico in 1982 that was widely reported as an attack on American 'cultural imperialism'. He criticized the erosion of cultural autonomy and identity, experienced not only by poorer countries but also by France (Lang 1983: 116). To reverse the trend, Lang said: 'we have doubled the budget for culture; we are irrigating the whole country through a vast network of centres of creation; we are encouraging all forms of creation, and giving support to national cultural industries in such domains as cinema, publishing and record production'. This was a strategy both of cultural policy 'proper', in the sense of supporting cultural activity ('*creation*') materially, and also of display in so far as it projected the combined cultural and economic interests of the French nation. In successive negotiations of the General Agreement on Tariffs and Trade (GATT) and its successor, the World Trade Organization (WTO), France would generally go along with the flow of neo-liberalism while, at the same time, insisting on 'the cultural exception'. Free trade in culture had to be resisted on national and economic grounds.

There is no greater recent example of cultural policy as aggrandizing national and, indeed, metropolitan display than Mitterrand's expensive *grands projets*, such as the Louvre pyramid, the Opera Bastille and a new national library; in effect, a series of controversial memorials to his presidency. Mitterrand was not unusual among French presidents, however, in bequeathing such cultural monuments to the nation. Georges Pompidou was responsible for and gave his name to the modern art museum and public library at Beaubourg, and Giscard d'Estaing presided over the extraordinary transformation of an old railway station into the Musée d'Orsay. Mitterrand had also wanted to put on an international exposition in Paris to mark the bicentenary of the Revolution in 1989. For economic and political reasons this did not happen. It went to Brisbane in 1988 instead (T. Bennett 1995). Jean-Paul Goude's bicentennial celebration on 14 July 1989 was another feature of Lang-Mitterrand cultural policy as display, representing the French nation in its (post)-modernizing moment with the black opera singer Jessye Norman dressed in the tricolor belting out 'La Marseillaise' on the Champs Élysées.

From the Left, Alain Finkielkraut (1988 [1987]) complained that Lang had made everything cultural (*le tout culturel*), to the extent that the true values of a universally humanistic culture had become dissipated. From the Right, Marc Fumaroli (1991) pointed out that the embrace of an undifferentiated consumer culture by a Socialist government had resulted in a discourse of cultural policy indistinguishable from market speak, the popular articulation of neo-liberalism.

Jeremy Ahearne (2002: 22) suggests that between them Lang and Mitterrand had instituted a 'new cultural policy matrix' which combined culture and economy. He cites Jacques Renard's (1987) defence of this new matrix on not just cultural but on less flimsy economic grounds. Renard stated the now very familiar, albeit somewhat tenuous, economic justifications for extravagant cultural expenditure: boosting national creative business, job creation, urban regeneration and so forth. Here, again, we see the peculiar combination that characterizes cultural policy as display, national aggrandizement and economic reductionism, given a modernizing twist, which so often turns out to be more a matter of blind faith than of solid evidence. There is a nagging suspicion that the costs of such a policy matrix may outweigh the benefits in its own terms. This can be illustrated by the remarkable case of the French government's subsidy for the Walt Disney Company.

In his book, *Once Upon a Time an American Dream – The Story of Euro Disneyland*, Andrew Lainsbury (2000) recounts in detail how Disney built a theme park near Paris. Originally named 'Euro Disney', it had to overcome local opposition, intellectual objections, lower than expected visitor numbers in the early years and a series of financial crises that brought it close to bankruptcy before achieving the successful turnaround that is now known as 'Disneyland Paris'. On 15 December 1985 French Socialist Prime Minister Laurent Fabius signed a letter of intent with Disney's Chief Executive, Michael Eisner. The following March the Socialists lost office, though they were back two years later. In the interim period key decisions were made. Disney executives had immediately gained support for their project from the incoming Centre-Right Prime Minister, Jacques Chirac, who was later to become President of France, cohabiting with yet another Socialist government, that of Lionel Jospin, at the turn of the Millennium.

Chirac is said to have approved the project because of its potential for job creation. However, the planned theme park was not universally popular among the people of Marne-la-Valle where it was to be sited. There was opposition to turning valuable farming land into an entertainment venue that would destroy the local rural economy of small farmers and villagers. Moreover, the government was not interested in consulting with local people. Their land would be bought under a law that allowed compulsory purchase in 'the public interest', or seized without compensation if need be. Resistance organizations sprang up, not so much to stop the development (that was thought to be impossible by the leaders) but in order to get the best deal for local people in terms of employment and preservation of their way of life. However, public demonstrations expressed utter hostility to Disney. Pitchforks were put through effigies of Mickey Mouse and the slogan, 'Stay Home, Mickey', articulated popular feeling. Travelling carnival and small park operators also campaigned against the likely impact of a Disney theme park on their businesses. Nevertheless, on 11 July 1986, the Île-de-France's regional council approved the project by a vote of 112 to 20 with only communist members opposing it.

On 24 March 1987, Chirac and Eisner agreed a $7.5 billion contract for the Euro Disney resort. The Disney Company was determined to strike a much harder bargain with the French than it had done with the Japanese over Tokyo Disneyland. In Japan, the contract was for only 45 years and limited Disney's cut to 10 per cent of admissions, and 5 per cent of food, licensing and merchandizing revenue. The French government did restrict the company's ownership of the Euro Disney theme park to 49 per cent; the rest was to be issued through European stock exchanges. However, Disney struck a much better bargain on revenue percentages in Paris than it had done in Tokyo.

Of at least equal significance and, in fact, more so from a cultural policy point of view, the French government supported the Euro Disney project lavishly with a generous loan, subsidy and expenditure on infrastructure. It provided a twenty-year loan of $960 million at, for then, the very low interest rate of 7.85 per cent and arranged other loans with syndicates and the state bank. The government sold 4841 acres of land to Disney at the knockdown price of just $5000 per acre. State and regional governments paid for the extension of railway lines to the site. Central government spent $400 million on electricity, water and other services for the site. Furthermore, it cut the standard rate of 18.6 per cent for value-added-tax to 7 per cent for theme-park tickets. It is not surprising, then, that Gilles Smadja subtitled his book, *Mickey*, on Euro Disney, *The Sting* (Lainsbury 2000: 32).

Still, in spite of, arguably, taking the mickey out of the French government, Euro Disney nearly failed, returning losses for the first few years after opening in 1992 until it eventually went into profit from the mid-1990s onwards. It is unnecessary here to consider how the 'turnaround' was achieved. From a cultural business perspective, Lainsbury (2000) attributes it mainly to smart marketing under Philippe Bourgignon, thus telling the kind of managerial success story that typically begs more questions than it answers. Curiously, much of the recent commentary on French cultural policy has little to say about the Euro Disney/Disneyland Paris saga. The cultural debate around its significance is, of course, usually mentioned. Was it or was it not a 'cultural Chernobyl', in the theatre director Ariane Mnouchkine's memorable phrase? The high-minded complaints of Finkielkraut and Fumaroli are normally discussed. Yet, the French government's massive financial commitment to establishing a Disney theme park near Paris is hardly, if at all, mentioned. In that sense, the case of Disney in France is a profound illustration of Williams's argument that cultural policy as display in its most material variant, as a business proposition, is perhaps too obvious to notice, rather like Edgar Allan Poe's purloined letter on the mantelpiece.

Exhibiting

The operations of cultural policy as display – combining national aggrandizement and economic reductionism – may be illustrated further by reference to the succession of *expositions universelles*, great exhibitions and world's fairs from the mid-nineteenth to the mid-twentieth centuries. Paul Greenhalgh (1988) calls them 'ephemeral vistas', short-lived spectacles of European industry and empire, especially in the British and French cases, yet not so very different in the American variants. Maurice Roche (2000) uses a broader category of 'mega-events' that encompasses Olympics and World Cups. There are analytical problems in categorizing these phenomena in general and identifying their peculiarities, similarities and differences. Historical and international comparisons are necessary in order to trace the ascent and – particularly with regard to the older tradition of international exhibitions – descent of ephemeral vistas and mega-events. While appreciating that the globalization of sport is of immense significance and developed historically on occasion in relation to expos, this section focuses specifically upon Greenhalgh's ephemeral vistas rather than on Roche's mega-events in the broad sense.

The grand-daddy of them all was, of course, the Great Exhibition of the Works of Industry of All Nations, housed in the Crystal Palace at London's Hyde Park between May and October 1851. It undoubtedly put the exhibiting of industrial design and manufacture in an international context, albeit dominated by 'the workshop of the world'. The tradition did not, however, have only British origins. As early as 1797, the Marquis d'Aveze and François de Neufchateau put on a display of goods in the forecourt of the Louvre, and this was followed by similar events in Paris and other French cities during the early nineteenth century. The organization of such exhibitions was actually motivated by a fear of British industrial might and its threat to France's prowess in tastefully designed goods. In fact, the Great Exhibition of 1851 itself was not only an expression of Britain's strength in manufacturing but also an implicit recognition of its weakness in design compared to France. 'The English' were capable of producing cheap goods on a massive scale for supply to other national markets, promoted by the ideology of *laissez-faire*, but Britain's advantage was not necessarily secure. Despite the rhetoric of peaceful cosmopolitanism, international competition was the major impetus for great exhibitions, universal expositions and world's fairs, with Britain, France and the USA respectively in the vanguard, followed by other countries, especially those with a growing imperial interest like Belgium and Holland.

In Britain, the Society for the Encouragement of Arts, Manufacture and Commerce – which became the Royal Society for the Arts in 1847 on recognition by the monarchy – organized industrial exhibitions, including, most famously, the great one of 1851. The principal aim of such an institution, in Greenhalgh's words, was 'promoting the principle of display'. He goes on to comment: 'In the first instance this was to be a device for the enhancement of trade, for the promotion of new technology, for the education of the ignorant middle classes and for the elaboration of a political stance' (Greenhalgh 1988: 3). The educational purpose was to be realized by showing exemplary objects and bodies in an accessible and didactic manner, such as in the tableaux display techniques initiated by American world's fairs. The ideology of progress realized through technological innovation was at the heart of the tradition as it developed from the mid-nineteenth century on both sides of the Atlantic. These were collaborative ventures that were supposed to extol general principles, not particular interests. Financing differed, however: in France, the state took financial responsibility, whereas private enterprise clubbed together in the USA. The British preferred 'public subscription' to the more direct forms of state control in France and business control in America through funding.

Two major trends in the unfolding of the tradition from the late nineteenth century are worthy of special note with regard to entertainment and imperialism. Each successive exhibition, exposition or world's fair typically sought to out-do the previous one in scale and specularity. The sites and buildings themselves were wonders to behold, perhaps best exemplified by the 1889 Eiffel Tower, emblematic of temporariness turning into permanency. The 1893 Chicago ferris wheel was another great structure to be copied endlessly. Artistic and scientific enlightenment may have been the original aim of organizers but 'family entertainment' came to predominate. In a pre-televisual age, there was much to see that would not otherwise have been seen by the mass of visitors, middle class and working class. The display of empire is especially significant in this respect.

Britain's industrial might was intimately connected to its imperial power in terms of sourcing raw materials and opening up markets. The imperial aspect of British exhibitions actually grew and became more swaggering as the gigantic empire that had been put together began to show signs of cracking apart in the first half of the twentieth century. Exhibitions in this period were called 'Empire Exhibitions', the last one taking place in 1938 (Crampsey 1988). These were stock-takings of UK Ltd's colonial possessions, particularly showcasing 'the jewel in the crown', such as at Wembley's India Palace in 1924. Disraeli's famous speech of 1872 extolling the benefits of high imperialism to the masses had actually been delivered in the Crystal Palace.

France as well as Britain showcased its imperial possessions, particularly Algeria. As Greenhalgh (1988: 65) remarks, 'The exhibitions came, by 1889, to expose both countries as spoiled children attempting to out-boast each other with their vast and priceless toys'. The USA also joined in the imperial swagger, for instance by showing off its command over Puerto Rico, the Virgin Islands, Hawaii, the Philippines and Samoa at the Paris Exposition Internationale Coloniale in 1931 (Greenhalgh 1988: 78).

Social Darwinism was an integral feature of international exhibitions during the era of high imperialism. The West's claim to be at the peak of 'civilization' was underscored by the display of 'primitive' peoples such as Africans in Europe but not in the USA, where 'Red Indians' were the prime object of the imperial gaze. Displaying colonial bodies and ways of life was accompanied by the emergence of the discipline of anthropology, the intellectual handmaiden to empire. French expositions perfected the display of 'the native village' that was peopled by colonial subjects who were also required to parade through the site on a daily basis. Black bodies and scanty clothing were the signs of inferiority and backwardness. Nevertheless, there was a certain fascination and pleasure for Europeans and Americans in looking at exotic peoples and their strange ways.

For Greenhalgh (1988), the decline of an exhibitionary tradition, which virtually terminated at the beginning of the Second World War in New York, is related to the eclipse of high imperialism. However, as he makes clear, the tradition was complex and, to an extent, contradictory, in the play of nationalism and internationalism, and in providing sites for aesthetic experimentation and public debate. For instance, American feminism was a lively presence at a number of world's fairs. Moreover, the tradition did not end with the Second World War. There has been a steady succession of more or less successful major expositions since then (see, for instance, Harvey 1996, on Seville 1992), up to and including Hanover 2000 and London's peculiarly national-istic New Millennium Experience in the same year. The trouble is that nobody is quite sure exactly what the point of these ephemeral vistas is now, an issue that will be taken up in the next section.

It may well be that the international exposition no longer has a clearly defined function to perform. However, even the 'original' function may not have been entirely clear. There are differences of analytical perspective on the historical meanings and purposes of great exhibitions. In an article first published in 1988, Tony Bennett (1995) gives a Foucauldian account of what he calls 'the **exhibitionary complex**', which exemplifies that theoretical perspective's preoccupation with 'the conduct of conduct'. Taking issue with his mentor, Michel Foucault, however, Bennett points out that newer – 'modern' – procedures of social control were not just about incarceration in asylums and prisons for disciplinary purposes, the removal of problematical subjects from public view. Modern governmentality is also about making public that which was hitherto hidden from view through spectacular display, as in exhibitions and museums; in effect, a means of achieving order through educative regulation. Bennett (1995: 63) defines the exhibitionary complex as 'a set of cultural technologies concerned to organ-ize a voluntary self-regulating citizenry'. And, 'the exhibitionary complex provides a context for the *permanent* display of power/knowledge' (66). Again, following Roland Barthes (1979), the Eiffel Tower is emblematic for Bennett:

> To see and be seen, to survey, yet always to be under surveillance, the object of an unknown but controlling look: in these ways, as micro-worlds rendered constantly visible to themselves, expositions realized some of the ideals of panopticism in transforming the crowd into a constantly surveyed, self-watching, self-regulating, and, as the historical record suggests, consistently orderly public – a society watching over itself.
>
> (1995: 69)

Panopticism (Foucault 1977 [1975]) – seeing all around – is not restricted to the surveillance and docile conduct of the confined but is also a mechanism for regulating work and consumption in the wider society. After all, who would make the goods and buy them if everyone was locked up? Bennett stresses the role of expositions in 'rational recreations' in contrast to more unruly popular sites and pastimes, such as traditional fairs and modern amusement parks. The most important implication of this analysis is that the exhibitionary complex contributed to the production of the conforming customer and consumer culture generally.

The role of great exhibitions in the formation of consumer culture is pointed up yet more sharply by Thomas Richards's (1991) *The Commodity Culture of Victorian England*. Richards's analysis is classically Marxist in comparison with Tony Bennett's post-Marxist position which hardly mentions capitalism as such, so concerned is it with a generalized notion of modern governmentality. According to Richards (1991: 3), 'The Great Exhibition was devised by a think tank expressly to become a sort of semiotic laboratory for the labour theory of value.' After all, the exhibition was a celebration of manufacturing that did, to an extent, acknowledge 'the dignity of labour'. However, it is a feature of consumer culture that the process of production is eventually obscured by the glittering magic of commodities, as Karl Marx argued. Richards's analysis is also very much influenced by a latter day critique of mature consumer culture:

> In particular this book draws upon the work of Guy Debord, a founding member of the Situationist International and a major theorist of the aborted revolution of May 1968. Laid out in the manner of Marx's 'Ten Theses on Feurbach' as an open sequence of propositions rather than a closed argument, *Society of the Spectacle* (1967) is the *Communist Manifesto* of the twentieth century. In it Marx meets Saussure. Marx had viewed the commodity as a slippery thing, 'abounding in metaphysical subtleties and theological niceties.' Debord brings to Marxist analysis the powerful tool of semiotics, which enables him to see the commodity as a dense locus of signification.
>
> (T. Richards 1991: 13)

In studying expositions, it is necessary to read how they signify the times in their historical nuances. Richards does this by tracing the role of the Great Exhibition in the early formation of consumer society. He argues that the Great Exhibition articulated 'six major foundations of a semiotics of commodity spectacle' (T. Richards 1991: 58). These are as follows:

1. autonomous iconography;
2. commemoration;
3. democratic ideology for consumerism;
4. transformation of the commodity into language;
5. figuration of a consuming subject;
6. myth of the achieved abundant society.

(T. Richards 1991: 59–66)

Richards's Debordian analysis of the materiality and meanings of the Great Exhibition provides a more comprehensive account than Tony Bennett's Foucauldian analysis, though they are not necessarily at odds with one another. However, both are vulnerable to a critique of determinism in the sense that neither addresses the sheer precariousness of the phenomenon under study and offer little insight into its loss of manifest function now. As Roche (2000: 34) quite rightly notes, 'Bennett's conceptualization underplays the dramaturgical or performative aspects of producing and consuming in "the exhibitionary complex" '. Roche proposes the alternative notion of a '**performative complex**' in the construction of cultural modernity around mega-events. The implications of such an argument are twofold. First, research into ephemeral vistas and related mega-events needs to pay close attention to the historical specificity of particular cases. Second, such research needs to take into account the multidimensional complexity of such phenomena. Recent research on the Great Exhibition (Auerbach 1999; J. Davis 1999) manifests a more empirical approach than that of Bennett and Richards. The issue at stake here, however, is not to do with the respective merits of empiricism and theoreticism. Instead, it is to do with the value of multidimensional analysis that draws upon a range of perspectives, a principled eclecticism, rather than seeking to demonstrate the ultimate superiority of one perspective over others, Foucauldian, Debordian or whatever (Kellner 1997).

Jeffrey Auerbach's (1999) *The Great Exhibition of 1851 – A Nation on Display* is an exemplary case study. From a methodological point of view, it is important to appreciate that the book is divided into three parts: 'Making', 'Meaning' and 'Memory'. He traces the processes of production, representation and reception in detail, concluding that:

> Embedded within the exhibition was a multiplicity of meanings and identities that can be disclosed only by reinserting it into the historical context from which it emerged, by refusing to regard its creation in a teleological manner, and by giving credence not only to those who supported and promoted the event, but also to those who opposed . . . It is a misnomer, then, to speak of the 'meaning' of the exhibition, for it has many meanings, and its meanings have changed over time.
>
> (Auerbach 1999: 231)

Auerbach views the Great Exhibition as a fiercely contested event, the construction and consequences of which were never inevitable. In this respect, he calls into question accounts of the exhibition as simply the triumphant expression of the Victorian bourgeoisie's attitudes and interests. Its class composition and range of meanings were much more complex than that. There was class segregation regulated by ticket pricing, out-pricing the working class at weekends, but working-class visitors made the best of it and were not cowed by bourgeois prejudice. Moreover, middle-class anxiety about working-class insurgency at the exhibition, in the event, was ludicrously unwarranted.

In effect, Auerbach tells an alternative 'story of reluctant manufacturers, nationalistic and jingoistic rivalries, petty political disputes, and, in many areas of Britain, outright antipathy to the exhibition' (1999: 4). The Great Exhibition became a hugely popular success by any measure. It drew 6 million visitors in just over 5 months, many on their first excursion by railway to London. This success was achieved, not guaranteed: it occurred in the face of much criticism, dissent and scepticism. The Crystal Palace – Paxton's giant greenhouse – was astonishing in itself. The goods, machinery and materials on display in the glass building were startling. Britain hosted the products of the world, demonstrated its own vanguard position in manufacturing and extolled the benefits of free trade. However, it was not just a boast. As Auerbach (1999: 3) notes, 'the Great Exhibition was designed less to celebrate Britain's economic success than to locate and remedy its deficiencies'. There were doubts concerning the quality of British design and manufacturing. And a heated debate on the respective merits of 'culture' and 'commerce' took place over the exhibition. The surplus of £186,000 – a very large amount of money in 1851 – was spent on the site in South Kensington where a famous set of arts and science buildings is now located, including the Victoria and Albert Museum, the Natural History Museum, the Science Museum, the Royal College of Art, the Imperial College of Science and Technology, and the Royal Albert Hall – 'a lasting legacy' indeed.

Nationalism and internationalism were in a complicated interplay at the Great Exhibition, resulting in the solidification of a particular version of Britishness, the arrogant and insular feeling that the British are uniquely different from 'foreigners' in general and, implicitly, superior to everyone else. That is not, perhaps, an exclusively British delusion and is probably more generally characteristic of popular imperialism whether consciously avowed or simply taken for granted. It did, however, have an historical content. Auerbach (1999: 167) sums up the components of that specific identity construction: 'Britain was seen as industrial and commercial, its people energetic and enterprising, its social and political system based on freedom, justice and liberty.' This was a strong and widely shared sense of national identity, the persistence of which became seriously debilitating for Britain during its century of decline (Gamble 1994b [1981]), something that was supposed to have been arrested at least symbolically by New Labour's Millennium Experience, considered in the next section. Before passing on to that event, however, it is worth pausing for a moment to recollect how the Great Exhibition was funded.

Before Prince Albert was secured as figurehead for the exhibition in the role of President of its Royal Commission, the Royal Society made a deal with Messrs James and George Munday, a public works contractor, to put the show on the road. For £20,000 investment, the Mundays would get the profit, which was subsequently estimated conservatively, as it turned out, at £100,000. The deal was attacked in sections of the press as 'jobbery' and 'corruption'. Critics argued that the exhibition should not be a vehicle for private profit since it was a matter of national dignity. In response, the contract with the Mundays was rescinded and replaced by the gathering of not-for-profit 'public subscriptions', aided by the prestige of the monarchy in the person of Prince Albert as promoter-in-chief of the Great Exhibition. Auerbach comments:

The controversy of the contract had a number of implications. First, and most importantly, it determined a strategy for funding the exhibition. The outcry over the prospect of a national event being funded by private capitalists who might potentially benefit from public funds forced the organizers and commissioners to make the exhibition a truly public and national undertaking. The opposition forced the organizers to appeal not to the government or to the wealthy few, but to people of all classes, a step which turned the fund-raising for the Great Exhibition into a tribute to the principle of voluntarism. It is important as well to recognize the notions of nationalism here, as the exhibition was transformed from a private and sectional to a public and national event.

(1999: 36)

While jobbery was considered a bad thing at the height of liberal capitalism in the mid-nineteenth century, it had become a normalized feature of neo-liberal governance by the end of the twentieth century.

Amazing

The publicity slogan for the exposition in a dome-shaped tent at Greenwich during the year 2000 – the centrepiece of Britain's 'New Millennium Experience' celebrations – was 'one amazing day'. M. & C. Saatchi's television advertisement for the opening showed a child being amazed by the marvellous spectacle on offer. Within the Home Planet Zone, two alien guides descended to Earth, Gaia and her son Max. Passing through various elemental forces of nature until the human variety of different peoples is reached, young Max asked his mother repeatedly, 'Is this the amazing thing?' Good question.

Responding to critics of the project, long before it opened, in his 'People's Palace' speech of February 1998, Prime Minister Tony Blair had himself promised amazement:

Picture the scene. The clock strikes midnight on December 31st, 1999. The eyes of the world turn to the spot where the new Millennium begins – the Meridian Line at Greenwich. This is Britain's opportunity to greet the world with a celebration that is so bold, so beautiful, so inspiring that it embodies at once the spirit of confidence and adventure in Britain and the spirit of the future in the world. This is the reason for the Millennium experience. Not a product of imagination run wild, but a huge opportunity for Britain. It is good for Britain. So let us seize the moment and put on something of which we and the world will be proud.

Then we will say to ourselves with pride: this is *our* Dome. *Britain's* Dome. And believe me, it *will be* the envy of the world.

It doesn't surprise me that the cynics have rubbished the idea. They are in good company. They are part of an inglorious strand of British history: like those who said St Paul's would be a calamity, that the 1851 exhibition would have no visitors and that the 1951 Festival of Britain would never be finished on time.

(Blair 1998: 1)

On adopting the Dome project from the outgoing Conservative government in June 1997, Blair said he had set down five criteria for it. First, 'the content should inspire people'. Second, 'it should have national reach'. Third, 'the management of the project should be first rate'. Fourth, '[it] should not call on the public purse'. Fifth, 'there should be a lasting legacy' (2). He went on to say:

> It will bring the nation together in common purpose – to make a difference. It will unite the nation. It will be a meeting point of people from all backgrounds. It will be an event to lift our horizons. It will be a catalyst to imagine our futures.
>
> (Blair 1997: 3)

Blair claimed the New Millennium Experience would be an educative guide to conduct. He said, 'I want today's children to take from it an experience so powerful and memories so strong that it gives them that abiding sense of purpose and unity that stays with them through the rest of their lives' (4). The demotic and personalizing quality of Blair's rhetoric is well known and has been analysed carefully (Fairclough 2000). Yet, the idea that such an exposition might actually influence popular conduct in a fundamental way was well beyond its sell-by-date. The amazing thing about the Millennium Dome was not so much its impact on the conduct of conduct but that it was done at all and in the way that it was done.

Although visitors to the Millennium Dome generally approved of it, there was little expression of amazement except for the building itself (McGuigan and Gilmore 2001 and 2002), as anticipated in *The New Yorker* (Goldberger 1998). It was not a dome in the traditional sense but closer to a suspension bridge in engineering terms (Wilhide 1999), designed by the Richard Rogers Partnership. It was, in fact, a big tent – a very big tent with teflon coating. Built on the partially reclaimed and still deeply toxic site of an old coal-fired gasworks at Greenwich Marsh (Irvine 1999), the Millennium Dome was indeed massive, in the words of the Queen, 'the largest enclosed space on earth' (NMEC 2000: 5). It dominated a south-eastern peninsula of the Thames where the Prime Meridian cuts across the tip of the peninsula like a circumcision. However, it did not dominate the cityscape in the way the Eiffel Tower looms above Paris. Tucked far away down the river in East London, the Dome could just about be glimpsed from the top of the London Eye ferris wheel, which was also built to mark the Millennium, on the other side of the Thames from the Palace of Westminster. Unlike British Airway's (BA) London Eye, the Millennium Dome provided no panoramic view of London. The greatest sights on offer were to be inside. As an icon of the Millennium, the Dome was best seen in aerial photography, through mediated rather than direct vision. The world was supposed to be amazed.

More amazing than the thing itself or its image circulating globally was how the project was constructed as a display of Britain's 'greatness' at the turn of the Millennium. It was an artefact of the National Lottery that was introduced by John Major's Conservative government in 1994. Some of the proceeds from the Lottery were to be spent on celebrating the Millennium. A Millennium Commission of 'the great and the good' was set up to plan the celebrations (Rocco 1995). Deputy Prime Minister Michael Heseltine, the politician who had been responsible for bringing about the overthrow of his bitter enemy Margaraet Thatcher, was a key figure on the Millennium Commission. He had a ministerial record of promoting urban regeneration schemes. Heseltine (2000) regretted that Greenwich had been neglected in the docklands regeneration of the 1980s, the most prominent aspect of which was the Canary Wharf office complex across the Thames from the Greenwich peninsula. In choosing Greenwich for the Millennium Dome, Heseltine had sought to make amends for its earlier neglect.

Claims are made, of course, for the local regenerative effect of the project (McGuigan and Gilmore 2001) but, in 1996, Heseltine enunciated an even grander purpose for putting on a Millennium Festival with Greenwich at its core:

> I want millions of visitors to visit the country, share in the festival and go away deeply impressed, much excited by British achievements. The excellence of UK companies, the pre-eminence of the City of London as a financial centre, the technological prowess, the innovative genius will leave an indelible impression.
>
> We can do that only in partnership with our leading companies. It is not a bureaucratic concept of central government, or a whim of the Millennium Commission. It is about selling ourselves and our country.
>
> (quoted by Nicolson 1999: 2)

Heseltine is especially noted for his patriotic capitalism, which was the cause of his conflict with the Atlanticist Thatcher. For Heseltine, the Millennium Dome was to be a re-run of the Great Exhibition.

Strenuous efforts were made to bring 'British' business on board. No private company, however, not even BA, would agree to run the project. Instead, the New Millennium Experience Company (NMEC) was set up as a curious hybrid of a limited company and a 'non-departmental public body'. The single shareholder in the company was to be the minister charged with overseeing its operations. When the New Labour government was persuaded to adopt the project from the outgoing Conservatives, the minister given responsibility for the Millennium celebrations was not the Secretary of State for Culture, Media and Sport – Chris Smith – but, instead, the arch 'spin doctor' – Minister Without Portfolio, Peter Mandelson. He immediately started spinning on behalf of the Dome: 'Greenwich is the home of time. The meridian line runs through the exhibition site. It's a chance for Britain to make a big statement about itself and the rest of the world' (quoted by L. Harding 1997). Mandelson was well aware that the Dome was a tricky proposition, already hugely controversial long before opening (S. Richards 1997). Its funding was the principal matter of concern. An initial National Lottery grant of £200 million would have to be increased to £450 million, Mandelson realized on entering office. Eventually, £628 million of Lottery money would be spent on the New Millennium Experience, in addition to nearly £200 million of 'taxpayer's money', spent by the regeneration agency English Partnerships on buying and reclaiming the site. Another significant source of funding was corporate sponsorship, which was not so readily forthcoming as Heseltine had hoped.

Mandelson – like Heseltine – was one of the leading characters in the Dome drama. Its continuous and interweaving story lines were distinctly soap operatic over the years up to, including and beyond 2000. The Dome's unfolding narrative also had features of situation comedy, with a cast of eccentric characters stuck together for a succession of disasters and temporary resolutions. Mandelson's maternal grandfather, Herbert Morrison, had overseen the post-Second World War Labour government's Festival of Britain in 1951 (Banham and Hillier, 1976). This, rather more than Heseltine's Great Exhibition, was a constant reference point for Mandelson in promoting the Dome. He was, however, to be accused of wishing to dumb down the exposition on visiting Disney World in Florida for inspiration (Bayley 1999). When Mandelson was forced to resign from the government for the first time in December 1998 over a loan scandal, 'Mandy's Place' (B. Lewis 1999) became the responsibility of another comic character, Lord Charles Falconer, the old school pal of Tony Blair. Mandelson was eventually welcomed back into government but had to resign for a second time when he was accused of selling passports to the Hinduja brothers for their sponsorship of the Dome's Faith Zone. The media had a field day with this 'scandal' and other endlessly entertaining story lines.

The fact of the matter is that the Millennium Dome was the biggest news story in the British media during the year 2000, if only because of the sheer volume of broadcast time and column inches devoted to the crisis-ridden exposition (McGuigan 2002). Journalists at Canary Wharf were constantly reminded of the Dome when they glanced out of their office windows just across the river. It took a lorry drivers' protest at the price of petrol, which threatened to close down the British economy, to topple the Dome from lead news story in September on radio and television and in the press. Yet, even at the height of the fuel crisis, the problems of the Dome's sell-off and its need for further lottery subsidy to keep open occupied second place in the news media.

Years of public scepticism concerning the good sense of the project seemed to be confirmed on the opening night of 31 December 1999. National newspaper editors, the BBC's director general and many other guests for the launch party were detained at Stratford Underground station for a security check that lasted up to three hours before they were bussed into the Dome at North Greenwich. The news media immediately dubbed it 'a fiasco'. The New Millennium Experience itself was soon attacked as a cultural 'disaster' by leading commentators in the press. The amazing thing was very quickly judged to be distinctly uninspiring in both broadsheet and tabloid journalism (McGuigan 2003b). The Dome itself became the object of incessant popular conversation and, indeed, derision. NMEC's management had lost the public relations battle straight away. Then, it transpired that, while the Dome had opened on time, it had not opened on budget. The company's contingency fund had been depleted in order to meet escalating costs as time ran out before opening. Only one-third of the expected number of visitors for January went to the Dome that month. Just over half the predicted 12 million for the whole year visited the Dome. On opening, several sponsors had not yet paid up and some of them had not even concluded contracts with NMEC. By the end of the first month, the company was virtually bankrupt.

NMEC asked for and received £60 million of additional Lottery money from the Millennium Commission in February, at the time described as a 'loan' but with little likelihood of ever being repaid. This was the first of four extra tranches of Lottery funding through the year. Another £29 million was agreed in May. On the Millennium Commission's deal to sell the Dome to the Japanese investment bank Nomura for £105 million, £43 million was made forthcoming in August as an advance on the sale's proceeds. When Nomura pulled out of the deal in September because of confusion over contractual ownership of properties at the Dome, the Millennium Commission awarded it another £47 million to keep going until the end of the year (McGuigan and Gilmore 2001). A 'city troubleshooter' was appointed the third chair in succession of NMEC in order to bring about solvent liquidation of the project. This involved selling off the contents at knockdown prices in February 2001.

It is not surprising, then, that the key theme of media coverage was that the Dome was a waste of public money which would have been better spent on genuinely good causes. That was particularly embarrassing for the New Labour government since it had prided itself on being more fiscally prudent than Old Labour. In September, the Prime Minister issued an 'apology' which, however, blamed the disaster on inadequate management rather than the concept and production of the New Millennium Experience as such. Back in January, a group of sponsors had defined the problem as a managerial one and demanded that something should be done about it. They commissioned research that purportedly showed that association with the Dome was bringing them bad publicity, though it did not demonstrate a loss of sales. Long queues at the high-street chemist Boots's Body Zone, for instance, had been widely reported as indicative of poor management. In effect, the sponsors' revolt brought about the sacking of the chief executive officer, Jennie Page, former civil servant and previously head of the Millennium Commission. She was replaced as NMEC's CEO by a 34-year-old former vice president of Disneyland Paris, P.-Y. Gerbeau. He was inaccurately reported as the man who had been responsible for 'turning around' Disney's French operation. The idea was that Gerbeau would do the same with the Dome. Gerbeau had, in fact, been in charge of ticketing and car parking at Disneyland Paris. It was his mentor, Phillippe Bourgignon, the CEO, who had presided over the turnaround at the Disney theme park outside Paris.

The replacement of Page with Gerbeau certainly did result in a shift of managerial style. Page was the epitome of the public bureaucrat who had no experience of running a visitor attraction and blamed the problems of the Dome on political interference (Page 2000). As Blair later argued on television and at the October Labour Party Conference, it was essential to bring in commercial expertise for running a visitor attraction in a business-like manner, which is exactly what Gerbeau represented. He was imbued with the new managerialist 'philosophy' of customer service and flat organizational structure. A stratum of middle management disappeared. Gerbeau was a showman who became a popular figure in the media and was said, as well, to be popular with the black-and-yellow-clad hosts, the front-line workers suffering from the flak being flung at the Dome on a day-to-day basis. Changes were made more or less cosmetically, such as the issuing of time-slot tickets for visiting the Body Zone. Gerbeau knew whom he had to please first and foremost: the sponsors. He redefined them as 'partners' (interview with the author). Under the Gerbeau regime, large placards were erected in front of sponsored zones, making corporate beneficence quite clear to the visiting public. Access to the Dome's main entrance was cordoned off in order to route visitors through 'the sponsors' village' of shop units and past BSkyB's Skyscape cinema, where the *Blackadder Back and Forth* film was screened at regular times during the day.

While Gerbeau ensured that corporate logos were given more prominent display than previously, it would be quite wrong to assume that he was responsible for the overweening presence of sponsorship at the Dome. Corporate sponsorship was integrally related to the whole project from hesitant beginning to bitter end. Page had said that she would not allow the exposition to become 'Logoland', yet it already was so before the advent of Gerbeau. For example, McDonald's sponsored Our Town Stage, where children from around the country had their day performing at the Dome. McDonald's had sought copyright in the performances but had to settle for copyright of recordings. Involvement in the New Millennium Experience's National Programme, in effect, facilitated McDonald's' incursion into schools. Furthermore, McDonald's was a massive presence at the Dome. On the outside, directly across from the main entrance, was the largest McDonald's in Europe. There were two more McDonald's eateries inside. In January, before the regime change, an advertisement appeared on television asking, 'What's in the Dome?' The answer: 'McDonald's'.

Moreover, it is quite inadequate to explain the Millennium Dome's manifest 'failure' – or even its latent 'success' – as simply a matter of management, particularly the lack of private-sector skills for running a public-sector project on opening. That the Dome picked up increasing numbers of visitors towards the end of the year and that approval ratings were high are perhaps grounds for the managerial argument. However, as visitor research shows, a sceptical response to its damnation in the media was a more pronounced motive for visiting the Dome than awareness of improved management. Gerbeau himself admitted in interview that the changes he brought about were not fundamental.

Various different accounts of the Millennium Dome were given before it actually opened, ranging from managerial analysis (Lewis, Richardson and Woudhuysen 1998) to *belle-lettreiste* critique (Sinclair 1999). While controversy still raged, the Dome was attacked as symptomatic of New Labour's disingenuous populism by a former Conservative politician (Walden 2000). There are several other insightful and largely journalistic accounts of the Dome's cultural disaster (such as Martin 2000 and Morrison 2000). None of them, however, apply a rigorous method of cultural analysis or a critical suspension of partial judgement.

In accounting for such a phenomenon as the New Millennium Experience, it is important to look at it in the round, that is by taking into account the multiple determinations and agencies in its production, representation and consumption. There are diverse kinds of cultural analysis that focus on particular aspects of production, representation and consumption (for instance, the political economy of cultural production, textual analysis of cultural artefacts and audience research). All of them are valid in their own terms and exemplify a practical division of labour as well as the contest of rival paradigms in cultural and media studies. However, there is a case for a combined approach that traces various moments in the circulation of culture and their interrelations in order to grasp the **ontological complexity** of a specific phenomenon. For instance, the Open University's study of the Sony Walkman (du Gay et al. 1997) adds identity and regulation to the trinity of production, representation and consumption in a circuit of culture analysis. Such analysis can only be sketched in here (see McGuigan and Gilmore 2002 for greater empirical detail and McGuigan 2003b for further reflections on the Dome study).

What, then, are the key features of the Millennium Dome's production, representation and consumption? Consideration of the role of corporate sponsorship is at the heart of explaining how the Millennium Dome turned out. Sponsorship eventually amounted to less than one-fifth (around £150 million) the amount of public money spent on the New Millennium Experience (around £800 million, including £628 million of Lottery money). Yet, corporate sponsors had a decisive impact on the exposition's focal concerns, design and management. Typically, sponsors were associated with a particular thematic zone: so there was BT's Talk; Ford's Journey; Manpower's Work; Marconi and BAe Systems's Mind; Marks and Spencer's Self Portrait; the main zones discussed here. Some zones did not attract sponsorship, such as Living Island and Play. Living Island was critical of environmental pollution. Play lost its sponsor, BSkyB, because it was not designed to publicize that company's products.

An obvious motive for sponsorship was commercial promotion to the public. This was manifestly evident in the cases of BT's Talk Zone and Ford's Journey Zone. Both companies negotiated 'turnkey' contracts with NMEC, which meant they were allowed to design, build and run their own zones, in effect with minimal interference from NMEC. The only motor cars in Journey were Ford. BT and Ford spent a great deal more on their zones than was normally spent on the zones ostensibly under NMEC's control. On the other hand, several sponsors quite evidently paid less than the official tariff for association. And, 'value in kind' – equipment and so on – was often supplied instead of money, such as Coca-Cola's ice rink.

NMEC had editors allocated to zones and a 'Litmus Group' of luminaries from the entertainment industry to advise on the representational aspects of the exhibition. There was a great deal of hiring and firing of designers in the production of the Dome's contents. But, even in these cases, it is evident that NMEC relinquished a great deal of control to sponsors. Some sponsors brought in designers that they had worked with before on product launches. In fact, many of the zone designers came from the world of corporate communications rather than museum design. Also, in the Work Zone, for example, its sponsor, the American employment agency Manpower was permitted to put up a display of jobs on offer through the agency as well as extolling the brave new world of flexible labour.

Left-wing critics of the Millennium Dome attacked its promotional culture, for instance Jonathan Glancey (2001: 26): 'The Millennium Experience, its entrance flanked by a branch of McDonalds, proved to be an exhibition of corporate sponsorship.' This was an accurate criticism to a certain extent, but not very deep in accounting for the political economy or ideology of sponsorship at the Dome. With a few notable exceptions, such as Greg Palast (2001) in *The Observer*, journalists hardly penetrated the deeper motives of corporations for sponsoring parts of the Dome. It is easy enough to see why Boots took the opportunity to promote pharmaceutical products, but harder to see why BAe Systems put money into the Mind Zone, the most intellectual of zones, designed by deconstructionist architect Zaha Hadid. One of the largest arms manufacturers in the world, BAe Systems does not sell Hawk jets directly to the public.

Unlike the brazenness of several other sponsor/zone relations, Mind did not manifestly promote BAe's core business. Instead, the ostensible purpose of the zone was to represent modern engineering and encourage the education of engineers. However, like a number of other sponsors, BAe may have had ulterior motives for supporting the Dome. In 1997 the New Labour government promised to pursue an 'ethical foreign policy', which might have meant not sanctioning the sale of weapons to dictatorships such as the genocidal Suharto regime in Indonesia. Soon, this 'unrealistic' policy was quietly dropped since the production of armaments is one of the few remaining buoyant sectors of British manufacturing and exports in what is said to be a 'weightless' informational economy. The government's U-turn on foreign policy – the unrestrained issuing of export guarantees to armaments manufacturers and the conduct of diplomacy on their behalf – was of more than incidental benefit to BAe Systems. This was of greater significance than the much commented upon allegation that the Hinduja brothers' modest donation to the Faith Zone bought them British passports, a story which, incidentally, brought the journalists who broke it the journalism of the year award.

The Hinduja passports-for-sponsorship scandal was only the tip of an iceberg, the greater part of which the news media largely ignored. As the former marketing director of one of the corporate sponsors remarked in interview, everyone had a political deal. This was evidently so for the Work Zone's sponsor Manpower in building its business in Britain. Manpower handled human resources for the New Millennium Experience, hiring, training and relocating employees on closure. Yet more significantly, in association with Ernst and Young, Manpower won nine out of fifteen contracts for the management of employment zones around the country, a little remarked upon feature of the New Labour government's privatization of public agencies. This may perhaps be coincidental.

There are several other coincidences to note. The supermarket chain Tesco – sponsor of the Learning Zone and heavily involved in promoting its business through computing in schools – must have been pleased when the government decided to withdraw its proposed legislation for taxing out-of-town car parking at retail estates. BA and BAA (British Airports Authority) – co-sponsors of Home Planet, the closest thing to a ride at the Dome – must have appreciated the government's sanctioning of Terminal Five at Heathrow in face of popular protest on environmental grounds by locals. It came as something of a surprise when Camelot – sponsor of Shared Ground – had its National Lottery contract renewed by a Labour government that had vowed to replace its profit-making operation with a not-for-profit operator. Rupert Murdoch's BSkyB – sponsor of Skyscape – benefited from the government's light-touch policies on broadcasting and digitalization, not to mention its relaxed press policy. There are other examples. It may all just be coincidence. However, it is reasonable to infer that sponsorship of the New Millennium Experience was more than a publicity exercise.

In carrying out the present multidimensional analysis, it is necessary to demonstrate that the role of corporate sponsorship was not only about behind-the-scenes deals but had consequences for the ideological construction of meaning at the Dome. John B. Thompson (1990) identifies a number of different modes of ideological representation (legitimation, dissimulation, unification, fragmentation and reification) each with their typical strategies of symbolic construction (such as displacement and euphemization for dissimulation). Examples of all these ideological modes and strategies could be found scattered around the Dome, of which only a few brief illustrations can be given here.

Thompson treats ideology as a matter of symbolic domination and subordination, thus avoiding questions of interest and distortion. This is unfortunate since interest and distortion in the critique of ideology (Lovell 1980) are manifestly pertinent to analysing the construction of meaning in representation at the Dome, especially in sponsored thematic zones. However, it is not necessary to claim that some essential truth was masked over at the Dome or that 'real' reality was simply misrepresented. Instead, it is possible to argue the case from the dialogic perspective of critical theory that not only questions the form and content of the Dome's attractions but also imagines what might otherwise have been there. The potential articulation of alternative views in the spirit of rational-critical debate (McGuigan 1996) could reasonably have been expected from an exposition that was very largely funded by the public in a democratic polity and only marginally by corporate sponsors.

Ideological representation with regard to corporate sponsorship worked differently in different parts of the Dome. Sponsorship was extremely intrusive in some cases, for example in Manpower's Work Zone. In other cases, it was comparatively unintrusive, as in Marks and Spencer's Self Portrait Zone. The Mind Zone came in between. And, in yet other cases, it was entirely absent, as in the Millennium Show. Moreover, in the interstices and on the edges, there were signs of something different from 'an exhibition of corporate sponsorship', for example in artworks such as Antony Gormley's *Quantum Cloud* out on the River Approach.

To take the most straightforward example first: Manpower's Work Zone. This was crudely propagandistic for both the agency and government policy on vocational training. Visitors were told didactically to assemble 'new skills' for a flexible labour market in which there are no more 'jobs for life' – communication, literacy, and so on – and test them out in the games room at the termination of the zone. 'Old work' was reified as pure drudgery compared to the excitements of 'new work'. Furthermore, there was no mention of past labour struggles to establish worker rights or the extreme exploitation and oppression of sweated labour in the world today.

Quite different from the crude propaganda of Work, the Mind Zone was very subtle. Its primary ideological mode was dissimulation, in that the arms industry was displaced ostensibly from its focal concerns. Instead of representing technologies of warfare, the emphasis was on communications and the networking principle so thoroughly analysed by Manuel Castells (1996). Euphemism is commonly used in discourses of war; and this was replete within the Mind Zone. With its postmodern art, Internet and ant colony, the Mind Zone was a curiously dehumanized zone, a celebration of 'the inhuman', in Jean-François Lyotard's (1991 [1988]) term (see Sim 2001), the coagulation of body and machine, alongside the superior yet uncreative powers of artificial intelligence. There was, however, a startlingly humanistic exception in the middle of the zone: Ron Mueck's sculpture, the enigmatic *Boy*. In criticizing the Mind Zone, it is necessary to imagine what might have been said. It would have been reasonable for the Dome to contain a War Zone that looked critically at the history of military conflict as it has developed into the virtual reality and inhumanity of high-tech warfare. Instead, there was the intellectual obscurantism of Mind.

The editorial relation between business and design in the Millennium Dome case illustrates an important distinction and a significant transition occurring in a cultural project that was funded largely by the public. It is necessary to distinguish between **associative sponsorship** and **deep sponsorship**. Associative sponsorship is the standard form in the arts and public sector of cultural provision. Sponsors accrue kudos through association with artistic culture, particularly prestigious events, but are not supposed to influence content. As critics have argued (such as Shaw 1993), this is not what actually happens in practice. Sponsorship exerts all sorts of subtle pressure on editorial decision-making, programme selection and so forth. Nevertheless, the norms of associative sponsorship are still claimed and defended officially in order to protect cultural integrity: for instance, sponsors of Tate Modern are not supposed to select the artworks and dictate exhibition policy, though donations of money and work, of course, are gratefully received. On the other hand, the purpose of deep sponsorship is, unashamedly, to actually construct culture in the interests of corporate business. This is evidently so in, for instance, product placement in Hollywood films and sponsorship of sporting events, where corporations have even sought to change the rules of the game. The most extreme form of deep sponsorship is autonomously created culture, usually of a popular kind so that the form itself is a vehicle for advertising, merchandizing and public relations. Disney was a pioneer in this respect. Corporations' construction of children's culture both in entertainment and education is perhaps the most profound and widespread instance of deep sponsorship.

Several zones at the Dome were instances of deep rather than associative sponsorship, perhaps most notably Tesco's Learning Zone that connected its display to the supermarket chain's long-standing sponsorship of computer-aided education. Other examples of manifestly evident editorial command include BT's Talk Zone, Ford's Journey Zone and Manpower's Work Zone. Gerbeau did not initiate deep sponsorship at the Dome; he merely justified it in his fashionable rhetoric of 'public-private partnership' and, specifically, in his argument that you cannot just take money off sponsors without allowing them to influence what is on display. Yet, the vast majority of funding did not come from corporate sponsorship but, instead, from 'the public purse'. Lottery money, in this sense, is a kind of public subscription that was disbursed by the Millennium Commission but which failed to police editorial integrity at NMEC's Dome.

Clearly, the Dome was a site of tension over public and corporate control – in effect, regulation. That there were notable instances of associative sponsorship and, also, examples of the absence of sponsorship demonstrate the tensions in play. An example of associative sponsorship is Marks and Spencer's Self Portrait Zone, which dealt with British national identity. In this zone contradictions were set up by the juxtaposition of placards extolling the virtues of Britishness – 'creativity', 'fair play' and so on – with Gerald Scarfe's sculptures representing the darker side of Britishness. There was, for instance, Bootman, the thug with a boot for a head, and a vicious but ostensibly respectable racist. It would have been unlikely, to say the least, for this zone to point out that Marks and Spencers was a 'quality' and hitherto 'patriotic' retail chain in deep trouble at the time. It was currently losing custom precipitately and turning towards outsourcing products from sweatshop labour around the world as part of the solution to its business problems. The sponsor did, however, allow a questioning of Britishness and an opening up of debate over national identity to be articulated in its zone; and did not manifestly promote its own products there (see McGuigan 2004a for a fuller discussion of Self Portrait).

According to visitor research, the most popular feature of the Dome was the Millennium Show in the Central Arena, an aerial ballet choreographed by Mark Fisher and with music by Peter Gabriel, which told an allegorical love story linked to the emergence, destructiveness and collapse of industrialism. The pivotal motif of a rising and falling gas holder recalled the previous use of the Dome site. There was also a spectacular light show. It is interesting to note that the Millennium Show had no sponsor. Moreover, 'a lasting legacy' from it was intended and perhaps realized. Young people had been selected and trained in the performance skills associated with the Canadian troupe Cirque de Soleil, leaving a greater pool of modern circus talent than had previously existed in Britain.

Analysis of a cultural phenomenon such as the Millennium Dome must take into account its consumption – visitor experience, not just mass-mediation – as well as the political economy of production and the ideology of representation. Although it only attracted 6.5 million, instead of the possibly unrealistic projection of 12 million, those who actually visited the Dome generally said they liked it (see the discussion of MORI polling for NMEC in McGuigan and Gilmore 2001). A great many people did choose to find out for themselves whether or not the Dome was any good, in spite of the media damnation. NMEC claimed, with some good reason, that it was an under-reported 'success'. MORI polling revealed high approval ratings, stretching into the region of 90 per cent of visitors who had a good day out at the Millennium Dome. However, the visitor experience at the Dome was not just about numbers and bald approval ratings. How did visitors experience the Dome?

There are bound to be differences of orientation, interpretation and appreciation. This is worth thinking about in terms of qualitative differentiation rather than just crude percentages for satisfaction and dissatisfaction. The marketing model of museums, exhibitions and entertainment tends to use customer typologies which stereotype differences of orientation, for instance, 'streakers', 'strollers' and 'readers' (Perin 1992). NMEC had such a classification of visitors, as 'divers', 'swimmers' and 'paddlers'. Divers were the clever ones who could penetrate the deep meanings of the Dome. Paddlers would not really be concentrating due to their intellectual deficiencies or having to deal with screaming kids. Swimmers were identified as coming between the extremes of 'brainy' and 'thick' (Parton 1999). It is necessary for cultural analysis to go beyond such stereotyping in order to explore the actual texture of visitor experience. The following typology, developed for the Arts and Humanities Research Board (AHRB) project, 'The Meanings of the New Millennium Experience', identifies two major coordinates of visitor orientation, *generosity* and *reflexivity* (McGuigan and Gilmore 2002). **Generous and reflexive visiting** are not mutually exclusive categories or crude stereotypes. On the one hand, you could be generous and reflexive or generous and unreflexive. On the other hand, you could be reflexively or unreflexively ungenerous. Cross-hatched, these distinctions produce four general modes of visitor orientation. The point of such a typology is to create a general framework for exploring the complex and different ways in which attractions like the Dome are negotiated by visitors and, in the case of ungenerous and unreflexive perhaps, non-visitors.

Table 3.1 Typology of Visitor Orientation

VISITOR ORIENTATION	Generous	Ungenerous
Reflexive	1. Generous reflexive	3. Reflexive ungenerous
Unreflexive	2. Generous unreflexive	4. Ungenerous unreflexive

The typology facilitated the conduct and analysis of conversational interviews with visitors to the Dome (see McGuigan and Gilmore 2002 for details of this visitor research). Visitors to the Dome were typically found to be generous in their orientation, willing to give the benefit of the doubt and keen to make the best of what was on offer. For example, there is the case of a family from Middlesbrough – 300 miles from London – who visited the Dome in March 2000. A grandmother, a mother, a toddler and a boy of about 10 had set off by coach from the North East at 4 in the morning and were going on to the London Eye after the Dome before returning to Middlesbrough at 2 the following morning. The adults and the boy did not say much except that they were having a great time, which is just as well, considering the sheer expenditure of time, money and effort they had put into their 'one amazing day'. If you went at all, you were likely to make the best of it.

Visitors were well aware of the controversial nature of the Millennium Dome. Sceptical of its damnation, they came, in the spirit of practical criticism, to see for themselves. As one visitor summed it up, 'it is nothing like the disaster you read in the newspapers'. Typically, the general experience of the visit exceeded expectations. For some, the Millennium Show was worth the price of the entrance ticket alone. Hosts, however, mentioned a small minority of visitors who had come to confirm their expectation of just how bad it was.

Three general conclusions can be derived from the visitor research for the AHRB project. First, it has to be registered that visitors did not complain much about the role of sponsorship. That does not necessarily mean they approved of it or that it was inconsequential for their experience. Instead, it is reasonable to suggest that many people these days simply take the **logoscape** for granted, rarely questioning its significance so normal has it become under present conditions. Second, it was not unusual to find visitors expressing approval for the Dome in general, the building and its central attraction of the show, rather more than its particular elements, especially the thematic zones. As a visitor experience, the Dome amounted typically to more than the sum of its many tainted parts. Third, the under-reported success that the Dome did, arguably, achieve in terms of visitor response was due more to the generosity of visitors, determined to have a good day out, than of sponsors determined to have their pound of flesh.

Among the determining factors of the Dome 'disaster', the role of corporate sponsorship – economically, ideologically and politically – was decisive. It is an extreme case of the impact of corporate sponsorship on public culture, illustrating the inordinate power symbolically as well as materially of business in liberal-democratic polities today. For a small fraction of the public money spent on it, sponsoring corporations were permitted to have the loudest say in most of the Dome's thematic zones. The role of corporate sponsorship was actually more important ideologically than financially. The four extra tranches of National Lottery money spent to keep the Dome going throughout 2000 amounted to more than the value of sponsorship. It might have been possible, albeit ideologically inconceivable, to have put on an exposition without any sponsorship at all. That would have been contrary to the whole point of the project from a governmental perspective, which was to represent Britain as a nation of corporations instead of a democratic people engaged in debate over their time and place in history.

There is a paradox, however, that needs to be explained, between the publicly mediated 'failure' of the New Millennium Experience – 'the disastrous Dome' – and evidence of an under-reported 'success' according to expressions of visitor approval. Many visitors brought levels of hopeful anticipation and intellectual engagement to the Dome that much of its contents did not actually merit. The Millennium Dome was, to put it mildly, a disappointment in spite of the strenuous efforts made by visitors to make it better than it really was. Visitor generosity and reflexivity towards an ideologically distorted exposition in a big tent at Greenwich are symptomatic of the imperilled standing of the public cultural alternative to commercial speech today. In the face of the taken-for-granted dominance of neo-liberal values and corporate machinations, there is little mass-popular resistance.

It is a sad coda to the project that the Dome and its site were literally given away to corporate business in the end. A series of failed attempts were made to sell off the place before and after closure. Had the Dome been demolished, the land would have been more profitable to developers. To let that happen, however, would have been a final admission of failure for its flagship project by the New Labour government. The place was eventually given away to the Meridian Delta consortium in the summer of 2002 in the vague hope that the government might at some time in the future receive a share of the profits. Profit is to be made from use of the Dome as a sports and entertainment venue by the American Anschutz Corporation and property development around it by Quintain Estates and the Australian Lend Lease Real Estate Group.

Perry Anderson (2000: 11) has remarked, 'the Third Way' of New Labour politics 'is the best ideological shell of neo-liberalism today'. The Great Exhibition of 1851 represented the original liberalism of free trade, with imperial Britain in a commanding position. The 1951 Festival of Britain represented a post-imperial, nationalistic social democracy, a vision of the future that was eventually given concrete form in the South Bank arts complex. The 2000 Millennium Dome turned out to be an ideological shell for neo-liberalism. The British Labour Party, having been out of power for 18 years, relinquished the substance of social democracy while retaining some of its rhetoric in order to subsume neo-liberalism in a governmental project that has reasonably been labelled 'post-Thatcherite' (Driver and Martell 1998). It not only inherited the neo-liberal agenda from the preceding regime; it inherited the Dome. New Labour's Millennium Experience, in effect, represented the government's subordination to the imperatives of big business at great expense to the public.

Conclusion

This chapter has elaborated upon Raymond Williams's brief but suggestive distinction between cultural policy 'proper' and as display. The very category of cultural policy 'proper' is questionable since it is rooted in a sense of post-Second World War governmental propriety in subsidizing the arts, regulating the media and representing identity that may now be *passé*. Already, there was a problem with this category when Williams was talking about it in the 1980s – the nation-state framework for policy was drifting into doubt due to internationalizing and localizing trends. These and other trends – including the shift from state to market regulation – have put 'the welfare-state model' of cultural policy in crisis. Still, however, cultural policy is conducted and rationalized on nation-state grounds. The example of French cultural policy up to and including the 1990s indicates the persistence of the old model, which is also a symptomatic example of cultural policy as display, national aggrandizement and culture as a business proposition. That aspect of cultural policy is not new. Its history is exemplified in this chapter by the tradition of *expositions universelles*, great exhibitions and world's fairs. These extravagant displays were about promoting national business in a complex interplay with other nations and in the context of trade rivalry.

The case study of the Millennium Dome further illustrates the operations of cultural policy as display. It is an extreme instance both of nationalistic hubris, particularly considering its failure to articulate a sufficiently multicultural Britishness, and of corporate exploitation of publicly funded culture. That an exposition on this scale should have been mounted at all in the same year as the official successor to the international tradition, Hanover 2000, is peculiar to say the least. Interestingly, Hanover 2000 met with a similar fate to the Millennium Dome. It attracted only 16 million of a projected 40 million visitors and was an object of persistent criticism and public debate. The corporate presence was massive at Hanover as well. However, unlike the British exposition, it played host to countries from around the world, although the USA refused to participate. Hanover 2000 still represented a world of nations, whereas the Millennium Dome represented a nation of corporations. The Dome was a vehicle for old delusions of national grandeur allied to corporate power. Commenting in the 1960s on what he considered then to be the terminal decline of the tradition, Umberto Eco (1987b [1967]) remarked prophetically, 'The bug of grandeur kills invention.'

4

RHETORICS OF DEVELOPMENT, DIVERSITY AND TOURISM

Introduction

'Development' and 'diversity' are cardinal terms in contemporary rhetorics of cultural policy as broadly conceived. In effect, they bring together economy and culture, a profound site of which coming together is tourism. It is a massive industry across the world. This chapter interrogates the interplay of development, diversity and tourism.

First, it is necessary to say something about rhetoric and why it is relevant to the critical and reflexive analysis of cultural policy. The ancient art of rhetoric was propounded by Aristotle (1991) in fourth-century BC Athens where the virtues of debate in philosophy and politics were regarded highly. 'Rhetoric' refers to the persuasive use of words. Aristotle sought to clarify its various modes and techniques. Acquiring rhetorical skills was considered essential to elite forms of education in Europe until the nineteenth century AD, though the art of public speaking was hardly neglected subsequently in the preparation of leaders. To some extent, however, it became discredited, which is summed up now in the commonplace phrase, 'mere rhetoric'. In the twentieth century attempts were made to revive its explicitly educational and analytical value. In 1936, I.A. Richards (1965 [1936]: 23) called for 'a revived Rhetoric' as the 'study of verbal understanding or misunderstanding'. In 1983, Terry Eagleton concluded his magisterial survey, *Literary Theory*, with the recommendation that the study of Literature in the narrow sense of a canon of consecrated texts should be superseded by the study of rhetoric. To quote him:

Rhetoric, which was the received form of critical analysis all the way from ancient society to the eighteenth century, examined the way discourses are constructed in order to achieve certain effects. It was not worried about whether its objects of enquiry were speaking or writing, poetry or philosophy, fiction or historiography: its horizon was nothing less than the field of discursive practices in society as a whole, and its particular interest lay in grasping such practices as forms of power and performance. This is not to say that it ignored the truth-value of the discourses in question, since this could often be crucially relevant to the kinds of effect they produced in their readers and listeners.

(Eagleton 1983: 205–6)

Michael Billig (1996 [1985]) has put the case for 'a rhetorical approach to social psychology', which stresses linguistically mediated interaction and the wider social and power contexts of attitude and belief. His arguments are as applicable to cultural analysis as to social psychology (Billig 1997). In fact, for him, 'argument' is the very stuff of public communication. Billig traces the value and, indeed, reality of argumentativeness back to Protagoraean sophistry. Sophists were often dismissed in ancient Greece for their sheer peskiness and accused of deception, perhaps unfairly. They are still treated with suspicion, not only in Greece. Whether honestly or dishonestly, sophists ask awkward questions, as did Socrates, and refuse to let the debate rest at some point of spurious agreement.

Protagoras emphasized 'the two-sidedness of human thinking' and insisted that there were 'two contrary sides to every question' (Billig 1996 [1985]: 71). In ancient Greek terminology, 'logos' is always accompanied, no doubt to the chagrin of logocentrics, by 'anti-logos'. Anti-logos, words against words, is not just the sign of personal awkwardness and anti-social cussedness; it is constitutive of how we make sense and move the argument on, through contradiction: the endless process of claim and counter-claim. Bureaucratic modes of thought, including governmental and commercial, would prefer it to be otherwise, but to little avail.

It is characteristic of bureaucratic rhetoric to suppress difference either by discounting it, by pretending not to have noticed it, or by incorporating it and thereby showing that it is not so different after all: this latter may be the function of the rhetoric of 'diversity' in contemporary policy discourse.

What is the meaning of words? 'Development', with its connotations of 'bringing out', 'evolutionary growth' and 'progress' might be regarded universally as signifying a good thing, but it is not necessarily so in reality. In Jean-François Lyotard's writing, 'development' was a code word 'for advanced capitalism (and such high-profile aspects of this phenomenon as the multinationals), whose sole concern is with expansion of its operations', according to Stuart Sim (2001: 76). Sim goes on to remark, 'Such expansion demands continual improvement of the system's productive efficiency, hence the appropriation of techno-science to its cause.' Lyotard's post-humanist desire to retrieve something of humanism from the ravages of anti-humanism and the inhuman effects of technocapitalism castigated 'development': 'The inhumanity of the system [. . .] is currently being consolidated under the name of development (among others)' (Lyotard 1991 [1988]: 2). The negative sense given to the term 'development' by

Lyotard is not shared typically by public policy discourse, of course, whether exclusively economic in orientation or tempered by social considerations.

In the peculiarly cultural turn of recent development rhetoric it is connected to 'diversity', with positive connotations of 'The condition or quality of being diverse, different or varied' in contrast to the older negative connotations of 'oddness, wickedness, perversity [. . .] contrariety, disagreement' (*Oxford English Dictionary*). You would not expect policy rhetoric to be anything other than upbeat, however vacuous it may be.

One of the major sources of development today, especially in poorer countries, is tourism, constituting a key site of disputation over culture and economy, the dialectic of sameness and difference, the imbroglio of growth and exploitation. Issues to do with tourism – especially **ecotourism/ecotravel** – are interrogated in the final section of this chapter.

Developing

'Development' frequently appears in rhetorics of cultural policy as narrowly conceived, that is, in terms of subsidizing the arts and heritage but not so much, strictly speaking, for specifically *cultural* development. It is worth pausing for a moment to consider why the development of art and cultural heritage is not widely held to be an end in itself. There is a crisis concerning assumptions of aesthetic authority and hierarchy in the West that has been going on since the 1960s. Established criteria of valuation were called into question to the extent that public support for the arts as a set of superior values to mass-marketed culture was no longer regarded as self-evidently justified whether on grounds of preservation or dissemination. From this point of view, art and culture have no intrinsic worth. Art and culture are either to be valued aesthetically by relative rather than absolute criteria of judgement which vary wildly according to the contingencies of prevailing taste in time and place or on criteria extrinsic to aesthetics as such. The latter are most typically economic and/or social considerations these days, not by so explicitly political *diktat* as in Nazi Germany and the Soviet Union during the 1930s.

Since the 1980s public cultural investment has been justified increasingly and perhaps predominantly on economic grounds. John Myerscough's (1988) neo-Keynesian *The Economic Importance of the Arts in Britain* and his related city-based studies were influential not only in Britain but also throughout Europe. He sought to demonstrate that investment in the arts had a knock-on effect in stimulating economic activity generally, and urban regeneration particularly, in a period of de-industrialization. Public subsidy to the arts was not a luxury, a wealthy extravagance, a waste of tax-payers' money, but had an instrumental value beyond the arts themselves. As Peter Rodgers (1989: i) remarked at the time, 'The issues now should be not whether the arts have a significant economic importance, but how great is it, how can it be further encouraged and exploited, and how should arts policy be related to wider economic aims?' While there was some scepticism about the actual economic impact of the arts on urban regeneration, sceptics tended to argue for a broader notion of social impact (Bianchini and Parkinson 1993) that met up with a more diffuse discourse of 'human development'.

Although the arts might still be regarded as a means of levering economic development, by the late 1990s, the argument had shifted on to the social as well as economic impact of public investment in this area. François Matarasso's *Use or Ornament? The Social Impact of Participation in the Arts* (1997) claimed to present conclusive evidence of the social impact of arts funding. He says, 'This research was designed to add a dimension to existing economic and aesthetic rationales for the arts by looking at their role in social development and cohesion' (Matarasso 1997: vi). To an extent, this was a re-run of the 'access' discourse of the 1970s but less concerned with the battle over cultural value than promoting arts funding as a solution to 'social exclusion', the problem which the European Union wishes to combat in addition to strengthening Europe's economic competitiveness. That illustrates how the range of 'cultural policy' has been extended as a solution to all problems, the principal concern of this chapter. However, it is worth considering in passing the narrower rhetorical function of the *Use or Ornament?* research report. It aims to be useful, but is it merely ornamental?

The role of 'impact' is vital here. Survey evidence is deployed to claim that public funding for 'participatory arts' impacts upon personal development, social cohesion, community empowerment and self-determination, local image and identity, imagination and vision, health and wellbeing. The apparently overwhelming evidence of such impacts presented by Matarasso is largely derived from asking participants whether arts participation has had these impacts upon them. Matarasso's research has been submitted to rigorous methodological critique by Paola Merli (2002: 108), who says, 'My first criticism is that Matarasso's research has no internal validity, i.e. the data collected cannot support conclusions about the hypotheses of the research project.'

Merli points out that Matarasso's hypotheses are framed by concepts so abstract that they are not actually observable or measurable. The ostensibly objective survey method used to establish impact is, in fact, irredeemably subjective. Moreover, it does not even explore the complexly subjective meanings of arts participation that in-depth interviewing might do. This is a fundamental fault of attitudinal surveying as a means of studying what actually happens.

However, the question has to be posed: does a rather basic critique of the validity of Matarasso's method really matter in 'the real world' of cultural policy. Probably not a jot since its most important function is rhetorical rather than that of disinterested empirical science. In such a case, an elementary apparatus of empiricism is used to justify a reductive politics of measurable impact.

That became an especially salient characteristic of evidence-based policy-making in Britain towards the end of the twentieth century and into the twenty-first century. For instance, in order to circumvent a pre-election commitment to the previous

Conservative government's spending plans, the 1997 Labour government gave the Arts Council of England an extra £5 million for a New Audiences development fund (Hewison 2001). A condition of the extra funding was that it be supported by impact research that proved the money was not to be wasted.

Whether the rationale is economic, social or residually cultural, 'development' is the cardinal term, weaving together any number of disparate purposes. As the editors of a recent collection of articles from Australia on cultural development observe, 'cultural development gives priority to the building and enhancing of cultural capacity for the twin purposes of both social and cultural inclusion *and* industrial development' (Gibson and O'Reagan 2002: 5). Cultural development in this wide-ranging and ambitious sense was launched by the 'creative nation' agenda of the Australian Labour government in the early 1990s (Commonwealth of Australia 1994). Since then there has been a greater recognition of 'multiculturalism' and the promotion of 'cultural industries' has shifted into a much broader notion of 'creative industries' which brings together cultural policy with information-society policy in a heady mixture. As Tom O'Reagan (2002: 22) remarks wryly, 'I think those of us involved in cultural policy formation and cultural policy studies failed to recognise the consequences of success.' Indeed, since cultural policy has blurred into economic policy, in effect, it becomes the object of really serious business and governmental politics. Now that culture has been snatched from the hands of reformed cultural critics wanting to be practical, they must adapt to a 'new reality' to stay there or die. Stuart Cunningham (2002) registers the problem of running cultural industries policy into creative industries policy, the latter a catch-all for the production and circulation of 'knowledge' generally that is driven by the post-industrial economy. Yet, he also stresses the economic value to Queensland of developing a small business strategy that operates on a local/global nexus across information and culture. 'One of the ways forward is to centre new policy around a small business development agenda which potentially has as much to do with a portfolio like industry, IT and the information economy as it has with culture and the arts', according to Cunningham (2002: 61).

As cultural policy immaterializes into economic policy in rich countries, curiously, it becomes a new way of thinking about development for poorer countries, which arguably obscures the realities of economic inequality and political domination. 'Development' in postcolonial 'Third World' countries during the 1960s and 1970s had been about economic development first and foremost from a governmental perspective, closing the gap in living standards with the capitalist 'First World' and the communist 'Second World'. It was a major concern of rich countries, especially the USA, while the Cold War raged. Even then, however, American development economics placed great emphasis on social and cultural factors, with its Parsonian distinction between 'tradition' and 'modernity' according to 'pattern variables'. As Jan Nederveen Pieterse (2001: 21) comments, 'modernization is defined as a movement from particularism to universalism, from ascription to achievement, from functional diffuseness to functional specificity, and from affective roles to affective-neutrality'. In order to become modern,

Third World people were required to change their attitudes as a prelude to changing their behaviour and their societies.

It is often said now that the problem with such modernism is that it presented a single, one-size-fits-all model of culture and society, which is not quite true in that capitalism and communism at least ostensibly represented rival modes of development. Many Third World countries sought to develop in a non-aligned manner. Nevertheless, it was assumed across the board that state intervention and public-sector development were key to **modernization** whether capitalist, communist or somewhere in between. Governments were lent money and given advice on this assumption. Marxist critics argued, however, that such development resulted in 'dependency', repeating the process of 'underdevelopment' initiated by capitalist imperialism (for instance, A.G. Frank 1971).

Today, it is widely assumed that the kind of development theorized and practised in the 1960s and 1970s failed, that poverty was not eradicated and that grandiose state-sponsored and aided schemes for a great leap forward were often mistaken. For instance, the writer Arundhati Roy has criticized the obsession with building dams in India since independence:

> There was a time when everybody loved Big Dams. Everybody had them – Communists, Capitalists, Christians, Muslims, Hindus, Buddhists. They did not start out as a cynical enterprise. They began as a dream. They've ended up as a nightmare. It's time to wake up.
>
> (Roy 2002 [2001]: 51–2)

As 'monuments of Modern Civilization', the thousands of large dams built from 1947 onwards turned out to be spectacular failures, according to Roy. More areas are drought prone now while there have also been several flood disasters. One-fifth of the Indian population in the twenty-first century is without safe drinking water and two-thirds do not have basic sanitation facilities. Well-off city dwellers enjoy Western standards of living and millions of lower-caste Indians have been displaced from their traditional farming lands.

There has been a loss of confidence in modernization in both theory and practice. Paradigms of development have shifted, at least theoretically, from modernist thought to postmodernist scepticism and anti-modernity of one kind or another (Schech and Haggis 2000; Nederveen Pieterse 2001). For instance, Arturo Escobar (2002 [1995]) deconstructs the discourse of development with regard to 'the problem of poverty', which it constructed and, simultaneously, failed to solve. He presents a Foucauldian analysis of power–knowledge relations in the field that challenges the scientific pretensions of developmental modernization as well as its Utopian promise. The standard criticisms typically refer to the homogenizing and teleological features of Western modernity in general, that is, discursive oppression. There is a tendency in such reasoning to play down comparatively recent changes in the actual political economy of development and particularly the rise of neo-liberal globalization.

Joseph Stiglitz (2002), formerly chief economist at the World Bank, has no doubt where the fundamental fault lies. It derives from the 'Washington consensus' on the utter superiority of free-market economics over protection for vulnerable nations that is put into practice by its aid and trade agencies, the International Monetary Fund (IMF) and the World Trade Organization (WTO). He traces their devastating impact on poorer parts of the world from the neo-liberal turn of Reagonomics and Thatcherism in the 1980s. The gulf between rich and poor has widened dramatically since then with few exceptions, most notably the 'tiger economies' of East Asia which have benefited, in fact, from considerable state intervention. Stiglitz himself, an unreconstructed Keynesian, partly absolves the World Bank *for Reconstruction and Development* from the evangelical ruthlessness of the other agencies. According to him, the World Bank looks closely at the particular circumstances of countries in request of aid, whereas the IMF has a single solution for all: market liberalization and privatization of state-owned infrastructure and services. In the 1980s, developing countries were required to restructure according to the principles of neo-liberal globalization that inevitably favour rich and powerful countries, most obviously the USA itself. This 'market fundamentalism' became the new common sense for governments around the globe. It has met with little resistance from nation-state governments since the collapse of communism and virtual implosion of social democracy. Apart from anti-globalization protest, only trading blocs, especially the European Union, put up any serious obstruction. That is particularly so for trade in cultural goods and services where issues of identity combine, to some extent, with considerations of economic expediency.

From the late 1980s, through GATT (General Agreement on Tariffs and Trade), its successor since 1995 – the WTO – and GATS (General Agreement on Trade in Services), the USA has sought to exert its economic power in communications and culture. It is not surprising why, as Toby Miller and George Yudice observe:

> The services sector of the developed world expanded massively over the 1990s, to the point where it comprised 70% of gross domestic product in the industrialized nations and 50% in much of the Third World, accounting for US $ 1 trillion a year in trade, perhaps a fifth of the global total.
>
> (Miller and Yudice 2002: 173)

In truth, there is little popular resistance or governmental, for that matter, to the import of American and other 'global' cultural products and services in countries rich and poor around the world. They have great appeal at the point of consumption: at the point of production too. The **New International Division of Cultural Labour** (**NICL**), moreover, involves the location of cultural manufacture and service work in comparatively low pay economies, supported by governments with tax breaks and other gifts. Hollywood not only gives pleasure to global audiences; it employs global workers in a complex system of production and circulation (see Miller et al. 2001).

The actual reduction of the cultural to the economic and its seemingly indisputable realism, oddly enough, has provoked an argumentative response, ostensibly a contrary rhetoric, that of *cultural development* but not that of economic underdevelopment. 'Development studies' love affair with political economy and neo-liberal economics is beginning to wane. Culture is coming back onto the agenda, displaced by the centrality of the market over the last twenty years', say Susanne Schech and Jane Haggis (2002: xiii). This does not only represent the alternative love affair with Foucault and post-structuralism in the groves of especially Australian academe but also is at the heart of **UNESCO (United Nations Educational, Scientific and Cultural Organization)** rhetoric since its 1990s decade of cultural development and recent international debates on cultural policy generally.

Diversifying

The report of UNESCO's World Commission on Culture and Development (WCCD 1996 [1995]), *Our Creative Diversity*, is said to have marked a 'paradigm shift' in the theory and practice of cultural policy. As stated in the Council of Europe's follow-up report to UNESCO's deliberations on culture and development, this meant, in the European context, bringing both the socially excluded and cultural policy 'in from the margins' of political and economic governance (European Task Force on Culture and Development (ETFCD) 1997). These reports initiated a great debate and a series of declarations on the role of 'diversity' in cultural development, such as the *Action Plan for Cultural Policies for Development* (see Kleberg 1998; and also Wright 1998). The Bank of Sweden Tercentenary Foundation, in association with other bodies, funded seminars and conferences aimed at formulating a research agenda within the framework of the new paradigm (see Knutsson 1998). Carl-Johan Kleberg (2000: 49), of the Tercentenary Foundation, points out that the new paradigm employs 'a wide anthropological definition of culture'. He acknowledges, however, that moving cultural policy from a narrow preoccupation with the arts and directly related matters puts it into a potentially boundless arena. This should be checked, according to the Council of Europe's *In From the Margins*, by including, in Kleberg's term, 'popular mass culture', but not absolutely everything that could be included by the anthropological definition of culture. That is a reasonable and, indeed, essential limitation. Yet, if you actually read the reports of the new paradigm you will not find such a strict adherence to this limitation on cultural policy discourse and rhetoric.

UNESCO's summary on its web site says, the 'central argument' of *Our Creative Diversity* is that 'development embraces not only access to goods and services, but also the opportunity to choose a full, satisfying, valuable and valued way of living together, thus encouraging the flourishing of human existence in all its forms and as a whole' (unesco.org). Such a statement suggests that the purpose of the new paradigm of culture and development is to contest economic reductionism in human affairs or at least qualify it substantially. Culture wishing to check economy has a very old and Romantic provenance. In effect, however, when looked at closely, it becomes evident that the emerging paradigm hovers uncertainly between a counter-discourse to global neo-liberalism, inspired by cultural humanism, and a consensual orientation that seeks to absorb it into a more humane set of principles.

There is hardly a word in the reports, action plans and universal declarations of the new paradigm of cultural development and diversity with which I personally would want to disagree. It all seems so very reasonable and decent. That makes me feel uneasy.

In his forward to *Our Creative Diversity*, Javier Perez de Cuellar (1996 [1995]: 8) remarks upon 'a need to transcend economics, without abandoning it'. So it is not just that all we need is love. But, we do need more mutual respect and understanding. This does not quite amount to Habermasian discourse ethics of dialogue and negotiation. What is called for is a 'global ethics', a set of principles that we can all share. In the executive summary to the report, it is made clear that global ethics must avoid the 'dual pitfalls' of ethnocentrism and cultural relativism. The difficulty is, however, to identify universal principles in a divided world. Presumably, it must be assumed, then, that Christianity is not alone in believing we do not live on bread alone. Purely economic development is soulless. Human rights, democratic legitimacy, public accountability and evidential proof are the foundations of a global ethics, according to *Our Creative Diversity*. Cultural pluralism, recognition that there are many voiceless in a 'media-rich world', gender equality, appreciation of youth and cultivation of children, preservation of heritage and protection of the natural environment: all of these constitute the substance of a global ethics. Who could possibly disagree?

Towards the end of *Our Creative Diversity*, sticking points are mentioned. For instance, 'the globalisation of cultural tastes and styles has limited the role government can play in the provision of cultural products' (WCCD, 1996 [1995]): 237). The old instruments of national cultural policy are worn out, incapable of dealing with the predominance of global culture. Hence, the need for universal principles of, shall we say, *cultural resistance*? But, to what exactly? Could it possibly be neo-liberal globaliza-tion? Benjamin Barber's (1996 [1995]) *Jihad vs. McWorld* is cited as a key indication of where the tensions lie and, since 9-11 (Chomsky 2001), it reads as an especially poignant citation.

Perhaps it is in the very nature of the genre that reports like *Our Creative Diversity* and *In From the Margins* tend to a certain opacity when it comes to the object of their rhetorical critique. Instead of naming the source of trouble unequivocally, these reports opt for a positively idealistic advocacy of cultural development. It becomes, thus, a rather vague solution to problems that are not made quite clear. This is not, however, to deny the good intentions of the new paradigm or is it to undervalue the work of mapping a greatly extended, though over-stretched, space for cultural policy theory and practice in the world today.

In From the Margins is rather more explicit than *Our Creative Diversity* in question-ing neo-liberal globalization by associating it with US interests. Europe is in competi-tion with the USA. However, Europe has its own internal problems as well with which to contend: loss of conviction in state intervention and the problematic unity of European culture. The problem of the state is especially acute for cultural policy. This is partly due to the newly installed conventional wisdom that mass-popular culture, exemplified by American commercialism, can no longer be regarded as inherently inferior to the great European heritage of high culture, the market failures of which the state had sought to ameliorate. It is vital, then, that cultural Europeanness is reconceived in complex diversity instead of a simple and largely mythical unity. This is necessary not only because of differences of national culture but also – and more urgently – because of ethnic differences that cut across national borders. European labour markets have attracted economic migrants from former colonies and relatively poor countries like Turkey adjacent to European affluence. The problem is further complicated by the integration of formerly communist Eastern Europe into the capitalist club of the European Union.

The question of European diversity would seem, however, to be secondary to

> the key question which this report seeks to address: to what extent should the development of the arts and culture, and especially their impacts into overall development, be left to market forces and, if and when public intervention is deemed to be necessary, on which areas should it focus and what forms should it take? In other words, what should be the criteria for assessing the proper role of public intervention?
>
> (ETFCD 1997: 239–40)

So, 'the key question' turns out to be a very old one for cultural policy. Loss of conviction in hierarchical standards of cultural value in the face of the sheer dynamism of commercial culture and its popular self-financing appeal make it very difficult to answer the question. This is the question of cultural policy from the point of view of the state and alliance between states with ostensibly shared interests that are primarily economic, not necessarily cultural at all, under the pressure of global competition. Does this mean, then, that public cultural policy no longer has a role to perform? Not a bit of it, for *In From the Margins*. In fact, cultural policy is more important now than ever, apparently. Its object becomes the promotion rather than the suppression of 'diversity'. Implicit here is another old assumption, that mass-popular culture, driven by commerce, is homogenizing. Against that, it is the task of public agencies to embrace heterogeneity. Somehow, then, cultural policy will solve the problem of social exclusion. How it is supposed to do that is left somewhat unclear, although it has something to do with the revival of civil society. The way forward is to 'manage change', in the managerial terminology of *In From the Margins*, not to hark back to older solutions, increased welfare and the like, or surrender to the ineluctable force of neo-liberal globalization. After all, this is a matter of principle: principles such as Identity, Creativity, Participation and, of course, Diversity – buzzwords without referents.

In an ongoing debate the leaving of loose ends at various points along the way is really only to be expected. To pick up the loose ends, the Council of Europe commissioned a cross-national study including participation from Austria, Belgium, Bulgaria, Luxembourg, Switzerland and the UK, *Differing Diversities – Cultural Policy and Cultural Diversity* (T. Bennett 2001). Edited by Tony Bennett and introduced by his essay, 'Differing Diversities – Transversal Study on the Theme of Cultural Policy and Cultural Diversity', like *Our Creativity Diversity* and *In From the Margins*, this report contains a wealth of useful information and suggestive analysis. As well as the introductory essay, which I shall consider in a moment, *Differing Diversities* contains seven research position papers ranging across media policy, cultural planning and copyright law. One of the papers examines the relationship between cultural diversity and biodiversity. If there is unity, like similar reports, it is unity in diversity. To draw out the underlying assumptions and key arguments from such work is to do a certain kind of symbolic violence to the complexity and variety of deliberation that characterizes recent cultural policy discourse and rhetoric. This really is a time of debate rather than the enunciation of fixed positions.

Bennett's introduction epitomizes the in many ways refreshing absence of fixity, open-endedness and, no doubt, for some less charitably disposed towards the language of official reports, the vague, all-encompassing abstraction of bureaucratic rhetoric. It is declared confidently that 'Cultural diversity, in all its forms, is posing a profound challenge to traditional formulations of cultural policy, and to our understanding of the public interests served by this policy' (T. Bennett 2001: 12). Essentially what follows is a categorizing and classifying exercise on cultural diversity 'in all its forms'. The sources of diversity are identified: 'sub- or multinational', 'autochthonous', 'diasporic' and 'indigenous'. There are 'civic', 'administrative', 'social', 'economic' and 'conceptual' contexts of diversity. Issues of concern include 'public spheres', 'changing social dynamics', 'markets', 'everyday life' and 'culturally appropriate quantitative and qualitative forms of assessment'. Bennett counts four 'principles' of 'entitlement': 'equal opportunity', providing 'all members of society' with 'the cultural means of functioning effectively', nurturing 'sources of diversity through imaginative mechanisms' and 'obligation for the promotion of diversity to aim at establishing ongoing interactions between differentiated cultures' (20). The priorities are:

i.   Decentralisation and cultural planning approaches to diversity . . .
ii. Cultural entrepreneurship and diversity . . .
iii. Culture and the management of conflict . . .
iv. Cultural diversity in everyday life . . .
v.   Majority/minority public spheres.

(T. Bennett 2001: 67)

Again, nothing much to disagree with there by anyone from almost any persuasion. That is the trouble with such rhetoric: it all seems fine and inoffensive but curiously insubstantial.

Perhaps there is more in the method, which Bennett calls 'transversal', than in the substance. It derives from 'transversal politics', described by Cynthia Cockburn and

Lynette Hunter (1999: 88–9) as 'the practice of creatively crossing (and re-drawing) the borders that mark significant politicised differences'. Nira Yuval Davis (1999: 94–5) says that it has three notable characteristics. The first, 'standpoint epistemology', assumes that all knowledge is perspectival and that 'truth' only emerges in dialogue between different positions. The second assumes that difference and equality must be reconciled with one another. The third assumption is that while people might categorize themselves as different from others they may share something with others and differ in some respects from those within their own category.

Such thinking is opposed to bigotry and in favour of dialogue. If cultural policy can help in fostering mutual understanding then indeed it should. In Europe and elsewhere, it is perennially necessary to combat both hard and soft racism. Work like the Parekh Report, *The Future of Multi-Ethnic Britain* (Runnymede Trust 2000), is especially valuable in revealing the taken-for-granted racism implicit in assumptions concerning nationhood and cultural heritage (see McGuigan 2004b). It is not so clear, however, what this has to do specifically with the challenge of neo-liberal globalization. Unlike in the shadow boxing of *Our Creative Diversity* and *In From the Margins*, it is not even a shadowy presence in Bennett's essay, *Differing Diversities*. That is probably because neo-liberal globalization and exclusionary racism are, to a significant extent, separate problems for cultural or any other public policy. It is certainly difficult to see quite how the gentle approach of cultural development and diversity can deal with the harsh problems associated with neo-liberal globalization. It is as though a solution has been displaced from one problem, that of racialized social exclusion, to handle another one, that of the oppressive dominance of economic power and reasoning in every aspect of life.

Interestingly, however, a recent contribution to the genre of reports on cultural development and diversity, Colin Mercer's (2002) *Towards Cultural Citizenship – Tools for Cultural Policy and Development*, quotes Denise Meredyth and Jeffrey Minson's observation concerning the relationship between cultural policy and neo-liberalism approvingly. 'Studies of cultural policy are centrally concerned with [. . .] modes of neo-liberal governance, which work between public institutions and private lives and at both national and international levels, shaping civic or civil habits, tastes, and dispositions in ways that are all the more effective for not being experienced as obtrusive' (Meredyth and Minson 2001: xi–xii). For these students of cultural policy, there seems to be a happy coincidence between neo-liberal 'structural adjustment', marketization and privatization, on the one hand, and civic democracy on the other hand. And, as Mercer (2002: xix) comments, 'This being so, and we strongly believe that it is – increasingly so in a globalised world – the question of "resourcing citizens" becomes very important and strategic'. The task of the new cultural policy, from that perspective, would thus appear as the cultivation of citizens suitably disposed for life in a neo-liberal world, not quite what was implied by the UNESCO report – *Our Creative Diversity* – or the Council of Europe report – *In From the Margins*. Neither of them envisaged a neat fit with neo-liberalism but, instead at the very least, a counterweight to it, however timidly expressed.

The bulk of Mercer's *Towards Cultural Citizenship*, which was produced for the Bank of Sweden's Tercentenary Foundation and allied organizations, is actually unobjectionable when viewed from a perspective critical of neo-liberalism. In fact, it is rather more in line with the protocols of the administrative state – leaning towards Adorno's totally administered society – than the supposed freedoms of the market. Like similar reports of its ilk, *Towards Cultural Citizenship* is concerned with turning principles into practice. That is to be achieved by drawing up innumerable and endless lists of indicators. A bureaucratic nightmare is conjured up of research and assessment overseeing and, if ever plausibly put into comprehensive practice, swamping policy formation and implementation: all in the name of *cultural* development. For instance, Mercer cites Arundhati Roy's critique of the Narmada River Sardar Sarovar Dam project, alluded to earlier in this chapter:

> This major infrastructural project has caused massive displacement and hardship to communities in the area affected. Doubtless the project was subjected to an Environmental Impact Assessment in order to gain funding and formal approvals.
>
> It is unlikely, however, that there was anything like a Cultural Impact Assessment which would measure its effects on ways of living, lifestyles, the identities, the value systems and beliefs of the communities affected. Such factors are crucial to the acceptability and, more importantly, the sustainability of any development process. We have learned this for the environment. Can we also learn it for culture?
>
> (Mercer 2002: 88)

Once more, in this passage, the concept of culture is being stretched to breaking point, to the point where the *material* impact of a development scheme on people's livelihood can only be talked about in oddly displaced *cultural* terms.

On a more charitable note, *Towards Cultural Citizenship*, might be read as merely calling for a cultural statistics bureau tooled up on a global scale that is large enough to inform thoroughly every detail of policy-making. It would contribute to the growth of nothing less than – or other than – the cultural policy research industry itself. However large and lavishly funded, though, it is not likely to ask the more interesting questions from a critical perspective on cultural policy.

Touring

From the point of view of development, tourism is the biggest game these days. Travel and tourism make up the largest industry in the world in terms of gross domestic product, exports and employment; and it is growing at the rate of nearly 5 per cent a year, according to the WTO at the turn of the Millennium.

For developing countries, tourism constitutes a crucial comparative advantage because such countries still have a mainly non-industrialized environment that can be represented as a pre-lapsarian paradise to those from more economically developed countries. Moreover, the debt crisis that broke out in the 1980s brought tourism increasingly to the fore as a foreign currency earner and generator of employment. This fitted neatly into the neo-liberal paradigm of development. The way forward for developing countries was no longer to be confined to state-sponsored mimicry of advanced industrial states but, instead, carving out a niche in the global economy whereby the poor might more efficiently service the rich by concentrating on what they were good at. That suited the discerning Western consumer very nicely, not only in clothing but also in getaway places.

The rhetoric of tourism addressed to the consumer of any kind always emphasizes escape from the drudgery of everyday life, whether the promise is realized or not. Yet, it is well known that tourism has a down side, that paradise ceases to be paradise when flooded with vulgar tourists. The search is on, therefore, for a kind of holiday unspoilt by tourists. Educated members of the middle class are especially attracted to such a prospect, to a culture or environment where they may search for themselves. Randomly selected, on the 'Escape' section's front page of *The Observer*, Sunday, 5 January 2003, the reader is offered 'Holidays that will change your life'. These consist of 'luxury spas', 'monastic retreats', '15 holidays to sort your head out', 'an idyllic new Andalusian retreat' and a 'family round-the-world adventure'.

There are, of course, different kinds of tourism from the point of view of the tourist. They include the kind of mass tourism characteristic of the British invasion of the Costa Brava, the cultural tourism of visiting great cities and historic sites that harks back to the European 'grand tour', and the rediscovery of 'nature' in ecological travel and tourism. For some reflexive selves, you may be a 'tourist' but I am a 'visitor' or a 'traveller'. Tourism is a positional practice, a means of distinction not just a getaway for the self-conscious.

Still, tourist development is a controversial matter that is not reducible to the subjectivity of the tourist but is an issue of public policy, as Dean McCannell pointed out some time ago:

The development of an area for tourism has given rise to two new and distinctive political positions. A protagonist position is held by many planners of marginal economies who look to tourism as a new way of making money. An anti-touristic position is held by urban and modernized liberals and third world radicals who question the value of touristic development for the local people. They point out how tourism irreversibly alters local tradition, and the capital that is siphoned off by large corporations (hotel chains and airlines) and returned to its point of origin in the rich countries and cities.

(1989 [1975]: 162)

Jennifer Craik (1997) argues that the recent association of cultural development with tourism tends to exacerbate rather than ameliorate established tensions concerning benefit culturally as well as materially. Typically, the tourist's perception of the host culture is mystified, constructed by preconceived notions and exotic fantasies bearing little relation to actuality. Otherness is thus consumed unknowingly more often than not.

Whatever way you look at it, tourism is a contradictory phenomenon. This was registered both by UNESCO's *Our Creative Diversity* and in the Council of Europe's *In From the Margins*. Neither of these reports had much to say about tourism, which is strange when its close link to cultural development is considered. Nevertheless, what they did have to say is largely critical. *Our Creative Diversity* commented upon the great hopes invested in tourism by developing countries and, at the same time, mentioned its seamier side, most notably the growth of sex tourism (WCCD 1996 [1995]: 142). More generally, the UNESCO report referred to how rich countries plunder the cultural resources of poor countries (199, 238). It certainly did not endorse tourism unreservedly as the cutting edge of cultural development.

In From the Margins acknowledged that tourism 'creates jobs, but it can also degrade the heritage and the environment in the process' (EFTCD 1997: 96). This report was also concerned about 'distortions of traditional lifestyles and cultural identity' (97). Furthermore, the European Task Force remarked upon how city-centre developments to attract tourism are often accompanied by neglect of local neighbourhoods in the city (100). The Council of Europe's report concluded, however, that it was equally mistaken to try and stop such development as to give up on trying to control it. The task, then, is to 'manage change'.

In the circumstances, that is empty rhetoric. Change is occurring and, indeed, it is being managed: but how and with what effects? As John Urry (2002 [1990]: 56) notes, 'the effects of tourism are highly complex and contradictory'. While the fascination of the developed world with the still comparatively underdeveloped world has increased, the actual economic benefits accruing to poorer countries are a great deal less than might be expected. For instance, in Mauritius, '90% of foreign exchange earned from tourism is repatriated to companies based elsewhere' (Urry 2002 [1990]: 57). Urry poses the crucial question:

> It must be asked: development *for whom*? Many of the facilities that result from tourism (airports, golf courses, luxury hotels and so on) will be of little benefit to the mass of the indigenous population. Likewise much indigenous wealth that is generated will be highly unequally distributed and so most of the population of developing countries will gain little benefit. This does of course depend on patterns of local ownership. Finally, much employment generated in tourist-related services is relatively low-skilled and may well reproduce the servile character of the previous colonial regime, what one critic has termed 'flunky training' . . .
>
> (Urry 2002 [1990]: 57)

Urry himself sees no way out of this situation: 'it must be asked whether many developing countries have much alternative to tourism as a development strategy' (57).

Urry usefully elaborates upon the experience of work in tourist resorts yet his classic, *The Tourist Gaze*, is much less concerned with the host than with the guest. Primarily, his aim is to explain the experience of tourism from the point of view of the tourist. For him, tourism is not to be defined as a search for authenticity, as McCannell would once have had it, but as something fundamentally mediated and specular in character. Urry is concerned with, in Roland Barthes's (1971) phrase, 'the rhetoric of the image'. However, his main theoretical source is not so much Barthes as Michel Foucault's (1977 [1975]) theory of vision and power. This was originally applied to the management of prisoners. It has been generalized as a key feature of the command of the Occident over the Oriental 'Other' – or, more generally, the West over the Rest – by Foucauldians (see my discussion: McGuigan 1999).

In *The Tourist Gaze*, Urry identifies several attributes of tourism, ranging from the opposition between work and leisure, journeying to new places, temporariness, symbolic mediation, collecting signs, and professional management of tourist spectacles. Tourism is not defined according to its developmental attributes for host communities. It is always seen from the point of view of the tourist. Urry distinguishes between 'collective' and 'romantic' tourist gazes, the former associated with being in a crowd, the latter associated with solitary contemplation. He examines the segmentation and specialization of post-Fordist tourism and the reflexivity of postmodernist tourism; and speculates upon the scope of and the possible limits to constructing objects for the tourist gaze.

McCannell (2001) has produced an incisive critique of Urry's tourist gaze thesis. He appreciates how Urry dissects the experiential meanings of tourism but he finds the general approach too narrow and somewhat complacent. According to McCannell (2001: 26), 'Urry's tourist gaze, in the precise way he has formulated it, is a blueprint for the transformation of the global system of attractions into an enormous set of mirrors to serve the narcissistic needs of dull egoes'. It simply marks out the illusory freedom of the tourist. MacCannell invokes 'a *second gaze* that is capable of recognizing the misrecognition that defines the tourist gaze' (30). He argues that tourists are aware of the constructedness of what they are shown and alert to signs of something else that may be disconcerting. It is difficult for the comparatively wealthy tourist – that is all tourists from all developed countries in developing countries – not to glimpse poverty in paradise, though it is assiduously hidden away.

In his studies of various kinds of tourism, McCannell (1992, for instance) retains a critical eye. However, his critique of Urry, arguably, does not go far enough in deconstructing the tourist gaze by recourse to the second gaze, a way of looking for 'reality' beyond the façade. It remains, like Urry's own preoccupations, an essentially phenomenological interpretation of tourist experience, a more or less exclusively subjectivist position and one, indeed, mainly confined to the subjectivity of the tourist. It neglects the subjectivity of hosts and, yet more seriously, the material conditions of affluent tourism in relatively poor countries.

Raoul Bianchi (2002: 16) observes, 'In a world of hyper-mobile capital, instantaneous communications and the mass movement of people, international tourism encapsulates the contradictory forces at play in today's world.' These are 'mobility and freedom for the wealthy few, and immobility and impoverishment for the disenfranchised many'. Again, Urry (2001) tends to focus on only one side of this picture, the astonishingly 'mobile life' led by the wealthy few. Recent terrorist atrocities against Western tourists in the hedonistic resorts of poor countries, spurred on by anti-Western fundamentalism, are hardly surprising in the circumstances. 'What is surprising is that tourists themselves, when it happens, are surprised', remarks David Nicholson-Lord acidly. Violence, however, is rare. There are many sources of resistance on the ground, mostly peaceful, and including Western campaigners opposed to the pillaging of cultures and environments:

> What unites all these strands of resistance is the dawning realisation that tourism is the cutting edge of Western development and that, like much of Western development, it doesn't work – or at least it doesn't work anything like as well as it was supposed to. It destroys landscapes and natural resources. It brings in foreign currency earnings, but much of these are sucked back out again because tourist facilities are often owned by multi-national companies – in less developed countries such losses have been put as high as 75%. Most of the financial benefits, in any case, accrue to national or local elites, accentuating income polarities. And the low-paid jobs it does create are not self-reliant: they can be blown away by distant tremors in financial markets.
>
> (Nicholson-Lord 2002: 24)

It is not just a problem of economic exploitation, however: there is cultural damage too, as Nicholson-Lord goes on to argue:

> Perhaps most offensive for those on the receiving end, tourism is a powerful cultural solvent; it takes customs and beliefs that are locally rooted and distinctive, puts them into the global blending machine and turns them into the liquefied gunk to which a mass market has been primed to respond. One consequence is the phenomenon known as 'staged authenticity' [MacCannell's concept], in which a cultural tradition, once celebrated for its own sake and out of a belief in its intrinsic value, turns into a tourist spectacle and thus, insidiously, into a performance.
>
> (2002: 24)

Nicholson-Lord's voice is strident but not an isolated one. Even *Our Creative Diversity* and *In From the Margins* pointed to such problems, albeit rather tamely. It is necessary to examine the grounds for criticizing tourist development as a neo-liberal panacea for enduring poverty and marginality in the global economy. Campaigners and critical academics have marshalled the arguments and, in case studies that go beyond the vague platitudes of official reports and mapping documents, substantiate a counter discourse to developmental ideology. Here, I shall consider a campaigning manifesto, Deborah McLaren's (1998) *Rethinking Tourism and Ecotravel* and Rosaleen Duffy's (2002) research on ecotourism in Belize, *A Trip too Far*.

Rethinking Tourism and Ecotravel is subtitled 'The Paving of Paradise and What You Can Do to Stop It'. McLaren's book represents opposition to neo-liberal globalization with regard to the development of tourism generally, but especially in the former colonies of the European empires. Postcolonialism has, in effect, been superseded by a neo-colonialism of global capital, led by the USA, McLaren's own homeland. She is not a Third World radical but a child of the First World alarmed by what it is doing to the rest of the world. It was from her own experience as a tourist that McLaren acquired a critical attitude to developmental tourism. She encourages other tourists to inform themselves and to act in ways that counter the damage done not only by mass tourism but also by 'alternative' practices, most particularly 'ecotravel', which is defined as follows:

> Ecotravel involves activities in the great outdoors – nature tourism, adventure travel, birding, camping, skiing, whale watching, and archaeological digs that take place in marine, mountain, island, and desert ecosystems [. . .]
>
> I use the term 'ecotravel' to encompass all forms of ecotourism, conservation-focused tourism, and other types of nature travel that market the earth. The popular term, 'ecotourism', is not limited to visits to natural areas. The number of tourists who travel solely to view natural surroundings or wildlife is actually quite modest. A majority of travellers also want an opportunity to experience a culture different from their own.
>
> (McLaren 1998: 97)

The important point here is that this kind of tourism – whether you call it 'ecotourism' or 'ecotravel' – is deemed superior to 'mass tourism' in that it is not supposed to damage host cultures and environments. Instead, it is supposed to aid 'sustainability'. Like Duffy, McLaren believes this not actually to be so. It enables tour operators and transnational hoteliers to 'greenwash' the holidays they supply. Yet, in practice, the development of new, ecologically responsible tourist haunts involves what Schumpeter called 'creative destruction' or reconstruction of places with destructive effects on ways of life and natural habitats. According to McLaren, the slogan of such tourism is 'Welcome to Paradise . . . before it's gone'.

While she may bemoan the impact of tourism, alternative as well as mainstream, on traditional ways of life and natural resources, McLaren recognizes the sheer scale of transformation wrought by developmental tourism; and which, in certain respects, may be considered positive rather than wholly negative. For instance, she notes how the Mexican government decided around 1970 to turn the tropical rainforest, Mayan pyramids and coastal region of Yucatan into a tourist destination. When McLaren was writing in the late 1990s, she noted that Cancun had gone from being a tiny fishing village of 426 inhabitants to a major tourist centre with 300,000 residents. By the time I visited the Yucatan Peninsula in August 2002, the population of Cancun had more than doubled to over 700,000. This is indeed impressive growth in terms of business and employment. Down the coast from Cancun is the Xcaret ('small inlet') theme park, epitomizing the conservation of nature and presentation of traditional culture as tourist commodity-experience. As the map for the Xcaret tour proclaims:

> Welcome! Xcaret was created to provide an environment where people can inter-act with nature and the cultural heritage of the Mayan world, providing both education and entertainment. Through our warm, family ambience we hope to share our love and wonder for nature and culture. We encourage all our guests to contribute, in their own ways, to nature and all cultural programs.

It would be mistaken to damn such development out of hand. It brings money and jobs to the area. In my experience, visitors and employees at Xcaret showed one another mutual respect. Nevertheless, a great deal of dissimulation on behalf of the locals is required in order to bring off the experience.

McLaren is interested in promoting what she calls 'people-to-people communica-tion' instead of the distortions, blind ignorance and misrepresentation that are associ-ated typically with tourism. She calls for greater knowledge and understanding, the unmasking of corporate propaganda and the monitoring of negative effects. Civil society organizations like Tourism Concern are vital in this respect. And, as we academics tend to say, more research needs to be done.

An excellent example of such research is Duffy's *A Trip too Far*, which displays the qualities of multidimensional analysis that characterize the best case studies of culture and policy (such as Auerbach 1999; and Dicks 2000). For her, ecotourism 'forms part of the legitimizing argument for the switch to free-market policies favoured by numerous global interest groups' (Duffy 2002: 2). We should not be blinded to this fact by ecological rhetoric in the tourism industry. However, there are different types of **environmentalism**. Duffy distinguishes between three positions: **blue-green**, **red-green** and **deep green**. According to her, blue-green environmentalism is entirely consistent with neo-liberal globalization. Red-green environmentalism challenges the exploitative and mystifying features of blue-green hegemony, though it is not against sustainable development, if that is what it really is, while being opposed, however, to over-consumption. It differs from deep green environmentalism, which is critical of both Left and Right anthropomorphism and can take an extremely conservative stance towards human intervention in nature and, with a romantic lack of realism, tourism as such. None of the critics considered here, including Duffy, go that far. As she says:

> Tourism presents the developing world with a series of challenges that include costs and benefits. The advocates of tourism as a development strategy are very closely allied to neo-liberal development theories that focus on market-led

measures, such as liberalization, earning foreign currency through international trade and privatization. The emphasis on tourism as a potential engine for growth and development is part of the resurgence of the popularity of modernization and neo-liberal economics. The criticisms of tourism as culturally, economically and environmentally damaging have led to an interest in alternative forms of tourism.

(Duffy 2002: 18–19)

The trouble is that some forms of 'alternative' tourism turn out to be just as bad as mainstream tourism in spite of the rhetoric.

The tiny Central American state of Belize (formerly British Honduras), adjacent to the second largest barrier reef in the world and a site of ancient Mayan civilization, is a favourite destination for ecotourists avoiding less discerning crowds of pleasure-seekers. Duffy provides a rounded account of ecotourism in Belize. One of the most distinctive features of her study is the evidence she gathered concerning the thought and practice of ecotourists themselves. Duffy conducted over fifty semi-structured interviews with ecotourists, individually, in couples and in small groups, in addition to interviewing participants in the Belizean tourist industry.

Ostensibly, ecotourists display the self-reflexivity of risk consciousness, that is, awareness of the unintended consequences of human action particularly upon the natural environment, consistent with Ulrich Beck's (1992 [1986]) 'risk society' thesis. Yet, Duffy found, such reflexivity was typically shallow among the ecotourists she interviewed. They tended to be much more concerned with themselves, their journey of self-discovery, than with their impact on the vacation environment, any conceivably negative aspects of which they denied. Duffy (2002: 39) observes, for instance, 'Reef conservation was clearly constructed and justified in terms of self-satisfaction.' Even for the most ecologically conscious, drug taking and sex tourism were major attractions in Belize. 'Roughing it' is part of the appeal of ecotourism but generally this is well organized for the tourist and not exactly uncomfortable. According to Duffy, ecotourism in places like Belize can best be understood in Bourdieuan terms as a matter of status distinction first and foremost, providing a distinguished enclave in Western consumer culture. Moreover, the involvement of local indigenous people, Mayans and Afro-Caribbeans, in Belize's tourist management is marginal and minimal. They merely provide the service.

As well as conducting ethnographic research on visitors and hosts, Duffy examined the political economy of tourism in Belize. She uncovers a 'shadow state' linked to the wider global economy in which illegitimate business is fronted by the legitimate business of blue-green ecotourism: 'the tourism industry has proved to be a place where illegitimate business interests can converge with corrupt public sector managers' (Duffy 2002: 137). Belize is an offshore banking centre, a convenient link for international drug trafficking and a good place to launder money through investment in tourist facilities. Duffy was fortunate not to have been found floating lifelessly over the coral reef.

Conclusion

This chapter has sought to interrogate rhetorics of development and diversity in recent cultural policy discourse. No statement, for or against, is rhetoric-free. This goes for the critics of tourist development as well as its exponents. In effect, whether we like it or not, we are engaged in a debate in which no position can be taken for granted as authoritatively true. However, it is striking how rhetorical in the pejorative sense is much official discourse on culture and development. There clearly is some doubt, however, as to the universal value of neo-liberal globalization. Practical people will always try to accommodate to the way things actually are. Yet, such accommodation usually lacks a sense of history. It naturalizes the present, forgets the past, and cannot imagine alternative futures. The practice of criticism at least recognizes the flux of time.

Debate may reach compromise and consensus or break down due to irreconcilable differences. It is hard to predict the likely outcomes. But without critical analysis and strongly worded arguments there is no debate at all. At present, the most powerful counter-discourse to the confluence of cultural development and neo-liberalism in policy rhetoric is in research on the ground that questions high-blown rhetoric. Rosalind Duffy's work is exemplary in this respect. It connects to broader arguments about the reduction of culture to a questionable economic realism and the subordination of issues of social justice to an excessively pragmatic politics.

CULTURE, CAPITALISM AND CRITIQUE

5

Introduction

This concluding chapter addresses questions of cultural value and economy from a critical perspective. Cultural policy is conceived here as a contested terrain both in terms of its public manifestations and latent conditions of existence. Decisions are made about what to do in circumstances where underlying forces shape actualities and possibilities. For example, the public debate over 'dumbing down' may raise important issues for cultural policy but it has little to say about the political economy of culture. Questions of value should, of course, be debated. Yet, such debate often fails to penetrate the economic and political determinations of culture, which in our day are largely those of neo-liberal globalization. A critical and reflexive cultural policy analysis, then, needs to engage in public debate as it is constituted and also to go beneath the surface to examine structures and processes that may not be immediately evident. It should ask awkward questions, the kind of questions that the powerful prefer not to be asked. Agendas that are set by capitalist and narrowly governmental interests must be interrogated with regard to how they frame, include and exclude issues of public interest.

In what follows I shall survey prevailing terms of cultural debate in the 'Western' world of mature capitalism and crumbling social democracy, the role of capitalism in cultural economy across the globe and the grounds for critical and reflexive research on issues of culture and policy in general. The point is not so much to reach definitive answers to questions of cultural policy that are already on the table but to consider how best appropriately critical questions might be formulated in an exploratory framework. In this sense, the approach is dialogic: it is open-ended, aimed at generating debate rather than closing it down; and directed towards encouraging critical and reflexive research on cultural policy in the public interest.

Dumbing down

Any discussion of public cultural policy – whether in the narrowest sense of arts patronage or in the broadest sense of reforming the social – must, at some point, address questions of value (see McGuigan, ch.2, 1996). Such questions stretch from the rigorous application of the most stringent criteria of aesthetic judgement to, at the other extreme, measuring indicators of social justice and wealth creation associated with specific cultural policies. The latter, instrumental approach conveniently avoids difficult questions of aesthetic value at the cost of evacuating the space of genuinely cultural debate.

Cultural debate is often constructed according to the binary opposition of elitism and populism. It is important to appreciate that, in practice, each of these terms is defined by the difference from its opposite rather than by some essential property. So, 'elitism' is defined by not being 'populist' and vice versa. Arguments from either side, then, are much clearer about what they are against than what they are for. Elitists know exactly what is wrong and should be opposed passionately: 'populism'. Hardly ever, these days, do they actually advocate **cultural elitism** in an explicit and unqualified manner. Both 'elitism' and 'populism' are defined by their negativity. Unlike elitists, however, populists may more likely declare their partisanship brashly if they so wish since populism is in the ascendancy. Now, it is much more acceptable to be a self-declared cultural populist than to be branded a cultural elitist.

Several years ago I gave the following definition of **cultural populism** in discussing the formation and development of cultural studies as an academic field. 'Cultural populism is the intellectual assumption, made by some students of popular culture, that the symbolic experiences and practices of ordinary people are more important analytically and politically than Culture with a capital C' (McGuigan 1992: 4). Quite apart from the fact that it does not make sense in German, this definition is too academic. Cultural populism is not confined to the academy. Much more consequentially, today, it is a ubiquitous assumption in the social world at large. The definition addressed cultural studies expressly and its object of study. I would still claim, in general, cultural studies as a field of study is distinguished by taking popular culture seriously along with its interdisciplinary orientation. Others have studied popular culture but not by arguing that it is more important than Culture with a capital C – quite the opposite, in fact.

F.R. Leavis and Denys Thompson (1933) urged teachers of English to teach about the products of mass-popular culture in order to demonstrate their crude techniques and pernicious effects. The aim was to win students over to the finer values of Literature with a capital L. Leavis and Thompson were realistic enough to appreciate that their view of culture was never going to capture the hearts and minds of the majority. This was a rearguard action on behalf of what they judged to be authentic culture against the onslaught of commercial entertainment and mass publicity. Leavis (1979 [1930]) had already proposed the standard version of cultural elitism, which did not by any means equate it with the residual values of the aristocracy and *haute bourgeoisie*. Instead, Leavis looked to a 'critical minority' of *petit-bourgeois* intellectuals like himself, educated in discrimination and who could tell the difference, that is in effect, a renewal of Coleridge's clerisy.

This was not a peculiarly British agenda. By the 1950s, the **critique of mass culture** had become intellectual common sense in the USA, exemplified by Bernard Rosenberg and David Manning White's 1957 collection of essays, *Mass Culture – The Popular Arts in America*, with contributions from such illustrious figures as Clement Greenberg and Dwight MacDonald. In those days the critique of 'mass culture' came from Left, Right and Centre. It not only differentiated mass culture from serious art and intellectual culture but also distinguished between mass culture and folk (that is, the 'real' popular) culture. So, it was nostalgic as well as elitist. Commercial interests would, of course, defend the value of mass culture in 'giving the public what it wants' rather than the so-called 'good' stuff that intellectuals liked and thought people should have. The unsatisfactory distinction between 'intellectuals' and 'ordinary people' is part of a network of binary oppositions that have framed and continue to frame the cultural debate. Especially bold about the emergence of cultural studies is that intellectuals of a Leftist persuasion began to privilege the popular in mass culture over high culture and, indeed, folk culture. To cut a long story short, this trajectory was taken to an extreme in the work of John Fiske. The consumer of mass-popular culture, from that perspective, is not to be treated as a passive recipient of standardized fare but, instead, as in active, self-realizing and sense-making control of what he or she chooses to consume (Fiske 1989 a and b).

The fact of the matter is that cultural populism is not just characteristic of much education and research in a comparatively marginal and still curiously controversial field of study, cultural studies and, to an extent, media studies. It meets up with the pervasive ideology of consumerism in late capitalism, which places the sovereign consumer at the centre of reality, and dovetails neatly with neo-liberal globalization (see McGuigan 1997a, for a fuller discussion of the homology between cultural populism and free-market ideology). The pincer movement of cultural populism in its one-dimensional attention to consumption and the marketization of everything that is promoted by neo-liberal globalization, the dominant ideology of the age, in effect, poses a big problem for public cultural policy, arguably undercutting its very reason to be. It is reasonable to ask, is there any point in cultural policy at all other than as an adjunct to economic policy?

There are some, however, who believe that questions of cultural value are not reducible to popularity and economic expediency. Nor are they reducible to the cruder forms of social engineering (see Smith 1998 for a governmental case in point). One of the founders of cultural studies, Richard Hoggart simultaneously encouraged the study of mass-popular culture, while discriminating between the 'lived' and the 'processed', and contributed to public cultural policy. His great work, *The Uses of Literacy* (1957), framed the agenda for cultural studies and, as a Professor of English, he established the Centre for Contemporary Cultural Studies at the University of Birmingham in 1963. His most notable contribution to cultural policy in Britain was as a member and guiding thinker of the Pilkington Committee in the early 1960s. Following the advent of ITV, the Pilkington report insisted that principles of public service broadcasting must override commercial considerations. This led to the setting up of BBC2 as a 'cultured' television channel instead of allowing a second advertising-funded channel at that time. Hoggart also worked for UNESCO and served as Vice-Chair of the Arts Council of Great Britain (see Hoggart 1992). By the 1980s, Hoggart had become troubled at the rise of 'populism' and 'cultural relativism' and saw a connection between this trend and the policies of successive Thatcher governments that transformed Britain in the 1980s from a European social democracy to a free-market economy copying the USA slavishly. As one of the few public intellectuals produced by cultural studies, Hoggart is still worth reading on these matters (see Hoggart 1995).

Similarly to the USA and elsewhere, a series of jeremiads on the state of the culture were issued in Britain around the turn of the Millennium in a suitably apocalyptic tone (see, for instance, Scruton 1998; Tusa 1999; Walden 2000). They came mainly from the Right of politics, unlike Hoggart's moderately Left position, but were critical of the combination of cultural populism and free-market economics which characterized both the Thatcher and Blair regimes. In one way or another, these critics argued that culture was going to the dogs or, in the current phrase of educated conventional wisdom, it was 'dumbing down'.

Towards the end of 2000, the *Guardian* newspaper devoted three successive weekly supplements to the dumbing-down debate (28 October, 4 and 11 November). The first of these supplements, '1066 and all what?' reported the findings of a survey which revealed a remarkable lack of knowledge about British history and literary heritage, particularly among young adults. A total of 97 per cent of 18–24-year-olds could not name the current poet laureate, Andrew Motion, yet 75 per cent of them could name the husband of the television presenter Anthea Turner, Grant Bovey. In subsequent issues the impact of television ('Down the tubes') and American globalization ('Everything for sale') were examined. The evidence presented by the *Guardian* did not point all one way, however. Examination papers for English over the past fifty years were surveyed. It was evident that they had become more, not less, sophisticated. On this evidence alone, the recurrent refrain of a decline in educational standards was called into question.

In every period, it seems, there are those who will claim that everything is getting worse. In his book *Hooligan – A History of Respectable Fears*, Geoffrey Pearson (1983) interrogated the claim that public spaces were safer 'twenty years ago' or 'before the war'. Tracing back to press reports of twenty years ago or before the Second World War, Pearson found the very same claims being made then. The first 'hooligan' panic, when the term was coined, occurred in the 1890s and even then it echoed longstanding fears about the 'dangerous classes'. Like the poor, middle-class anxieties concerning social disorder and cultural decline are always with us. So, it is wise to appraise recent assertions of dumbing down with some scepticism (see O. Bennett 2001 for a discussion of narratives of decline).

The term 'dumbing down' has an American provenance. In the country that so much commands the cultural landscape around the world, the USA, the reaction against it took fire most virulently in the 1990s. An exemplary text in this respect is the book edited by Katharine Washburn and John Thornton, *Dumbing Down – Essays on the Strip-Mining of American Culture* (1997). Washburn and Thornton acknowledge the earlier critique of mass culture with an anthology of passages quoted from critics of yore and, also, now: from the past, such as Hannah Arendt, Clement Greenberg and Dwight MacDonald; from the present, such as Saul Bellow, Jonathan Frantzen, the recently deceased Stephen Jay Gould, Robert Hughes and Simon Schama. These critics have had and still have penetrating points to make about 'the culture'. They are not a cabal of reactionary old fogeys. However, Washburn and Thornton's book as a whole does not measure up to the quality of some of the quotations. Several contributors denounce what is presently going on with precious little evidence and a great deal of manifest disdain for cultural democracy.

In their Foreword, Washburn and Thornton bemoan the entertainment industry's influence on social mores and 'the collapse of a social pyramid in which the high brow condescended to the low, while the low and high took shots together in the middle' (1997: 13). This recalls Dwight MacDonald's forty-year-old castigation of 'MidCult', where differences between high and low culture are ironed out, which anticipated the subsequently 'postmodern' blurring of boundaries and collapse of cultural hierarchy (see McGuigan 1999). Like Leavis and MacDonald before them, it is this mushy middle ground that annoys Washburn, Thornton and their contributors more than lowly mass culture as such. Washburn and Thornton attack the 'ugly notion of egalitarian "empowerment" ' (15) as a poor substitute for traditional civility when, presumably, everyone knew their proper place in the scheme of things. Washburn and Thornton do not like the 'marketing society' which involves 'carefully managed investigations into our tastes and preferences' (17). In this instance, they identify a current trend the effects of which are indeed worthy of criticism. The problem, however, is that Washburn and Thornton like most of their contributors set this against a mythical past that is supposed to have been better. The metanarrative is one of endless and irreversible cultural decline, backward looking and deeply pessimistic.

Here are some examples from Washburn and Thornton's edited collection of denunciatory statements. John Simon (1997) seeks to retrieve 'elitism' from its current status as a 'dirty word'. Gilbert T. Sewall (1997) attacks 'multiculturalism' in education as one of the causes of 'cultural decline'. And, Kent Carroll (1997) complains about 'the junk that is regularly published by New York trade houses'. There are exceptions to the general run of bilious material, such as an excellent essay by Carol Rifkind (1997) on the shopping mall and civility, but they are few and far between.

Equally dismal is a British collection edited by Ivo Mosley, *Dumbing Down – Culture, Politics and the Mass Media* (2000). As Mosley states in his Introduction, 'Never before in human history has so much cleverness been used to such stupid ends' (1) and 'elites are a necessity in human affairs of any great civilization' (1–2). This collection, however, is distinguished by two themes that are hardly present in the American collection: the dumbing down of democracy and the decline of religion. Son of the leader of the British Union of Fascists in the 1930s, Sir Oswald Mosley, Ivo Mosley is troubled by the circumvention of democratic process and the manipulation of public opinion, 'spin doctoring'. Mosley recruits the Labour Party politician Tam Dalyell (2000) to make the case. Dalyell is not the only peculiar presence in this particular anthology. Claire Fox (2000) of the Institute of Ideas and formerly *LM [Living Marxism] Magazine* has an insightful essay in it on what has been going on in British higher education. From the same political background, Mark Ryan (2000) attacks, in his opinion, the fake democracy of audience and consumer power. These are strange bedfellows indeed for the mainly conservative and, indeed, mystical critics of dumbing down.

Both left-wing and right-wing libertarians met up in opposition to the authoritarian populism of the Centre. Stuart Hall (1988) had used the term 'authoritarian populism' to characterize the ideology of Thatcherism, combining strong state and free-market economy, as Andrew Gamble (1994a [1988]) had also observed. Stephen Driver and Luke Martell (1998) characterized the programme of the 1997 New Labour government as 'post-Thatcherite', as representing continuity rather than a break with the eighteen previous years of unrelieved Conservative rule. The former Tory politician, George Walden, who had himself broken with Thatcherism but was not taken by Blairism, published a book, *The New Elites – Making a Career in the Masses* (2000), which attacked the disingenuous populism of New Labour and its camp followers, epitomized by the Millennium Dome fiasco.

Just before closure and before it transmogrified into the Institute of Ideas, *LM Magazine* (issue number 117, February 1999) organized a conference, directed by Mark Ryan, 'Culture Wars – Dumbing Down, Wising Up?' at London's Riverside Studios in March 1999. Dissidents from across the political spectrum spoke at it, such as the right-wing philosopher Anthony O'Hear and left-wing sociologist Frank Furedi, as well as bigger names from the liberal media like Kate Adie, Melvyn Bragg, John Mortimer and John Simpson. Stemming from that conference, a critique of the dumbing down of museums followed (Appleton et al. 2001).

Without delving into the motives of the organizers and their source of funding, such a forum of debate is hardly negligible. The arguments were many and various, none of them satisfied with the way things were going. This manifests something of a public sphere in which rational-critical argument is allowed free rein. In the same period, the PEER organization performed a similar role in stimulating debate over culture and policy, resulting in the publication, *Art for All? Their Policies and Our Culture* (Wallinger and Warnock 2000).

Still, the question remains, is dumbing down actual or imagined? Can the claims concerning dumbing down be measured? An attempt to do so has been made by Peter Golding and Shelley McLachlan with specific regard to the tabloidization of the serious press in Britain since the 1950s (Golding 2000b; McLachlan and Golding 2000). Golding (2000b) comments upon what he calls 'the communications paradox', characteristic of contemporary culture and politics: although there is more information and education around today, there is also an apparent decline of public engagement with the democratic process, judged by voting figure trends. Perhaps, this might be explained by dumbing down in the sense of a decline in quality coinciding with an increase in quantity, the old 'more means worse'. Golding and McLachlan studied the issue quantitatively with regard to the British national press since the 1950s. They looked at the range, form, mode of address and market structure of news reporting in both the 'quality' broad sheet press and the 'popular' tabloid press over a forty-five-year period. Their content analysis revealed a declining number of international stories in both *The Times* and *The Guardian* and an increase in picture content for the two papers. Also, there had been a sharp increase in the number of human-interest stories in these 'quality' newspapers between the late 1970s and the late 1990s. These may be indicators of 'tabloidization'. However, in the same period, there was a significant increase in serious news in the tabloids. Rather than a simple dumbing down of the serious press, then, there was a trend towards convergence between serious and popular newspapers. This might even be considered a 'smartening up', in Herbert Gans's (1999 [1974]) term, of tabloid journalism.

Behind the trend in content convergence, McLachlan and Golding (2000: 88) discerned a rather more worrying dynamic than the one identified by the critics of dumbing down and tabloidization: 'the conglomerate strategies and economic exigencies of a commercialized cultural apparatus of awesome power and reach and increasing integration'. A superficial attention to apparent cultural trends that may or may not be really significant does not grasp the structural processes that connect political economy to culture.

Another attempt to make sense of cultural change, also with a longitudinal dimension, is the second edition of Herbert Gans's classic *Popular Culture and High Culture* (1999 [1974]). Gans's book is comparable to Pierre Bourdieu's (1984 [1979]) *Distinction* as a serious disquisition on differences in taste and how we might evaluate them but, in his case, from a North American rather than a French experience. Gans began the first edition of *Popular Culture and High Culture*, in the 1970s, with a critique of the critique of mass culture. In the second edition, this is updated to take account of 'dumbing down' and 'infotainment'. Broadly speaking, high culture is creator-oriented, according to Gans, whereas popular culture is user-oriented. So, from an elitist point view, the producers of popular culture are suspect in seeking to please others more than themselves. That, to say the least, is a dubious deficiency. However, the mass culture critique goes further in making claims concerning the negative effects of popular culture on high culture itself, on the audiences for popular culture and on the society generally. Gans surveys the evidence for these claims and finds it wanting, for instance with regard to the alleged effects of representations of violence on social behaviour. Moreover, popular culture neither has a proven narcotic effect nor does it necessarily reduce standards. Typically, critics of mass culture compare the great work of the past with the worst of the present, thereby rigging the argument. There is an 'historical fallacy' built into the mass-culture critique, the myth of social decline resulting from urbanization and greater societal complexity. The effects of a greatly expanded field of mass-popular culture in the twentieth century, it could be argued, have been positive rather than negative, enabling ordinary people to gain more pleasure and self-understanding. However, the mass-culture critics hold ordinary people and their tastes in contempt. All this is reproduced by the dumbing-down thesis:

> The new cultural critique that bears the closest resemblance to the old mass culture critique is more a pejorative phrase than a formal critique. The phrase 'dumbing down' is used broadly and can suggest that the culture being supplied is less sophisticated or complicated, or tasteful, or thoughtful, or statusful than a past one, but it is also used to refer to the public or audiences being served, who are thought to have declined in taste, intelligence, and status.
>
> (Gans 1999 [1974]: 80)

In the first edition of *Popular Culture and High Culture*, Gans made a crucial move in countering the progenitors of dumbing down. He rejected a simple high/popular distinction and, like Bourdieu, constructed a more complex model of class-cultural differentiation in which he identifies five main 'taste publics'. First, there is *high-culture*, the creator-oriented culture which appeals mostly to highly educated people with its core theme of the individual's relation to society. Second, there is *upper-middle culture*, the culture of the professional-managerial upper-middle class, in effect, MacDonald's 'MidCult'. This is represented in particular by glossy magazines like *Harper's*, *The New Yorker* and *Vogue*. In 1974, Gans argued that it was the fastest growing taste public because of the expansion of higher education. The largest taste public numerically, however, Gans identified as *lower-middle culture*. It is particularly oriented towards reassurance, the resolution of conflict and so forth. Gans believed, in 1974, that this culture was fragmenting into traditional, conventional and progressive factions. The fourth is *low culture*, appealing mainly to skilled and semi-skilled factory and service workers, where the very word 'culture' itself is abhorrent. Fifth, there is *quasi-folk culture*, which still appealed to unskilled blue-collar and service workers.

Gans's original typology of taste cultures and publics has been revised and added to by him in taking account, for instance, of black culture's increasing importance, other ethnic and youth cultures. However, in the second edition of his book, Gans defends the centrality of class in the earlier formulation. And, he notes a further decline of high culture and expansion of high-middle, the terrain of postmodernism.

Gans recognizes the normative implications of his model of taste publics. He makes two value judgements, the effect of the second virtually cancelling out that of the first. Gans (1999 [1974]: 167) says that 'the higher cultures are better or at least more comprehensive and more informative than the lower ones'. Their appreciation requires high levels of education. But, Gans goes on to say, 'the evaluation of any taste culture must also take its public into account' (170). There follows a policy judgement: 'American society should pursue policies that would maximize educational and other opportunities for all so as to permit everyone to choose from higher taste cultures.' However, 'it would be wrong to criticize people for holding and applying aesthetic standards that are related to their educational background' (170). Gans names his position '*aesthetic relationism*', which is pluralistic with regard to taste cultures and publics. Politically, it is more important to pursue egalitarian economic policies than cultural mobility strategies. His specific recommendation for cultural policy is '*subcultural programming*' which is pluralistic, providing people with what they want rather than what is thought to be good for them from a superior position.

By the time he reached his postscript on evaluation and policy in 1999, Gans registers how things had changed since 1974, especially the attack on state intervention for the arts and worsening economic inequality in the USA. It has become more vital to defend 'the marginal, the deviant, and the innovative' (204) who had received support from the much weakened National Endowment for the Arts. Gans still did not want to privilege the already privileged taste public at the apex of the cultural hierarchy. In fact, he concludes, 'Inequality reduction is more urgent now than it was during the mid 1970s, when at least a partial antipoverty program still existed.' There are social issues more urgent than those of cultural policy; and, it is wrong to expect cultural policy to solve them.

Consuming

Neither in 'dumbing down' nor in 'aesthetic relationism' is there a satisfactory account of culture and economy; and, specifically, how this connection has become increasingly close and, indeed, inseparable. The critics of dumbing down, in practice, do little more than repeat the old Romantic opposition of culture to commerce as though nothing much had happened since the early nineteenth century. On the other side, Gans (1999 [1974]: 221) praises Tyler Cowen's (1998) *In Praise of Commercial Culture* – the most extreme free-market statement on cultural production and circulation – as 'a sprightly defence of popular culture'. If this is what Gans really thought of Cowen's argument – that there is no point in regulating the normal operations of capitalism in the field of culture since it would only stifle creativity – it is hard to see why he spent so many pages on cultural policy at all. It is quite usual these days, of course, to find resolutions of the tension between culture and economy that are uncritical of economic power in the production and circulation of culture and even the claim that it is now culture that dictates economy (for instance, du Gay and Pryke 2002).

Much thought and practice on cultural policy is marginal, to say the least, to understanding or acting upon the dynamics of culture and economy. The consumption of culture for most people most of the time has nothing to do with public subsidy for creative work and audience building. It is a side show to the big show, the performance of market-oriented cultural industries and mass-popular consumption (Garnham 1990). Quite reasonably, in the circumstances, many practitioners of cultural policy have learnt market speak and lost sight of the rationale for any alternative to capitalist ways of doing things, however modest. The issues are many and various, including the general operations of market economy, the particular operations of cultural industries, the ideology of consumerism and globalization.

A great deal of knowledge has been accumulated about cultural industries (Hesmondhalgh 2002). The object of enquiry was identified originally by Theodor Adorno and Max Horkheimer (1979 [1944]) of the Frankfurt School of Social Research, the progenitor of critical theory in sociology and cultural studies. They were German-Jewish Marxists exiled in the USA during the Second World War. As Hans Steinert (2003 [1998]: 9) points out, they meant by '**culture industry**' the production of commodity culture in general and by '*the* culture industry' those organizations that make cultural products industrially. For Adorno and Horkheimer, commodity exchange and serial production signalled the degeneration of culture under monopoly capitalism. The products of the cultural industries were formulaic and repetitive; and, they espoused pseudo-individualism. Once a successful formula was found – such as soap opera – it would be endlessly repeated in minor variations, thereby suppressing genuine creativity and originality. The message of culture industry was that everyone could achieve personal happiness through commodity consumption and by striving endlessly for individual success under capitalism. While individualistic values were promoted, in effect, individualism was suppressed. The catch phrase of the time was 'keeping up with the Joneses'. If your neighbour had something new – a television, a particular model of motor car – you had to have it too.

That was then but this is now. Adorno and Horkheimer were describing Fordism, without using Antonio Gramsci's (1971) term, a system of mass commodity production and standardized culture. Nowadays, it is often argued, cultural consumption is individualized by a much greater range of choice among products in fashion, music, television and so on. In the home, there is the on-line *personal* computer providing access to a cornucopia of informational and cultural commodities and shopping opportunities. The claim here is that we have shifted from a Fordist to a post-Fordist culture where 'being different from the Joneses' has replaced 'keeping up with the Joneses'. Speeded up production, distribution and marketing informed by customer feedback and facilitated by information and communication technologies, George Ritzer's (1998) 'new means of consumption' such as cash dispensers – and much else besides – free the individual to make himself or herself. However, it may be objected, that the present situation is more accurately described as neo-Fordist than post-Fordist, merely creating the illusion of abundance and choice – the fifty-seven channels but nothing to watch syndrome. You can choose from a vast range of models, colours, stylistic variations and add-ons for the Ford Focus, but it's still a Ford Focus.

In cultural studies, Adorno and Horkheimer are routinely dismissed as miserable old elitists – straw men easily knocked down from a populist position – yet, as Steinert

(2003 [1998]) argues strenuously, there is still much to learn from them. Ellis Cashmore (1997), for instance, has applied their approach to the Black culture industry, particularly by analysing the paradox of the global success of Black culture and especially popular music while the social conditions of most African-Americans have actually worsened. To say there remains something to learn from Adorno and Horkheimer, however, is not to say there are no faults or deficiencies in the culture industry thesis. There are plenty. Most notably, Adorno and Horkheimer treated the culture industry as an undifferentiated totality as well as displaying patrician disdain for mass-popular culture *per se*. French sociologists unpacked the notion of the culture industry from the 1970s, most notably in the work of Bernard Miege.

Miege (1989: 10) criticized the Frankfurt School's 'limited and rigid idea of artistic creation' which led to a conservative 'distrust for technology and artistic innovation'. He argued that 'the capitalization of cultural production is a complex, many-sided and even contradictory process' (12). Most importantly, Miege identified three competing logics of cultural production: the publishing, flow and press logics. The logic of publishing refers to the tasks of distributing and selling products of an ostensibly autonomous kind, such as literary novels. The flow logic characteristic of broadcasting involves sustaining a steady output of serial product and maintaining audience loyalty. The press logic is concerned with sustaining regular customer product with a rapid and routinely built-in obsolescence. As Nicholas Garnham (1990) noted, following Miege, the cultural industries have a peculiar problem to deal with. Cultural commodities proper – that is, bearers of meaning first and foremost – or, in Hesmondhalgh's (2002) formulation, 'texts', are not typically used up in consumption. You can re-read a book or watch a film on DVD over and over again. There is an enormous emphasis on novelty in the marketing of cultural commodities, therefore, persuading consumers that they must move on to the next thing. Moreover, it is extremely difficult to predict the potential market for cultural commodities. Hits have to pay for the many misses.

From a managerial point of view, Dag Bjorkegren (1996) has analysed the strategic problems of 'culture business'. For him, cultural businesses are characteristically postmodern in that they are, of necessity, multirational. Most businesses only pursue a single, commercial rationale whereas cultural businesses have to combine a specifically cultural rationale with commercial imperatives. The actual mix of culture and commerce varies from sector to sector in the cultural industries. However, the old stand off between culture and commerce no longer pertains so strictly, not only because cultural production and circulation have become more commercial but also because cultural awareness is influencing business management in general. Echoing Garnham, Bjorkegren points out that most cultural products fail in the marketplace. There is great uncertainty concerning demand. It is extremely difficult to plan ahead with any conviction in cultural business. Creativity and popular appeal are relatively unpredictable. Those performing the editorial function in the various cultural industries need, then, to be very alert to creative developments and shifts in taste. Judging what might work is a matter of aesthetic sensibility and sensitivity to current trends as much as quasi-scientific testing of product. There is, however, a spectrum in the cultural industries between the poles of cultural and commercial strategy. Traditional literary publishing, in the short run, privileges culture over commerce but, in the long run, it may prove very lucrative. For instance, the Parisian publishing house, Editions de minuit took a risk in publishing Samuel Beckett's novels and plays half a century ago yet they are still making money. At the opposite end of the spectrum, Hollywood tries every trick in the book to control the market for quick returns. Producers of Hollywood movies commission scripts and put together production and distribution deals based on educated hunches as much as on reliable market research. Nevertheless, movies are tested out routinely on sample audiences and sometimes they are recut and endings reshot according to evidence from audience response. On release, Hollywood movies have to be seen as immediately successful or else the publicity effort will be withdrawn and another 'turkey' will have resulted. It is all very risky even at the most commercial and lavishly financed end of the spectrum.

There is little doubt that a historical shift from cultural strategy on the artist's terms to commercial strategy on the audience's terms, as interpreted by the business, has occurred even in high culture: it was always thus in mass-popular culture. This is one feature of the accelerating timescale of late-modernity, its sheer impatience, which also should make us consider the relation of cultural economics to economics in general, as does David Throsby (2001). That is not only manifest in an ostensible victory of commerce over culture but also capital over the public interest, the global process of neo-liberalization.

The argument was put most forcefully by the late Herbert Schiller (1989) in his book *Culture, Inc.*, subtitled 'The Corporate Takeover of Public Expression'. He traced the development of American business corporations and their command over every aspect of US society and much of the world during the second half of the twentieth century. We tend to see the USA as home to the free market. However, it should be recalled that particularly from the 1930s there had been considerable state intervention in the economy in the interests of social justice and supported by a strong sense of the public interest, including some protection of communications and culture from capitalism. Communications and culture – especially telecommunications and computing – mushroomed up to become a gigantic part of the American economy by the end of the American century. Schiller (1989: 4) observes, 'One consequence of the increased importance of information in a corporate-managed society is that corporate speech, advertising in particular, has been granted fundamental, First Amendment protection.' In consequence, 'The corporate voice, not surprisingly, is the loudest in the land.' Directly relevant to even a narrow view of cultural policy: 'The sites where creative work is displayed – museums, theaters, performing-arts centers, etc. – have been captured by corporate sponsors.' That, however, is only the visible tip of an iceberg. Schiller refers to 'a marketing ideological atmosphere' (33) that defines reality Stateside and, increasingly, around the entire globe. I shall return to consideration of that pervasive ideology but, before doing so, the switch of information and culture from a public sphere resource to an exclusively marketable commodity requires further comment.

Schiller himself commented upon how the public library system in the USA was being undermined and sidelined by the privatization of knowledge and the commodification of information that had previously been more freely available to the public. Also, with regard to the American situation, Rick Prelinger (2002: 266) remarks, 'Intellectual property is our second most valuable export [after aerospace and armaments] and more and more of us labor to create, manage, distribute, sell and shrink-wrap what passes for "content" these days.' According to US law, intellectual property is copyrighted at the point of creation, which does not mean it remains the property of the creator. Intellectual properties are bought freely and sold over and over again. A crucial tension occurs around the newer reproductive and communicational technologies facilitating copying and distribution that are not easily policed by intellectual property owners, though they strive powerfully and in many cases successfully to do so. The big corporations are in constant battle with pirates of one kind or another, thereby seeking to contain the free circulation of culture and knowledge in the interests of profit, however, not necessarily to the benefit of their originators. Prelinger hypothesizes three possible scenarios: dystopian, diffuse and Utopian. The dystopian scenario, which is well advanced, puts a charge on everything. The diffuse scenario most accurately describes the present situation where public rights to information and culture still persist to a certain extent and there is opposition and resistance to repressive law. The Utopian scenario imagines the collapse of unwieldy corporate control over intellectual property and distribution of rewards to creators that somehow bypasses the corporations – Utopian indeed. Struggle over intellectual property has been rather neglected as a topic for cultural policy studies in spite of its enormous importance. Rosemary Coombes (1998), however, has combined legal expertise with cultural analysis in her wide-ranging study, *The Cultural Life of Intellectual Properties*. She is concerned with demonstrating how property rights regulate cultural economies and how various forms of resistance to the relentless commodification of culture represent citizenship interests.

Globalizing

It is commonplace to observe that processes of culture and economy are not confined to the nation-state, not even to such a commanding nation-state as the USA: they are global in reach. There is not the space here to discuss in any detail the relative merits of contending positions over globalization. These positions have been summarized usefully as hyperglobalist, sceptical and tranformationalist by David Held and his colleagues (see Held et al. 1999; and Held and McGrew 2000, for a comprehensive survey of debates on globalization). Although there is good reason to be sceptical about the excessive claims that are made concerning the novel extent of globalization and the depth of recent transformation, it is important, for present purposes, to register a critical view on globalization, of which Leslie Sklair (2001 and 2002) is a leading exponent.

Sklair does not doubt that globalization is happening and that its effects are immense. However, these effects are not wholly positive. According to Sklair, globalization cannot be explained simply as the increasing interrelatedness of nation-states. For him, there is a level of globalization that transcends the nation-state. This is driven by what he calls 'transnational practices (TNPs)' at the helm of which are 'transnational corporations (TNCs)' and a 'transnational capitalist class (TNCC)'. Although business corporations originate in particular countries and retain their bases in them, especially the USA, there is a sense in which global capitalism owes no necessary allegiance to any country. It will search out natural resources, cheap labour and new markets anywhere that offers favourable conditions to capital accumulation. The globalization process, however, is not only economic; it is also cultural.

> The actual study of globalization revolves primarily around two main classes of phenomena that have been increasingly significant in the last few decades. These are, first, the emergence of a global economy based on new systems of production, finance and consumption driven by globalizing transnational corporations (TNCs). [. . .] The second is the idea of a global culture, focused on transformations in the global scope of particular types of TNC, those who own and control the mass media (Herman and McChesney 1997), notably television channels and the transnational advertising agencies. This is often connected with the spread of particular patterns of consumption and a culture and ideology of consumerism at the global level. While not all globalization researchers entirely accept the existence of a global economy or a global culture, most accept that however we define globalization, significant economic, political, and culture-ideology changes are taking place all over the world because of it.
>
> (Sklair 2002: 36)

Globalization is secured ideologically, according to Sklair, by consumerism:

> The culture-ideology project of global capitalism is to persuade people to consume not simply to satisfy their biological and other modest needs but in response to artificially created desires in order to perpetuate the accumulation of capital for private profit, in other words, to ensure that the capitalist global system goes on forever.
>
> (2002: 62)

Sklair elaborates further on the culture-ideology of consumerism:

> The transformation of the culture-ideology of consumerism from a sectional preference of the rich to a globalizing phenomenon can be explained in terms of two central factors, factors that are historically unprecedented. First, capitalism

entered a qualitatively new globalizing phase in the 1960s. As the electronic revolution got under way, the productivity of capitalist factories, systems of extraction and processing of raw materials, product design, marketing and distribution of goods and services began to be transformed in one sector after another. This golden age of capitalism began in the USA, but spread a little later to Japan and Western Europe and other parts of the First World, to the NICs and to some cities and enclaves in the Third World. Second, the technical and social relations that structured the mass media all over the world made it very easy for new consumerist lifestyles to become the dominant motif for these media.

(2002: 108)

It may, of course, be objected that there is nothing wrong with consumerism; and, if globalization opens up a consumerist lifestyle for more people in the world, then, it is all to the good. Sklair, however, points to the undeniably negative consequences. Capitalist globalization generates two major crises: first, 'the crisis of class polarization' and, second, 'the crisis of ecological sustainability'. While some living standards are increased, others are actually reduced. There is greater economic inequality in the world today – disparities of wealth and income – than there was twenty or thirty years ago. During that period, more people around the world have been seduced by the culture ideology of consumerism but, for many of them, it is unrealized and possibly unrealizable, not least because capitalist globalization causes environmental havoc. Natural resources are used up in an unsustainable way and the health and living conditions of present and future generations put at risk. Business corporations may claim to be ecologically responsible and concerned about human rights but this is largely public relations rather than the truth.

Clearly, the phenomenon of globalization is of the most general significance. Because it raises so many issues, globalization is studied across the whole spectrum of the social sciences. It is of prime importance in media and cultural analysis; and is explored with regard to various communicational processes, ranging from television (Barker 1997 and 1999) to sport (Maguire 1999). One particular study stands out, from the point of view of cultural policy: *Global Hollywood*, co-authored by Toby Miller, Nitin Govil, John McMurria and Richard Maxwell (2001).

Global Hollywood stakes out a broad perspective on media and cultural studies while analysing a major example of globalization in communications and culture. The authors are dissatisfied with traditional screen studies, which largely derives from film studies. Much scholarship in this field is exclusively devoted to textual analysis and tends to display extraordinary indifference to not only actual contexts of consumption but also production. In this sense, the political economy of communications and culture is preferable in that it seeks to understand the institutional underpinnings of screen media. However, political economy has little to say about meaning. In this sense, it compares unfavourably to interpretative cultural studies. Miller and his co-authors combine political economy with cultural interpretation. They are also concerned with policy issues regarding screen culture.

There is no doubt that Hollywood is a global phenomenon. Throughout the world many people's very conception of cinema is that of the Hollywood product, the entertaining feature film and its various spin-offs in television programming, merchandising and so on. Hollywood has been around for a long time and it has been an international presence since the early twentieth century. Even so, in recent years, its global dominance has increased further. As Miller et al. note, Hollywood's share of the world's film market doubled during the 1990s.

National resistance to Hollywood has also been around for a long time with various protectionist measures, quotas and public funding for national film production and cinematic exhibition. Much of this resistance has either broken down entirely or simply become less effective, for instance, in France. That is both a matter of culture and meaning, on the one hand – the sheer popular appeal of Hollywood films – and a matter of economics and politics on the other hand.

Historically, Hollywood attained its commanding position over world cinema because of the size of its domestic audience, which meant that production costs could be recouped at home and films rented abroad cheaply. It was initiated by the virtual cessation of film production in Europe during the First World War and, again to some extent, during the Second World War. The Motion Picture Association (MPA) represented the interests of the American industry as a whole overseas. The promotion of Hollywood worldwide was motivated by economic considerations and cultural diplomacy – selling the American way of life – and, moreover, supported ruthlessly by successive US administrations. In recent years, through the General Agreement on Tariffs and Trade (GATT) and its successor, the World Trade Organization (WTO), American governments have sought to extend free-market policies to cultural commodities, including film and TV product, something that is still being resisted in Europe.

It is obvious that Hollywood is global at the point of consumption; not so obvious that it is global at the point of production. With the break-up of the old studio assembly lines from the 1950s, production of Hollywood films became increasingly dispersed nationally and globally, in effect, exemplifying the shift from Fordism to post-Fordism. In the 1980s, Susan Christopherson and Michael Storper (1997 [1986]) described this flexible structure as 'the city as studio; the world as back lot', by which they meant that the studios in Los Angeles were the front offices for the business whereas actual production occurred around the whole wide world.

Adapting the general thesis of the New International Division of Labour (NIDL), the authors of *Global Hollywood* formulate an argument concerning what they call the New International Division of Cultural Labour (NICL):

[W]e deploy the concept of the NICL [New International Division of Cultural Labour] to account for the differentiation of cultural labour, the globalisation of labour processes, the means by which Hollywood coordinates and defends its authority over cultural labour markets, and the role national governments play in collusion with MNCs [Multi-National Corporations]. The NICL is designed to cover a variety of workers within the cultural industries whatever their part in the commodity chain. So, it includes janitors, accountants and tourism commissioners as well as scriptwriters, best boys and radio announcers . . .

(Miller et al. 2001: 52)

This is partly to do with the exploitation of cheap labour abroad. American film workers are the most expensive in the world. It is cheaper to make a Hollywood movie even in a rich country like Britain, which offers relatively low wages as well as advanced technical skills and facilities for, most notably, special effects. In this respect, 'made in Britain' means films like *Star Wars* and *Saving Private Ryan*. Labour and facility in many other countries are cheaper still. *Titanic* was made in Mexico. Governments around the world are so keen to attract Hollywood film production to their shores on economic grounds but with immense cultural implications that they offer generous tax breaks as well as cheap labour and facility. The world at large is not only seduced by Hollywood pleasures but also by its money.

Capitalizing

While the global operations of culture industry are awesome both at the point of consumption and of production, it is yet more shocking to be told that the very cutting edge of capitalism now is culture, that we are entering a phase of 'cultural capitalism'. This is as yet perhaps a rather nebulous concept, particularly considering a book of that title (Bewes and Gilbert 2000) never actually defines it. Somewhat more satisfactory is Jeremy Rifkin's (2000) use of the notion, cultural capitalism, in his book, *The Age of Access – How the Shift from Ownership to Access is Transforming Capitalism*. This book presents a curious combination of futuristic managerialism and radical social criticism. It is tempting to surmise that the first part of *The Age of Access*, 'The Next Capitalist Frontier', is intended for the business-school reader eager to make a bomb whereas the second part, 'Enclosing the Cultural Commons', is for the social-justice movement activist eager to throw a bomb, metaphorically speaking. Still, the analysis proffered in the first half of Rifkin's book must be taken as framing the critical issues raised in the second half; so they need to be considered together.

In an article published in the British New Labour journal, *Renewal*, Jeremy Rifkin summarized his age of access and emergence of cultural capitalism thesis:

A new economic system is being born that is as different from market capitalism as the latter is different from the mercantilist system that preceded it. We are now in the early stages of a shift from property exchange in geographical markets to access relationships in electronic networks. This transformation is being accompanied by an equally significant shift from industrial to cultural commerce. The new forces of globalisation are being met, in turn, by a powerful counter-reaction in the form of a resurgent 'cultural politics', with profound implications for the future of society . . .

(Rifkin 2001a: 33)

The influence of Manuel Castells's (1996) network model in the age of information is discernible in Rifkin's age of access thesis. As he says in the book:

The age of access [. . .] is governed by a whole new set of business assumptions that are very different from those used to manage a market era. In the new world, markets give way to networks, sellers and buyers are replaced by suppliers and users, and virtually everything is accessed.

(Rifkin 2000: 6)

According to Rifkin, 'Cultural production is beginning to eclipse physical production in world commerce and trade' (8). This is the era of cultural capitalism. Rifkin notes that culture is becoming utterly commercialized. He has a very broad notion of culture that encompasses not only the practices and products of signification but social life itself. For him, culture in the sense of social relations precedes economic activity. When commerce swallows social life up it threatens the very source of culture off which it feeds. By cultural capitalism, Rifkin does not just mean the priority of a service economy over an industrial economy; he means the commercialization of experience itself. Arlie Russell Hochschild (2003) goes yet further in her analysis of 'the commercialization of intimate life'. Consumers of the new age of access, according to Rifkin, are less concerned with buying commodities and services than with buying experiences; hence, the centrality of culture in the broadest sense to current capitalistic developments.

The driving force, in Rifkin's account is, of course, technological innovation, the Internet and all that. In this high-tech world, networking and access to desirable experiences are becoming more important than producing and consuming things. Rifkin gives Hollywood as a cutting edge instance of network economy (the production and circulation of movies) and accessed experience (watching movies). All economy and culture is coming closer to this prototype culture industry. On to 'the Weightless Economy': 'the physical economy is shrinking' (Rifkin 2000: 30). The Nike model of outsourcing product is cited here as the exemplary business case. Nike does not own the factories. However, this is hardly symmetrical with Rifkin's claim that customers do not want to own the product; sneakers are sold, not leased or rented out. However, in other industries, that is increasingly so, certainly in the USA, such as the motor industry: 'If companies like Ford had their way, they would likely never want to sell another automobile again' (Rifkin 2001a: 35). As Rifkin (2000: 7–8) explains it, 'In business circles, the new operative term is "lifetime value" (LTV) of the customer, the theoretical measure of how much a human being is worth if every moment of his or her life were to be commodified in one form or another in the commercial sphere.' Furthermore:

The new idea in marketing is to concentrate on share of customer rather than share of market [. . .] Marketing specialists use the phrase 'lifetime value' (LTV) to emphasize the advantages of shifting from a product-oriented to an access-oriented environment where negotiating discrete market transactions is less important than securing and commodifying lifetime relationships with clients.

(Rifkin 2000: 98)

Instead of selling products to occasional customers, why not sign them up as lifetime clients who pay the rent? Then it gets really sinister. It is the goal of cultural capitalism to commodify human relationships *tout court*, catching them young and servicing their every need, deploying something called R (relationship) technologies. As Rifkin (2000: 100) remarks, 'In marketing circles, using R-technologies to commodify long-term commercial relationships is called "controlling the customer".'

The general analysis is summarized thus:

The birth of a network economy, the steady dematerialization of goods, the declining relevance of physical capital, the ascendancy of intangible assets, the metamorphosis of goods into pure services, the shift in first-tier commerce from a production to a marketing perspective, and the commodification of relationships and experiences all are elements in the radical restructuring going on in the high-tech global economy as part of humanity begins to leave markets and property behind on its journey into the Age of Access.

(Rifkin 2000: 114)

Rifkin, it transpires, is troubled by this brave new world of access. Adopting the metaphor of enclosure of common land in emergent capitalism, he discusses the enclosure of the cultural commons with the emergence of cultural capitalism. Capitalism is enclosing literal public space (for instance, the replacement of the town square with the shopping mall) and virtual public space (the sites of informational and cultural communication in general, including the Internet). Rifkin also discusses the depletion of cultural resources by their incessant mining, paralleling ruthless and unsustainable exploitation of nature. This is what marketing is ultimately about:

Not surprisingly, as cultural production becomes the high-end sector of the economic value chain, marketing assumes an importance that extends well beyond the commercial realm. Marketing is the means by which the whole of the cultural commons is mined for valuable potential cultural meanings that can be transformed by the arts into commodified experiences, purchasable in the economy.

(Rifkin 2000: 171)

Further on, he says, 'The culture, like nature, can be mined to exhaustion' (247). Rifkin, for instance, discusses the phenomenon of world music as a gigantic cultural mining and commodification of difference. 'Countercultural trends have been particularly appealing targets for expropriation by marketeers', notes Rifkin (174). In this respect, he also comments upon the role of 'cool hunters' among cultural intermediaries.

Similarly to the second chapter of this book, Rifkin distinguishes between state, market and civil society. The hope lies, for him, in civil society, 'the third sector', where ordinary sociality is formed and where the wellsprings of trust and meaning are located. Rifkin (2001a) points out that there are over a million not-for-profit organizations in the USA generating annual revenue of over six hundred billion dollars. Many non-commercial organizations in the third sector are cultural in the narrow sense of, say, arts companies; the rest are cultural in a broader sense, including churches: 'Today, the cultural sector exists in a kind of neo-colonial limbo between market and government sectors' (Rifkin 2001a: 44). This sector – this third leg of a three-legged stool – should be strengthened against the overbalancing weight of government, on the one side, and of capital on the other side.

Around the world, there is local cultural resistance to the unjust and homogenizing effects of globalization. The struggle for cultural diversity is twinned with the defence of bio-diversity in the politics of the twenty-first century. In this sense, Rifkin (2001b) is sympathetic to the movement for social justice, which is sometimes called the 'anti-capitalist', 'anti-corporate' or 'anti-globalization' movement. It represents 'a cultural backlash to globalization' which is of immense political significance. Rifkin, then, declares himself in favour of culture against commerce, though he also recognizes it is potentially reactionary as well as resistant, that is, fertile ground for backward-looking forms of fundamentalism.

Questioning

The questioning attitude of critical and reflexive cultural policy analysis is, in principle, unconstrained by immediately practical matters of administration and politics. In actual practice, such academic disinterestedness and independence is difficult to achieve, especially when conducting research for capital and the state. Commissioned research is usually framed by questions of an administrative or political kind that have been formulated prior to the research; and, for which, the researcher is supposed to come up with the answers, to furnish solutions to problems already identified. Critical researchers, however, tend to be more interested in picking up clues like a detective, piecing them together and formulating questions themselves than in answering questions asked by those whom they may regard arrogantly as clueless administrators and politicians. As the Singing Detective put it: 'All solutions and no clues [. . .] I'd rather it was the other way round. All clues. No solutions. That's the way things are. Plenty of clues. No solutions' (Potter 1986: 140).

Seldom, if at all, is independent research that pipes to no paymaster funded by agencies involved in practical politics, business and public administration. This is a 'real world' fact but one which exacerbates the tension between the production of 'critical knowledge', on the one hand, and 'instrumental knowledge' on the other hand. It is an old tension, one commented upon by Paul Lazarsfeld (1941) a long time ago in distinguishing between administrative and critical research on communications. As Jonathan Sterne (2002) has quite rightly observed recently, Lazarsfeld was not so much counter-posing the administrative and critical orientations to one another as identifying the opposite ends of a spectrum with various degrees of mixing in between.

Because I once posed the questions, 'how can critical intellectuals be practical?' and 'how can practical intellectuals be critical?' (McGuigan 1996: 190), I was accused of setting up an utterly implacable binary opposition, with each term defined irredeemably by its very opposite, in effect, locating an unbridgeable chasm between criticism and practicality (T. Bennett 2000). And, since I myself specialize in criticism, I was also accused of lauding critical thinking over practical action. Well, I certainly do believe that critical thinking is of value. In addition, however, I appreciate the circumstantial constraints of occupational practice in which things just have to be done. How could anyone surviving under the application of an excessive audit culture in British universities over recent years doubt it? The everyday working lives of cultural analysts and cultural managers may not be so very different from one another. Moreover, they both have an interest in culture and, for want of a better word, politics but not necessarily the same interest.

Jürgen Habermas (1972 [1968]) has distinguished between three kinds of knowledge interest, each in turn defined by their different orientations: *instrumental*, *mutual understanding* and *emancipation*. The orientation towards *instrumental* interest is to produce knowledge with utility, thereby functioning as a means of achieving ends other than knowledge itself, the most obvious being profit and, therefore, worthy of investment. Scientific research and development are heavily motivated by the imperative of applied knowledge, seeking technological innovation first and foremost. This instrumental category of knowledge interest is akin to Jean-François Lyotard's (1984 [1979]) performativity principle in that research is not so much a search for truth but, instead, the realization of measurable utility. It is debatable to what extent the humanities and, perhaps less problematically so, the social sciences can be driven by exclusively instrumental considerations. The second knowledge orientation identified by Habermas is towards *mutual understanding*. This is clearly the province of the humanities and the social sciences. And, indeed, culture in a general sense. Knowledge that is aimed at helping us to understand one another better may have no measurable utility and is typically regarded as frivolous and unworthy of expenditure by instrumentalists. Lyotard dismisses it as a stale and now inoperative myth. The third knowledge orientation is that of *emancipation*. From this point of view, research is conducted with the aim of contributing to equality and justice. Emancipation is the most obviously political orientation in that it tends to criticize prevailing arrangements in the interest of achieving constructive rearrangement. Instrumentalism is also political, however covert, but less controversially so in 'the real world'.

Habermas's orientation towards mutual understanding is not only a knowledge interest but also a fundamental communicative feature of ordinary social interaction and relationships. It can be related to the notion of a **cultural public sphere** (McGuigan 1998b, 2000 and 2004c), adapted from Habermas's (1989 [1962]) earlier concept of the literary public sphere. Habermas distinguished between the *political public sphere* and the *literary public sphere*. The literary public sphere of the eighteenth century, in Habermas's account, refers to the writings and discussion of the *philosophes* – who, among other vocations, were cultural critics (Eagleton 1984) – on how to live and order the conditions of existence. For instance, Voltaire's novella, *Candide* (1947 [1758]), originally inspired by his dissatisfaction with theological disputation concerning the Lisbon earthquake in which 50,000 people died, was an artefact of this emergent public sphere. The literary public sphere was not just about the immediate and transient topics of the day, the stuff of journalism, the normal operations of the political public sphere. Complex reflection upon chronic problems of life, meaning and representation transcends journalism and, arguably, constitutes the stuff of art and literature.

The cultural public sphere is not confined to a republic of letters and the fine arts but includes routinely mediated aesthetic and emotional reflections on how we live and imagine the good life. This is somewhat different from an exclusively critical focus upon the cognitive distortions of the political public sphere, the ideological selection and framing of information in the news, the machinations of 'spin doctors' and so on. The concept of a *cultural public sphere* refers to the articulation of politics, public and personal, as a contested terrain through affective – aesthetic and emotional – modes of communication. The cultural public sphere trades in pleasures and pains that are experienced vicariously through willing suspension of disbelief, for instance, in even the most mundane soap operas, identifying with characters and their problems, talking and arguing with our friends and relatives about what they should and shouldn't do. Our imagination of the good life and expectations of what we can get out of this life are mediated through entertainment and popular media discourses as well as serious art and literature; and, for most people most of the time, something like soap opera is more important than grand opera. In a revised Habermasian framework, then, affective communication helps us make sense of life-world concerns, however diffusely. The cultural public sphere provides us with vehicles for thought and feeling on salient issues that matter for whatever reason. Which is not to say there is no debate to be had over where these vehicles take us. Critical questions of distortion, mutual understanding and representation apply to the cultural public sphere as well as the political public sphere.

That culture is a valuable yet contested sphere in its own right is not, however, the only reason for cultural policy. Cultural policy itself and research on cultural policy are dominated by instrumental considerations. Geir Vestheim spells it out:

> Briefly defined, instrumental cultural policy can be said to mean *to use cultural ventures and cultural investments as a means or instrument to attain goals in*

other than cultural areas. Such goals may be investment and profit, creating places of work, preventing depopulation, creating attractive places to live, strengthening the creative ability of society (locally and regionally), attracting highly skilled labour, etc. The instrumental aspect lies in emphasizing culture and cultural ventures as a means and not an end in itself.

(1994: 65)

Eleonora Belfiore has examined the role of instrumentalism in British cultural policy. She poses the crucial questions:

[W]hat is exactly instrumental cultural policy? What historical circumstances does it originate from? And is there such a thing as a non-instrumental cultural policy? What are instrumental cultural policy's purposes and which forms does it take? And more importantly, what have been the impacts on the arts themselves of the increasing pressure to deliver a whole range of social and economic benefits?

(2003: 3)

Belfiore observes that instrumental rationales for cultural policy are not new. In fact, the modern formation of British State policy in this sphere was launched initially by the Great Exhibition of 1851, in particular, that funded the beginnings of the South Kensington complex. This was to eventually include Imperial College, the Royal College of Art, the Victoria and Albert Museum, the Natural History Museum, the Science Museum, the Albert Hall and Memorial and, later, the Serpentine Gallery. The original motive was economic, the concern of trade over the inferiority of British design to French design. Knowledge and culture were thus supposed to serve the interests of business. During the 1980s, with the rise of neo-liberalism, this became again the frank rationale for public investment in art, culture and education. Towards the end of the twentieth century, however, the rationale for cultural policy shifted at least partly from the economic to the social. It was now supposed to solve the problem of social exclusion as an addendum to stimulating enterprise. As Belfiore (2003: 11) notes, policy and practice were increasingly framed by the audit culture: 'Public "investment" in the arts is advocated on the basis of what are expected to be concrete and *measurable* economic and social impacts.' The function of research on cultural policy, from such a perspective, is to provide the evidence of its economic and social utility. Belfiore concludes that, while such instrumental reductionism was unquestioningly adopted as a necessary politics of survival in public arts funding, its actual effect 'might in fact turn out to be "politics of extinction", further undermin[ing] the legitimacy of the arts sectors' claims over the public purse' (18). So, the most practical and realistic thing to do in justifying subsidy could turn out ultimately to be autodestructive. If there are no manifestly measurable economic and social outcomes for specifically cultural policies, which may be in the very nature of the beast, what is the point of cultural policy at all in the terms of an instrumental rationale? Perhaps, it is as pointless as criticism.

There is, however, a point to critique. In arguing the case for critical social theory against the predictably dull routines of much empirical social science, which is represented in a great deal of instrumentalist research on cultural policy, Craig Calhoun says:

[C]ritical social theory [. . .] exists largely to facilitate a constructive engagement with the social world that starts from the presumption that existing arrangements do not exhaust the range of possibilities. It seeks to explore the ways in which our categories of thought reduce our freedom by occluding recognition of what could be.

(1995: xiv)

Critical thought and enquiry in this sense depart from simply describing and justifying the way things are presently constituted. It is, instead, oriented to questioning current arrangements through reflexive critique and the exploration of alternative arrangements in order to represent emancipatory knowledge interests.

A good example of such a rationale is the work of Alison Beale and her associates on the gender aspects of cultural policy in Canada and Australia (Beale and Van Den Bosch 1998; Beale 1999). This perspective is concerned with the position of women in cultural practice and policy. It involves calling into question not only more or less subtle and enduring forms of sexist discrimination and representation but also their relation to seemingly unrelated economic and political changes, offering 'a gender perspective on the economic rationalism and state neo-corporatism in capitalist democracies' (Beale and Van Den Bosch 1998: 2). With particular reference to Canada, Beale (1999: 436) discusses how 'new national and international structures of policy-making, deregulated technological change and the economic links between producers and consumers on a world scale, affect domestic policies including those responsible for (de)regulating employment and increasing income gaps'. While Canadian governmental rhetoric stressed a policy of social cohesion and fresh opportunity, the harsh material realities of the 'reprivatization' of public services and the corrosive effect of 'consumer sovereignty' were obscured. These developments impacted especially hard upon women in production and in consumption, most notably reducing childcare provision and thus increasing stress and strain at work and in the home. On a similar note, Judith Jones (1998) has commented upon the difficulties of working mothers in the British television industry that have been exacerbated by intensified competition, short-term contracts and long hours of work. The neo-liberal world of high-tech advance and lean organization is a tough masculine world in spite of the anti-sexist and upbeat rhetoric that typically goes with it.

As Beale observes:

[W]e are taught to celebrate the startup of website design firms by young women and forget about the transfer of telephone operators' jobs to cheap-labour locations (and the lowered unemployment insurance and family welfare provision that add to the burden of those workers). The assets of communications and cultural studies – intimate knowledge of the communications policy process, understanding of the relation between knowledge and media forms, and anti-elitist critique of the prescriptive cultural policies of liberal states – can be made useful in addressing these structured inequalities among citizens in the national and global cultural economy.

(1999: 453)

There are a number of general issues that need to be considered regarding **research orientation** in policy-oriented cultural and media studies. In deciding to write their controversial jeremiad against 'cultural compliance' in what they call 'media/cultural studies' and in social science generally, Greg Philo and David Miller say they had

two main purposes. We wished to analyze the changes in cultural life which had resulted from the new release of the free market. We then wanted to ask what had happened to intellectual debate such that it was not able to engage in any serious critique or explanation of these changes.

(2001: xiii)

Until the rise of the New Right in the 1980s, cultural and media studies had been greatly preoccupied with ideological critique – challenging the legitimization of the present order – yet, since then, criticism has diminished just when you might have expected it to flourish. Philo and Miller itemize what has happened and ought to be the focus of critical renewal in the field. Since the late 1970s, inequalities of wealth and income have widened dramatically around the world. Public assets have been sold off and the legitimacy of the welfare state undermined. Where full-scale privatization has not taken place public agencies are submitted to intensive auditing to ensure that they meet the supposedly exacting standards of the market and customer satisfaction. While the softer side of the state is turned back and put into check, the harder side is strengthened, resulting in the steady erosion of civil liberties. Ideological shifts have occurred that legitimize the neo-liberal order in terms of selfish individualism in everyday life and lavish praise for the winners, especially idolizing rich celebrities. And, for the media and broadcasting particularly, public service gives way to marketable sensation and outrage, including extreme violence in representation. It is irresponsible to assume that none of this has any negative effect on social conduct. Philo and Miller (2001: 32) remark, 'Given the state to which much social life has been reduced, there is no shortage of subjects which a critical cultural studies could address' relating to neo-liberalism and 'the real and often brutal power relationships which have transformed our cultural life' (33). These are not, however, the most compelling topics today in cultural analysis.

In practice much work in communications and culture has been confined to speculating about the latest 'popular' tastes. Academics have become culture industry groupies dedicated to excavating the most recent trends in music, fashion or popular culture and mistaking it for 'resistance' or viewing the transgression of boundaries as progressive political practice – cultural studies as a rationale for hanging out with what is cool.

(Philo and Miller 2001: 32)

Philo and Miller go on to complain, 'The drift towards relativism and the bracketing off of "truth" and even "accuracy" has characterized much contemporary cultural studies' (35). And, 'The distinctive influence of relativism in media studies is that the real is bracketed off – one interpretation of a text is in principle as good as any other' (38). The replacement of reality with discourse, ironic Baudrillardian commentary and the notion of a hyperactive consumer who can make something out of virtually anything are among the several faults in 'postmodern' cultural analysis identified by Philo and Miller. According to them, 'The problem with postmodernism is that it mistakes developments in market capitalism and public responses to it for an absence of defining structures' (46). Philo and Miller argue further that structural connections between lived experiences and underlying processes are missed entirely. In this respect, cultural analysis in academia compares unfavourably to 'a small number of critical journalists' who 'do the hard work of uncovering the truth and revealing corruption and abuses of power' (74).

Pulling their criticisms of mainstream cultural and media studies together, Philo and Miller list six major problems (75–6). First, there is little solid empirical research and much impractical theorizing. Second, the language games that are played by many cultural analysts lose sight of reality. Third, subjectivity constructed in discourse, derived from structural linguistics and psychoanalysis, eliminates the role of conscious human agency from social and cultural change. Fourth – and paradoxically with respect to the third point – the choices of the freewheeling and consumerist individual seem to transcend material interests and power relations. Fifth, there is no sense of the consequences of control over popular media and culture for public belief, power structures and the distribution of resources. Sixth, mainstream cultural and media studies have evacuated progressive politics.

Philo and Miller's critique of cultural and media studies is, no doubt, exaggerated and hotly contestable but it does raise important questions about the purposes of study and alternative research orientations. Four research orientations are identified each of which can be illustrated with reference to the actual practices of cultural analysis.

The first is 'government/state research designed to further the interests of policy' (Philo and Miller 2001: 77). This is the direction for cultural research that was advocated by Tony Bennett during the 1990s in Australia (1992a, 1992b and 1998): 'putting policy into cultural studies'. The strength of such a position was its critique of the political pretensions of a disconnected Gramscian and text-based cultural studies. However, the weakness of this pragmatic move is that, in wishing to be immediately useful, it jettisoned critique almost entirely. Bennett made tortuous use of the later Foucault's (1991 [1978]) notion of governmentality in order to provide policy-oriented cultural studies with a philosophical imprimatur that it hardly needed. 'Cultural policy studies', in this version, effectively turned a school of cultural critics into would-be management consultants who could only operate, however, as administrative researchers in a beleaguered public sector and with precious little credibility in the burgeoning private sector. Philo and Miller point out that publicly funded research in Britain has been increasingly required to serve current governmental agendas and contribute directly to economic competitiveness. A degree in business and management would, generally speaking, be more useful in fulfilling such instrumental demands than a degree in cultural and media studies. That is even truer of the next research orientation.

The second orientation, according to Philo and Miller, is 'commercial research designed for the interests of powerful players in the market and the "generation of wealth" ' (7). The pronounced emphasis on active consumption in populist cultural studies is not so very different from the sovereign consumer of free-market ideology. As Naomi Klein (2000a: xvii) remarks of North American universities in the 1990s, when she herself was a postgraduate, 'academic studies were starting to look more like market research'. In his book, *One Market Under God*, Thomas Frank (2001) notes that this relation is not so much that of resemblance but of actual convergence. In the 1980s and 1990s business became 'funky' (Ridderstrale and Nordstrom 2000) and was expounded in successive waves of 'revolutionary' management theory by the likes of Tom Peters. In all this, Frank argues, market thinking became virtually a religion, not just a principle of economic organization. It was extolled as *the* means of freedom, providing for every need and realizing every desire. The rhetoric was about popular liberation through consumption: capitalism was 'cool'. Much of cultural studies, having turned away from ideology critique, delivered roughly the same message.

> The signature scholarly gesture of the nineties was not warmed-over aestheticism, but a populist celebration of the power and 'agency' of audiences and fans, of their ability to evade the grasp of the makers of mass culture and their talent for transforming just about any bit of cultural detritis into an implement of rebellion.
>
> (T. Frank 2001: 282)

Frank goes on to register

> the fatal double irony of an academic radicalism becoming functionally indistinguishable from free market theory at exactly the historical moment when capitalist managers decided it was time to start referring to themselves as 'radicals', to understand consumption itself as democracy.
>
> (2001: 305)

In Frank's scathing opinion cultural studies was becoming the philosophical underlabourer for 'cool hunting' and, in effect, a way of doing market research.

'The third impetus for academic work is that generated from professional interests within a specific discipline', say Philo and Miller (77). It is not uncommon in any field of study for scholars and researchers to use a specialist language that only they understand. Theoretically oriented cultural and media studies especially is often criticized for talking incomprehensible jargon about issues that should be intelligible to everyone. After all, it is not rocket science. However, the objection must be lodged, a necessary feature of the field is to call into question common-sense understanding and to defamiliarize the taken-for-granted. As a still comparatively new field of study, moreover, seeking to establish credentials in what has often been a hostile academic environment, particularly in older universities, cultural and media studies may well have paid insufficient attention to the public translation of knowledge. That problem has been aggravated in Britain and elsewhere quite possibly above all by the sway of French theorists of guru status, the likes of Jean Baudrillard and Jacques Derrida, professors of 'Things-in General', as Raymond Tallis (1997) puts it derisively. There are also the circumlocutions of German *Kulturkritik* to contend with, another prominent target of Tallis's attack on cultural theory. Tallis's denunciation of cultural theory and scholarship in the humanities and social sciences more generally is in the main unfair but he does have a point in suggesting that casual use of excessively abstract theory and willingness to generalize without evidence have sometimes taken precedence over doing empirically valid research. And, possibly in terms of a sociology of academic game-playing, moves taken and positions staked out might have had greater motivating force than making sense of what is actually going on out there.

The fourth orientation identified by Philo and Miller is 'public issue research which focuses on the concerns and problems of a wider public' (78). They discuss 'a series of questions which a critical social science should address' around 'the consequences of "popular capitalism" ' (78). Philo and Miller stress research on economic and political policy, their ideological sources and material effects in the context of free and open debate concerning the actual and the possible.

> A critical social science must [. . .] analyze the key relationships which generate public issues and how these relationships can affect public understanding of the issues and the manner in which they can be resolved. It must analyze the ideological struggles over what is understood to be necessary, possible and desirable. The development of public policy and understanding is thus a central concern for public issue research.
>
> (Philo and Miller 2001: 78)

This orientation focuses upon controversial issues where conflicting interests are involved particularly in recognition of worsening social inequality and ecological crisis on a global scale. Where does cultural policy fit into such a critical agenda? First, by questioning its instrumental function, that is, its use in the service of economic and political interests that are not first and foremost cultural. In much cultural policy discourse and rhetoric today, the cultural has become an empty signifier that is articulated most typically for reductive economic purposes according to questionable politics. Second, the specificity of the cultural should be retrieved with regard to its complex communicative properties. It is not a question of returning to older rationales such as disseminating good culture to the masses, though there is a rational kernel even to that tired old rationale which needs to be reconsidered. The old certainties and unitary perspectives on what is good and bad no longer hold. Culture and the diverse value of cultures constitute an endless matter of debate, a site of disputation over the good life and the quality of this life. That's what makes the cultural and cultural policy interesting and consequential.

The cultural public sphere, like the political public sphere, is by no means secure. The management of public opinion in politics is accompanied by the manipulation of identity and desire in the cultural field. At present the most urgent issue from the point of view of cultural policy specifically is the corporate violation of public culture, which is manifest in sponsorship of the arts, broadcasting and education as well as sport. A commercial culture is one thing. It is the dominant culture in terms of scope and sway around the world. A public culture is another thing. It is not supposed to be reducible to business. Yet, a public culture is not just a public-sector culture. Realistically, there is perpetual interaction between the public interest in culture and the dynamic operations of commercial cultural industries. The cultural public sphere is the space for making sense collectively that is more than making a living or exercising power over others. In his book, *The Public Culture*, Donald Horne (1995 [1986]: 122), remarks, 'Especially in the English-speaking economies, there was a retreat into a kind of economic fundamentalism'. Such economic fundamentalism – referred to in this book summarily as neo-liberal globalization – is both reductive and idealist. Everything is boiled down to the economy. Yet, faith in market forces is a dogmatic creed, a set of beliefs expounded universally irrespective of their relation to particular social and cultural realities.

Conclusion

In concluding this chapter and the book as a whole, it is necessary to emphasize the insidious and often hidden connections between culture and power. This is a warning against being taken in by surface appearances. For instance, during the Cold War, the difference between the USA and the Soviet Union was defined in the West as 'freedom' versus 'totalitarianism'. On the surface, that was clearly evident in many ways, including cultural practice. In the Soviet Union, the artist was licensed by the state and constrained ideologically by communism. In the USA, artists were not licensed by the state and were allowed to express themselves freely. Many cultural workers escaped the oppression of soviet communism by fleeing to the West where they could express themselves without fear of punishment. However, the conditions of freedom in the West were not so straightforward as they appeared. In fact, for the USA, the country where state intervention in art and culture was apparently least practised, a well-funded public cultural policy existed behind the scenes. As Frances Stonor Saunders has revealed in her book, *Who Paid the Piper? – The CIA and the Cultural Cold War*:

During the height of the Cold War, the US government committed vast resources to a secret programme of cultural propaganda in Western Europe. A central feature of this programme was to advance the claim that it did not exist. It was managed, in great secrecy, by America's espionage arm, the Central Intelligence Agency. The centrepiece of this covert campaign was the Congess for Cultural Freedom run by CIA agent Michael Josselson from 1950 till 1967. Its achievements – not least its duration – were considerable. At its peak, the Congress for Cultural Freedom had offices in thirty-five countries, employed dozens of personnel, published over twenty prestige magazines, held art exhibitions, owned a news and features service, organized high-profile international conferences, and rewarded musicians and artists with prizes and public performances. Its mission was to nudge the intelligentsia of Western Europe away from its lingering fascination with Marxism and Communism towards a view more accommodating of 'the American way'.

(1999: 1)

So, even freedom came at a cost. Many critical intellectuals, who participated in the cultural fronts for subtle forms of propaganda at that time, were hoodwinked into thinking that freedom really was free.

Although the Cold War was won, the CIA still exists and presumably remains up to all kinds of tricks behind the scenes where US interests are involved. However, you do not need to be a conspiracy theorist these days, or even 'anti-American' – and, therefore, 'anti-freedom' – to be sceptical of the 'freedoms' we are supposed to have at the bequest of the free market and the enormous cultural apparatus of neo-liberal globalization, which needs no centrally directing agency. More starkly, however, since 9/11, the land of the free is protected by a Patriot Act that is used to stifle dissent and close the universe of discourse (Paretsky 2003). That is a matter of basic civil liberty and of cultural policy.

GLOSSARY

Associative sponsorship: the standard form of sponsorship, especially in the arts, where the sponsor is not supposed to influence content and programming. See **deep sponsorship**.

Branding: the marketing process whereby the social and cultural value of a product is enhanced by the name and logo of a company, such as Nike and the swoosh, which also involves the self-branding of the consumer as a distinction strategy.

Capitalism: an economic system based on exploitation of labour that produces great wealth, inequality and environmental damage.

Circuit of culture: cultural products pass through a cycle of interacting moments: **production, representation, consumption, identity** and **regulation**.

Citizenship: the rights and obligations of membership in a political community; and, by extension, social and cultural rights and obligations.

Commodification: the process whereby any product or service becomes the object of monetary transaction, including products and services that would otherwise be exchanged freely such as songs and childcare.

Commodity fetishism: when a product takes on a magical quality unrelated to its actual use, such as the devotion to branded commodities.

Consumerism: an ideology that enshrines commodity consumption as the meaning of life.

Consumption: the reception and use of products and services.

Cool: originally an alternative cultural stance to the mainstream, associated with Black American music (especially jazz) and style in the 1950s; now a word used widely by young people to mean little more than 'good' in a fashionable sense.

Criticism: various meanings but particularly in this book calling into question, from a perspective of emancipation, that which is taken for granted from the point of view of official discourse; in short, asking awkward questions.

Critique of mass culture: an intellectual tradition that is disdainful of mass-produced culture and popular taste. See **cultural elitism** and **dumbing down**.

Cultural capitalism: refers to the claim that the production and circulation of cultural goods and services are at the heart of latter-day capitalism.

Cultural and creative industries: 'cultural industries' is a descriptive term for organizations that produce and circulate products that are first and foremost meaningful; now being superseded in official discourse by 'creative industries' that include, for instance, advertising and information technology.

Cultural elitism: defined as the binary opposite to **cultural populism** with connotations of high-cultural preference and superior powers of discrimination, usually confined to a critical minority.

Cultural policy: deliberate action in the cultural field undertaken by governments but also including business operations and civil society campaigns around the conditions and consequences of culture.
- **proper**: manifest policies typically concerning public patronage of the arts, media regulation and cultural identity.
- **as display**: latent and sometimes quite manifest policies typically to do with national aggrandizement and the reduction of culture to economy.

Cultural populism: originally defined as an academic preference for the popular over elite culture in cultural studies yet now, evidently, the prevailing social attitude to cultural value: put summarily, if it is popular then it must be good.

Cultural public sphere: a development of the literary public sphere to include all aesthetic practices in which questions of everyday life and meaningfulness are given articulation.

Culture: in this book, confined to practices that are primarily about signification, communication, pleasure and identity rather than encompassing the social in general.

Culture industry: critical term that refers to the negative features of industrialized and commodified culture.

Deep sponsorship: where corporate sponsorship actually determines the form and content of cultural production.

Desetatization: French neologism usually translated as 'privatization' but which is perhaps broader in that it may also mean 'autonomization', where state control is relaxed but not transferred to the control of private business.

Determination: the setting of limits and exertion of pressure on cultural practices by, say, economic forces not reducible to an inescapable economic determinism over culture.

Development: signifying progress and improvement in human affairs.

Discourse: language in social context; a set of typical statements and forms of expression that characterize the signification of reality in particular contexts; for instance, market discourse.

Discourse ethics: respect for dialogic rules concerning statements of truth, truthfulness and sincerity; oriented towards mutual understanding.

Discourses of cultural policy: see **discourse**.
- **state**: in which the state is conceived of as the key agent in cultural policy.
- **market**: in which the free play of market forces is held to be sacrosanct not only in business but also in government.
- **civil/communicative**: emanating from civil society and concerned with democratization of communications and culture.

Discursive formation: the configuration of discourses in a particular historical conjuncture, such as neo-liberal globalization at present.

Diversity: recognition and respect for social and cultural differences.

Dominant ideology thesis: the claim that capitalism is reproduced through the inculcation of bourgeois beliefs and assumptions in the proletariat which has also been extended to explaining the reproduction of patriarchy, racial and sexual discrimination; now somewhat discredited in spite of the enormous ideological legitimacy of neo-liberal globalization.

Dumbing down: the common-sense version of **cultural elitism**, claiming that standards of communications and culture are in decline.

Economic reason: whereby all issues, including the production and circulation of culture, are ultimately reduced to the logic of economics.

Ecotourism/ecotravel: holidays that are not supposed to be detrimental to cultural and natural environments.

Enlightenment: the emergence of critical rationality in the eighteenth century which shaped modern consciousness in Europe and elsewhere.

Environmentalism: preservation and sustenance of natural habitats, especially
- **blue-green**: consistent with neo-liberal globalization in terms of development according to comparative advantage.
- **deep green**: fundamentally opposed to the human despoiling of nature, displaying a tendency towards mystical conservatism.
- **red-green**: in favour of development which is ecologically sustainable and socially fair and equitable.

Exhibitionary complex: cultural displays, such as expositions and museums, formed in the nineteenth century to inculcate appropriate attitudes and modes of conduct in the populace.

Exploitation: expropriation of surplus value (profits) from labour power (workers) involving poor wages and conditions for the actual producers of wealth.

Fordist: narrowly, the system of assembly-line production of standardized products developed in the motor industry and applied to other industries, including the classic Hollywood studio system that facilitated the rise of mass consumption in the early twentieth century; more broadly, the civilizational principle for organizing social production and consumption generally in the mid-twentieth century. See **post-Fordism**.

Foucauldian: ideas derived from the French historian of discursive formations, Michel Foucault; in this book, particularly the use of his **governmentality** concept in cultural policy studies and inspiration for differentiating between **discourses of cultural policy**.

Generous and reflexive visiting: a typology used to interpret orientations to visitor attractions like the Millennium Dome; referring, respectively, to the effort to make the best of an attraction and judging it with regard to publicity and personal experience.

Globalization: processes that operate at great speed and in a unitary time frame on a worldwide scale, including cultural, economic and political dynamics. See **neo-liberalism** for the predominant form of globalization.

Governmentality: the idea that modernity is best understood as a complex system for administering social conduct in minute ways; it is the focal idea of Australian cultural policy studies where the general aim is to adjust administration in a more equitable manner.

Hegemony: social leadership secured between contending forces which establishes the guiding ideological principle for the moment according to the interests of the most powerful, such as neo-liberal globalization.

Identity: the sense of self and social belonging.

Ideology: distorted ideas motivated by unequal power relations.

Information and communication technologies (ICTs): as referred to in this book, in the main, the relatively new wave of digital communications, storage and retrieval linking together, for instance, satellites, computers and mobile phones.

Instrumentalism: doing something not for its own sake but for another reason, such as investing in culture to achieve economic and political ends.

International Monetary Fund (IMF): the loan agency that demands 'structural adjustment' in the economies of debtor nations, which usually means **privatization** of public assets and the general observance of **neo-liberal** principles.

Keynesian: the economics of John Maynard Keynes, advocating public expenditure for economic growth and the welfare state, which prevailed in the capitalist world from the Second World War until the emergence of **neo-liberalism** in the 1970s.

Knowledge interest: Habermas distinguishes between three such interests: first, instrumental, which is particularly characteristic of natural and physical sciences and, to a lesser extent, the social sciences, where the outcome is the practical utilization of knowledge for purposes such as product development; second, mutual understanding, which is particularly characteristic of the humanities and social sciences that are concerned with making sense of the variety of life and experience; and third, emancipation, where the general aim is to bring about greater social equality and justice. See **research orientation**.

Logoscape: the ubiquitous presence of brand logs across public spaces.

Managerialization: the treatment of all problems as a matter of management irrespective of whether they are or not.

Marketization: the application of market principles to everything so that, for instance, public cultural policy that was supposed to make up for market failure becomes itself market-oriented.

Mobile privatization: the sheer mobility of life now – including virtual mobility through communication technologies as well as physical mobility – is simultaneously associated with increasingly private ways of living, such as watching television programmes broadcast from the other side of the world in the secluded space of the home.

Modernization: as discussed in this book, the goal of development in poorer countries, now called into question by postmodernism, which is critical of modernity.

Multiculturalism: both the fact and policy aspiration of ethnic diversity and heterogeneity in countries where a prevailing homogeneous culture neither really exists nor is desirable.

Multidimensional analysis: looking at the various dimensions of a phenomenon and how they interact with one another, such as taking account of **production, representation** and **consumption** in cultural analysis.

Neo-liberalism: the revival of nineteenth-century *laissez-faire* (free-trade) economics towards the end of the twentieth century, concerned with liberating market forces from state control and promoted around the world by the **IMF, World Bank** and **WTO**; in effect, the victory of capitalism over socialism. See **globalization**.

New international division of cultural labour (NICL): the globalization of cultural production that takes advantage of cheap labour and generally favourable conditions in poorer countries.

Ontological complexity: the actual multidimensionality of any object of analysis. See **multidimensional analysis**.

Panopticism: seeing all around; capacity to keep people under surveillance; originally the prison design of a viewing platform from where guards could look into each prisoner's cell.

Paradigm: in the Kuhnian sense of a framework of concepts and methodological procedures that are shared in the normal operations of science; in cultural studies and social science, specifically, it is similar to a theoretical perspective that may exist in rivalry with other perspectives.

Performative complex: of general significance but referring specifically in this book to coordination of the various aspects of a mega-event, such as the Olympics or an international exposition.

Political economy: the combination of political and economic forces that shape the material conditions of any social phenomenon, but especially in this book communications and culture.

Post-Fordist: whereas **Fordism** produced standardized products and fostered homogeneous lifestyles, post-Fordism is said to produce a greater range of products designed for lifestyle diversity and responsiveness to rapid changes in consumer taste; however, in practice, it may be considered neo-Fordist since freedom of choice might be more apparent than real.

Postmodernism: the field of a pervasive 'pick'n'mix' culture in which modern boundaries between forms, media and social activity are crossed routinely.

Power: command over others not only through physical force but also through material and ideological mechanisms.

Privatization: the selling off of publicly owned assets such as communications and transport systems.

Production: the actual making of that which would not otherwise exist.

Public sphere: the space(s) of rational-critical debate vital to democratic process.

Reflexivity: awareness of the conditions and consequences of a practice.

Regulation: the rules and conventions of operation that are subject to law.

Representation: referring to both how meanings are constructed in textual forms and how power is delegated to democratic representatives.

Research orientation: four alternative orientations are identified in this book: first, governmental/state research; second, commercial/market research; third, professional/disciplinary research; and fourth, public-interest research. See **knowledge interest**.

Rhetoric: originally the persuasive use of words in argumentative circumstances but which can be extended to the form of any communication, including visual images and scientific language.

Romanticism: historically, the critical response to excessive rationalism in favour of feeling and imagination.

Social Darwinism: a fallacious transfer of the principles of biological evolution to the evolution of societies and cultures, particularly prevalent in the late nineteenth century as an ideological justification for the imperial rule of advanced 'civilization' over backward 'primitivism'.

Technological determinism: the questionable yet widely held assumption that scientific discovery and technical invention are much more important determinants of social and cultural change than economics and politics.

Tourism: two main forms of which are mass tourism and, increasingly, niche-market ecological tourism. See **ecotourism/ecotravel**.

UNESCO (United Nations Educational, Scientific and Cultural Organization): the international agency – set up under the auspices of the United Nations after the Second World War – that is charged with responsibility for culture and cultural relations around the world.

World Bank: the banking arm of the international system of financial assistance to economic development put in place after the Second World War alongside the **IMF** and the General Agreement on Tariffs and Trade (GATT), which was the precursor to the current **WTO**.

World Trade Organization (WTO): Successor to the General Agreement on Tariffs and Trade (GATT), the WTO is the international forum for regulating trade between nations that has been the focus of demonstrations by the global justice movement due to its advocacy of free trade rather than fair trade.

REFERENCES

Abercrombie, N., Hill, S. and Turner, B. (1980) *The Dominant Ideology Thesis*, London, Boston and Sydney: George Allen and Unwin.

Abercrombie, N., Hill, S. and Turner, B. (eds) (1990) *Dominant Ideologies*, London, Boston, Sydney and Wellington: Unwin Hyman.

Adorno, T. (1991 [1978]) Culture and administration, in J.M. Bernstein (ed.) *The Culture Industry*, London and New York: Routledge, pp. 93–113.

Adorno, T. and Horkheimer, M. (1979 [1944]) *Dialectic of Enlightenment*, London: Verso.

Ahearne, J. (ed.) (2002) *French Cultural Policy Debates – A Reader*, London: Routledge.

Anderson, P. (2000) Renewals, *New Left Review* 1, 2nd series, pp. 5–24.

Anthony, P. (1994) *Managing Culture*, Buckingham: Open University Press.

Appleton, J. et al. (2001) *Museums for 'The People'?*, London: Institute of Ideas.

Aristotle (1991) *The Art of Rhetoric*, London: Penguin.

Arnold, M. (1932 [1869 and 1875]), *Culture and Anarchy*, ed. J. Dover Wilson, Cambridge: Cambridge University Press.

Arts Council of Great Britain (1985) *A Great British Success Story – An Invitation to the Nation to Invest in the Arts*, London: ACGB.

Auerbach, J. (1999) *The Great Exhibition of 1851 – A Nation on Display*, New Haven and London: Yale University Press.

Baldry, H. (1981) *The Case for the Arts*, London: Secker and Warburg.

Bangemann Report (1995) *Europe and the Global Information Society – Recommendations to the European Council*, Brussels: European Commission.

Banham, M. and Hillier, B. (eds) (1976) *A Tonic to the Nation – The Festival of Britain 1951*, London: Thames and Hudson.

Barber, B. (1996 [1995]) *Jihad vs. McWorld*, New York: Ballantine Books.

Barker, C. (1997) *Global Television – An Introduction*, Oxford and Malden, MA: Basil Blackwell.

Barker, C. (1999) *Television, Globalization and Cultural Identities*, Buckingham and Philadelphia: Open University Press.

Barker, M. and Petley, J. (eds) (1997) *Ill Effects – The Media/Violence Debate*, London and New York: Routledge.

Barthes, R. (1971) Rhetoric of the image, *Working Papers in Cultural Studies* 1, Spring, University of Birmingham Centre for Contemporary Cultural Studies, pp. 37–51. Reprinted in A. Gray and J. McGuigan (eds) (1997, 2nd edn) *Studying Culture*, London: Arnold, pp. 15–27.

Barthes, R. (1979) *The Eiffel Tower and Other Mythologies*, Berkeley, Los Angeles and London: University of California Press.

Bayley, S. (1999) *Labour Camp – The Failure of Style over Substance*, London: B.T. Batsford.

Beale, A. (1999) From 'Sophie's Choice' to consumer choice – framing gender in cultural policy, *Media, Culture & Society* vol. 21, pp. 435–58.

Beale, A. and Van Den Bosch, A. (eds) (1998) *Ghosts in the Machine – Women and Cultural Policy in Canada and Australia*, Toronto: Garamond Press.

Beck, U. (1992 [1986]) *Risk Society – Towards a New Modernity*, London and Newbury Park: Sage.

Beck, U. (1999) *World Risk Society*, Cambridge: Polity.

Belfiore, E. (2003) Instrumental cultural policy – the arts in the 'audit society', Workshop on Culture in Knowledge Society, Stockholm: Swedish Institute for Studies of Education and Research (SISTER), 20 pp.

Bell, D. (1973) *The Coming of Post-Industrial Society – A Venture in Social Forecasting*, London: Penguin.

Bennett, O. (1995) Cultural policy in the United Kingdom – collapsing rationales and the end of a tradition, *European Journal of Cultural Policy*, 1.2, pp. 199–216.

Bennett, O. (2001) *Cultural Pessimism – Narratives of Decline in the Postmodern World*, Edinburgh: Edinburgh University Press.

Bennett, T. (1992a) Putting policy into cultural studies, in L. Grossberg, C. Nelson and P. Treichler (eds), *Cultural Studies*, London and New York: Routledge, pp. 23–37.

Bennett, T. (1992b) Useful culture, *Cultural Studies*, 6.3, October, pp. 395–408.

Bennett, T. (1995) *The Birth of the Museum – History, Theory, Politics*, London and New York: Routledge.

Bennett, T. (1998) *Culture – A Reformer's Science*, London, Thousand Oaks and New Delhi: Sage.

Bennett, T. (2000) Intellectuals, culture, policy – the technical, the practical and the critical, *Pavis Papers in Social and Cultural Research* 2, Milton Keynes: Open University, 23 pp.

Bennett, T. (ed.) (2001) *Differing Diversities – Cultural Policy and Cultural Diversity*, Strasbourg: Council of Europe.

Bewes, T. and Gilbert, J. (eds) (2000) *Cultural Capitalism – Politics After New Labour*, London: Lawrence and Wishart.

Bianchi, R. (2002) Sun, sea, sand – and a sense of spectral danger . . ., *The Higher*, 26 July, pp. 16–17.

Bianchini, F. and Parkinson, M. (eds) (1993) *Cultural Policy and Urban Regeneration – The West European Experience*, Manchester and New York: Manchester University Press.

Billig, M. (1996 [1985]) *Arguing and Thinking – A Rhetorical Approach to Social Psychology*, Cambridge, New York and Melbourne: Cambridge University Press.

Billig, M. (1997) From codes to utterances – cultural studies, discourse and utterances, in M. Ferguson and P. Golding (eds), *Cultural Studies in Question*, London, Thousand Oaks and New Delhi: Sage, pp. 205–26.

Bimbaum, N. (1955) Monarchs and sociologists – a reply to Professor Shils and Mr Young, *The Sociological Review* 3.1, pp. 5–23.

Bjorkegren, D. (1996) *The Culture Business – Management Strategies for the Arts-Related Business*, London and New York: Routledge.

Blair, T. (1998) Why the Dome is good for Britain, People's Palace, Royal Festival Hall, 24 February, 5 pp.

Blazwick, I. and Wilson, S. (eds) (2000) *Tate Modern – The Handbook*, London: Tate Gallery.

Borrie Report, Commission on Social Justice/Institute for Public Policy Research (1994), *Social Justice – Strategies for National Renewal*, London: Vintage.

Bourdieu, P. (1984 [1979]) *Distinction – A Social Critique of the Judgement of Taste*, Routledge: London.

Bourdieu, P. (1991) *Language and Symbolic Power*, Cambridge: Polity.

Bourdieu, P. (1998a) A reasoned utopia and economic fatalism, *New Left Review* 227, January–February, pp. 125–30.

Bourdieu, P. (1998b) *Acts of Resistance – Against the New Myths of Our Time*, Cambridge: Polity.

Bourdieu, P. and Darbel, A. (1991 [1969]) *The Love of Art – European Art Museums and Their Public*, Cambridge: Polity. Original French publication, *L'Amour de L'Art – Les Musées d'art Européens*, Paris: Éditions de Minuit.

Bourdieu, P. and Wacquant, L. (1992) *An Invitation to Reflexive Sociology*, Cambridge: Polity Press.

Braden, S. (1978) *Artists and People*, London: Routledge.

Calhoun, C. (ed.) (1992) *Habermas and the Public Sphere*, Cambridge, MA and London: MIT Press.

Calhoun, C. (1995) *Critical Social Theory*, Cambridge, MA and Oxford: Basil Blackwell.

Carleheden, M. and Gabriel, R. (1996) An interview with Jurgen Habermas, *Theory, Culture and Society*, 13.3, pp. 1–17.

Carroll, K. (1997) The facts of fiction and the fiction of facts, in K. Washburn and J. Thornton (eds), *Dumbing Down – Essays on the Strip-Mining of American Culture*, New York and London: Norton, pp. 224–33.

Cashmore, E. (1997) *The Black Culture Industry*, London and New York: Routledge.

Castells, M. (1996) *The Rise of the Network Society*, Malden, MA and Oxford: Basil Blackwell.

Castells, M. (1997a) *The Power of Identity*, Malden, MA and Oxford: Basil Blackwell.

Castells, M. (1997b) An introduction to the information age, *City*, 7, 6–16.

Castells, M. (1998) *End of Millennium*, Malden, MA and Oxford: Basil Blackwell.

Caust, J. (2003) Putting the 'art' back into arts policy making – how arts policy has been 'captured' by the economists and the marketeers, *International Journal of Cultural Policy* 9.1, March, pp. 51–63.

Chippindale, P. and Franks, S. (1991) *Dished – The Rise and Fall of British Satellite Broadcasting*, London: Simon and Schuster.

Chomsky, N. (2001) *9–11*, New York: Seven Stories Press.

Christopherson, S. and Storper, M. (1997 [1986]) The city as studio; the world as back lot – the impact of vertical integration on the location of the motion picture industry, in A. Gray and J. McGuigan (eds), *Studying Culture*, London: Arnold, pp. 256–74.

Clarke, J. and Newman, J. (1993) The right to manage – a second managerial revolution?, *Cultural Studies*, 7.3, pp. 427–41.

Clarke, J. and Newman, J. (1997) *The Managerial State*, London, Thousand Oaks and New Delhi: Sage.

Cockburn, A., St. Clair, J. and Sekula, A. (2000) *5 Days That Shook the World – Seattle and Beyond*, London and New York: Verso.

Cockburn, C. and Hunter, L. (1999) Transversal politics and translation practices, *Soundings* 12, summer, pp. 88–93.

Colebatch, H.K. (2003, 2nd edn) *Policy*, Buckingham and Philadelphia: Open University Press.

Collins, R. and Murroni, C. (1996) *New Media, New Policies*, Cambridge: Polity.

Commonwealth of Australia (1994) *Creative Nation*, Canberra: Department of Communications and the Arts.

Coombes, R. (1998) *The Cultural Life of Intellectual Properties – Authorship, Appropriation, and the Law*, Durham and London: Duke University Press.

Couldry, N. (2000) *Inside Culture – Re-Imagining the Method of Cultural Studies*, London, Thousand Oaks and New Delhi: Sage.

Cowen, T. (1998) *In Praise of Commercial Culture*, Cambridge, MA. and London: Harvard University Press.

Craik, J. (1997) The culture of tourism, in C. Rojek and J. Urry (eds), *Touring Cultures – Transformations of Travel and Theory*, London and New York: Routledge, pp. 113–36.

Crampsey, B. (1988) *The Empire Exhibition of 1938 – The Last Durbar*, Edinburgh: Mainstream Publishing.

Crook, S., Pakulski, J. and Waters, M. (1992) *Postmodernization – Change in Advanced Society*, London, Newbury Park and New Delhi: Sage.

Cubitt, S. (1998) *Digital Aesthetics*, London, Thousand Oaks and New Delhi: Sage.

Cunningham, S. (1992) TV violence – the challenge of public policy in cultural studies, *Cultural Studies*, 6.1, pp. 97–115.

Cunningham, S. (2002) From cultural to creative industries – theory, industry and policy implications, *Media International Australia, incorporating Culture and Policy*, 102, February, pp. 54–65.

Curran, J. and Seaton, J. (1991 [1981]) *Power Without Responsibility – The Press and Broadcasting in Britain*, London: Routledge.

Dalyell, T. (2000) On the decline of intelligent government, in I. Mosley (ed.), *Dumbing Down – Culture, Politics and the Mass Media*, Thorverton: Imprint Academic, pp. 11–18.

Davis, J. (1999) *The Great Exhibition*, Stroud: Sutton Publishing.

Davis, M. (1993a) Who killed LA? A political autopsy, *New Left Review* 197, pp. 3–28.

Davis, M. (1993b) Who killed Los Angeles? Part two – the verdict is given, *New Left Review* 199, pp. 29–54.

Debord, G. (1994 [1967]) *The Society of the Spectacle*, New York: Zone Books.

Dent, G. (ed.) (1992) *Black Popular Culture*, Seattle: Bay Press.

Department of Culture, Media and Sport (1998) *Creative Industries – Mapping Document*, London: DCMS.

Dicks, B. (2000) *Heritage, Place and Community*, Cardiff: University of Wales Press.

Diggle, K. (1984) *Guide to Arts Marketing*, London: Rheingold.

Downey, J. (1999) Xs 4 all? 'information society', policy and practice in the European Union, in J. Downey and J. McGuigan (eds), *Technocities*, London, Thousand Oaks and New Delhi: Sage, pp. 121–38.

Driver, S. and Martell, L. (1998) *New Labour – Politics After Thatcherism*, Cambridge: Polity.

Duffy, R. (2002) *A Trip too Far – Ecotourism, Politics and Exploitation*, London: Earthscan.

du Gay, P. (1996) *Consumption and Identity at Work*, London, Newbury Park and New Delhi: Sage.

du Gay, P., Hall, S., Janes, L., Mackay, H. and Negus, K. (1997) *Doing Cultural Studies – The Story of the Sony Walkman*, London, Thousand Oaks and New Delhi: Sage.

du Gay, P. and Pryke, M. (eds) (2002) *Cultural Economy*, London, Thousand Oaks and New Delhi: Sage.

Eagleton, T. (1983) *Literary Theory – An Introduction*, Oxford: Basil Blackwell.

Eagleton, T. (1984) *The Function of Criticism – From the Spectator to Post-Structuralism*, London: Verso.

Eagleton, T. (2000) *The Idea of Culture*, Oxford and Malden, MA: Basil Blackwell.

Eco, U. (1987a [1967]) Towards a semiological guerrilla warfare, in his *Travels in Hyperreality*, London: Picador, pp. 135–44.

Eco, U. (1987b [1967]) A theory of expositions, in his *Travels in Hyperreality*, London: Picador, pp. 291–307.

Elias, N. (1994 [1939]) *The Civilizing Process*, Oxford and Cambridge, MA: Basil Blackwell.

Eling, K. (1999) *The Politics of Cultural Policy in France*, London: Macmillan, New York: St Martin's Press.

Enzensberger, M. (1977) Dziga Vertov, *Screen Reader 1 – Cinema/Ideology/Politics*, London: Society for Education in Film and Television, pp. 394–411.

Escobar, A. (2002 [1995]) The problematization of poverty – the tale of three worlds and development, in S. Schech and J. Haggis (eds), *Development – A Cultural Studies Reader*, Oxford and Malden, MA: Basil Blackwell, pp. 79–92.

European Task Force on Cultural Development (1997) *In From the Margins – A Contribution to the Debate on Culture and Development in Europe*, Strasbourg: Council of Europe.

Fairclough, N. (2000) *New Labour, New Language*, London and New York: Routledge.

Featherstone, M. (1991) *Consumer Culture and Postmodernism*, London, Newbury Park and New Delhi: Sage.

Ferguson, M. and Golding, P. (eds) (1997) *Cultural Studies in Question*, London, Thousand Oaks and New Delhi: Sage.

Field, A. (1983) Experiment and public accountability, in J. Shanahan (ed.), *Economic Support for the Arts*, Association for Cultural Economics/University of Akron, pp. 89–96.

Finkielkraut, A. (1988 [1987]) *The Undoing of Thought*, London and Lexington: Claridge Press. Original French publication, *La Defaite de la Pensee*, Paris: Gallimard.

Fiske, J. (1989a) *Understanding Popular Culture*, London: Unwin Hyman.

Fiske, J. (1989b) *Reading the Popular*, London: Unwin Hyman.

Foucault, M. (1977 [1975]) *Discipline and Punish – The Birth of the Prison*, London: Allen Lane.

Foucault, M. (1981) The order of discourse, in J. Young (ed.), *Untying the Text*, London: Routledge.

Foucault, M. (1991 [1978]) Governmentality, in G. Burchell, C. Gordon and P. Miller (eds), *The Foucault Effect – Studies in Governmentality*, Hemel Hempstead: Harvester Wheatsheaf, pp. 87–104.

Foucault, M. (2000 [1982]) Technologies of the self, in P. Rabinow (ed.), *Essential Works of Foucault 1954–84 vol. 1 – Ethics*, London: Penguin, pp. 223–51.

Fox, C. (2000) Education – dumbing down or wising up?, in I. Mosley (ed.), *Dumbing Down – Culture, Politics and the Mass Media*, Thorverton: Academic Imprint, pp. 245–52.

Frank, A.G. (1971) *Sociology of Development and Underdevelopment of Sociology*, London: Pluto Press.

Frank, T. (2001) *One Market Under God – Extreme Capitalism, Market Populism and the End of Economic Democracy*, London: Secker and Warburg.

Fraser, N. (1992) Rethinking the public sphere – A contribution to the critique of actually existing democracy, in C. Calhoun (ed.), *Habermas and the Public Sphere*, Cambridge, MA and London: MIT Press, pp. 109–142.

Frith, S. (1991) Knowing one's place – the culture of the cultural industries, *Cultural Studies from Birmingham* 1, University of Birmingham, pp. 134–55.

Fukuyama, F. (1989) The end of history?, *National Interest*, 16, pp. 3–18.

Fumaroli, M. (1991) *L'État Culturel – Essai sur une Religion Moderne*, Paris: Fallois.

Gamble, A. (1994a 2nd edn [1988]) *The Free Economy and the Strong State – The Politics of Thatcherism*, London: Macmillan.

Gamble, A. (1994b 4th edn [1981]) *Britain in Decline – Economic Policy, Political Strategy and the British State*, London: Macmillan.

Gamble, A. (2001) Neo-Liberalism, *Capital and Class* 71, autumn, pp. 127–34.

Gans, H. (1999 [1974]) *Popular Culture and High Culture*, New York: Basic Books.

Garnham, N. (1990) *Capitalism and Communication – Global Culture and the Economics of Information*, London: Sage.

Garnham, N. (1992) The media and the public sphere, in C. Calhoun (ed.), *Habermas and the Public Sphere*, Cambridge, MA and London: MIT Press, pp. 359–76.

Garnham, N. (1995) The media and narratives of the intellectual, *Media, Culture and Society*, 17.3: 359–84.

Garnham, N. (1998) Information society theory as ideology – a critique, *Loisir et societe/Leisure and Society*, 21.1: 97–120.

Garnham, N. (2000a) *Emancipation, the Media, and Modernity – Arguments About the Media and Social Theory*, Oxford: Oxford University Press.

Garnham, N. (2000b) The problem of culture in cultural studies and sociology, unpublished conference/seminar paper.

Gellner, E. (1996) *Conditions of Liberty – Civil Society and Its Rivals*, London: Penguin.

Gerbner, G. (1995) Television violence – the power and the peril, in G. Dines and J. Humez (eds), *Gender, Race and Class in the Media*, Thousand Oaks, London and New Delhi: Sage, pp. 547–57.

Gerbner, G. (1996) Why the Cultural Environment Movement?, http://www.cemnet.org

Gerbner, G. (1998a) Signs of hope – the Cultural Environment Movement, http://www.mediaed.org

Gerbner, G. (1998b) Saving our cultural environment – putting the vision back into television, http://newdimensions.org

Gibson, L. and O'Reagan, T. (eds) (2002) Culture – Development, Industry, Distribution, thematic issue of *Media International Australia*, incorporating *Culture and Policy*, 102, February.

Giddens, A. (1984) *The Constitution of Society – Outline of the Theory of Structuration*, Cambridge: Polity.

Giddens, A. (1999) *Runaway World – How Globalisation is Reshaping Our Lives*, London: Profile.

Gilroy, P. (1993) *The Black Atlantic*, London: Verso.

Girard, A. (1978) Cultural industries, in J. Ahearne (ed.), *French Cultural Policy Debates*, pp. 102–8.

Glancey, J. (2001) *London – Bread and Circuses*, London and New York: Verso.

Goldberger, P. (1998) The big top, *The New Yorker*, 27 April and 4 May, pp. 152–9.

Golding, P. (2000a) Forthcoming features – information and communications technologies and the sociology of the future, *Sociology*, 34.1, pp. 165–84.

Golding, P. (2000b) Assessing media content – why, how and what we learnt in a British media content study, in R. Pickard (ed.), *Measuring Media Content, Quality and Diversity – Approaches and Issues in Content Research*, Turku, Finland: Media Group, Turku School of Economics and Business Administration, pp. 9–24.

Goldman, R. and Papson, S. (1998) *Nike Culture*, London, Thousand Oaks and New Delhi: Sage.

Gorky, M., Radek, K., Bukharin, N. et al. (1977) *Soviet Writers' Congress 1934 – The Debate on Socialist Realism and Modernism*, London: Lawrence and Wishart.

Gorz, A. (1989 [1988]) *Critique of Economic Reason*, London and New York: Verso.

Gouldner, A. (1970) *The Coming Crisis of Western Sociology*, New York: Avon Books.

Graham, S. (1999) Towards urban cyberspace planning – grounding the global through urban telematics policy and planning, in J. Downey and J. McGuigan (eds), *Technocities*, London, Thousand Oaks and New Delhi: Sage, pp. 9–33.

Gramsci, A. (1971) *Selections from the Prison Notebooks*, edited and translated by Q. Hoare and G. Nowell Smith, London: Lawrence and Wishart.

Greenhalgh, P. (1988) *Ephemeral Vistas – The Expositions Universelles, Great Exhibitions and World's Fairs, 1851–1939*, Manchester: Manchester University Press; New York: St Martin's Press.

Grosshans, H. (1983) *Hitler and the Artists*, New York and London: Holmes and Meier.

Gumbel, A. (2001) Fashion victims – inside the sweatshops of Los Angeles, *The Independent*, 3 August, p. 13.

Habermas, J. (1972 [1968]) *Knowledge and Human Interests*, London: Heinemann.

Habermas, J. (1970) Toward a theory of communicative competence, in H. Dreitzel (ed.), *Recent Sociology no.2 – Patterns of Communicative Behaviour*, New York: Macmillan, pp. 115–48.

Habermas, J. (1979 [1976]) *Communication and the Evolution of Society*, London: Heinemann.

Habermas, J. (1987 [1981]) *The Theory of Communicative Action, Volume Two – The Critique of Functionalist Reason*, Cambridge: Polity.

Habermas, J. (1989 [1962]) *The Structural Transformation of the Public Sphere – An Inquiry into a Category of Bourgeois Society*, Cambridge: Polity.

Habermas, J. (1990 [1983]) *Moral Consciousness and Communicative Action*, Cambridge: Polity.

Habermas, J. (1992) Further reflections on the public sphere, in C. Calhoun (ed.), *Habermas and the Public Sphere*, Cambridge, MA and London: MIT Press, pp. 421–61.

Habermas, J. (1996 [1992]) *Between Facts and Norms – Contribution to a Discourse Theory of Law and Democracy*, Cambridge: Polity.

Hall, S. (1988) *The Hard Road to Renewal*, London: Verso.

Hall, S. (1997) The work of representation, in S. Hall (ed.), *Representation – Cultural Representations and Signifying Practices*, London, Thousand Oaks and New Delhi: Sage, pp. 13–74.

Hall, S. and du Gay, P. (eds) (1996) *Questions of Cultural Identity*, London, Thousand Oaks and New Delhi: Sage.

Haraszti, M. (1987) *The Velvet Prison – Artists Under State Socialism*, London: Penguin.

Harding, L. (1997) Laser lift-off for £750m Dome, *The Guardian*, 27 June, p. 3.

Harding, J. (2000) Blair's law of convergence, *Financial Times*, 17 October, p. 30.

Harvey, D. (1989) *The Condition of Postmodernity*, Oxford and Cambridge, MA: Basil Blackwell.

Harvey, P. (1996) *Hybrids of Modernity – Anthropology, the Nation-State and the Universal Exhibition*, London and New York: Routledge.

Hatton, R. and Walker, J. (2000) *Supercollector – A Critique of Charles Saatchi*, London: Ellipsis.

Held, D., McGrew, A., Goldblatt, D. and Perraton, J. (1999) *Global Transformations – Politics, Economics and Culture*, Cambridge: Polity.

Held, D. and McGrew, A. (eds) (2000) *The Global Transformations Reader*, Cambridge: Polity.

Herman, E. and McChesney, R. (1997) *The Global Media – The New Missionaries of Global Capitalism*, London: Cassell.

Herzstein, R. (1978) *The War That Hitler Won – The Most Infamous Propaganda Campaign in History*, New York: Putnam.

Heseltine, M. (2000) *Life in the Jungle – My Autobiography*, London: Hodder and Stoughton.

Hesmondhalgh, D. (2002) *The Cultural Industries*, London, Thousand Oaks and New Delhi: Sage.

Hewison, R. (2001) Cultural policy, in A. Sheldon (ed.), *The Blair Effect – The Blair Government 1997–2001*, London: Little, Brown, pp. 535–53.

Hochschild, A.R. (2003) *The Commercialization of Intimate Life – Notes from Home and Work*, Berkeley and Los Angeles: University of California Press.

Hoggart, R. (1957) *The Uses of Literacy*, London: Chatto and Windus.

Hoggart, R. (1992) *An Imagined Life – Life and Times Volume III, 1959–1991*, London: Chatto and Windus.

Hoggart, R. (1995) *The Way We Live Now*, London: Chatto and Windus.

Horkheimer, M. (1972) *Critical Theory – Selected Essays*, New York: Continuum.

Horne, D. (1995 [1986]) *The Public Culture – An Argument with the Future*, London: Pluto.

Irvine, A. (1999) *The Battle for the Dome*, London: Irvine News Agency.

Itzin, C. (1980) *Stages in the Revolution – Political Theatre in Britain Since 1968*, London: Methuen.

Jones, J. (1998) Passion and commitment – the difficulties faced by working mothers in the British television industry, in S. Ralph, J. Langham Brown and T. Lees (eds), *What Price Creativity?*, Luton: John Libbey, pp. 221–8.

Keane, J. (1998) *Civil Society – Old Images, New Visions*, Cambridge: Polity.

Kellner, D. (1995) Intellectuals and new technologies, *Media, Culture and Society*, 17.3, pp. 427–48.

Kellner, D. (1997) Critical theory and cultural studies – the missed articulation, in J. McGuigan (ed.), *Cultural Methodologies*, London, Thousand Oaks and New Delhi: Sage, pp. 12–41.

Kellner, D. (1999) New technologies – technocities and the prospects for democratization, in J. Downey and J. McGuigan (eds), *Technocities*, London, Thousand Oaks and New Delhi: Sage, pp. 186–204.

Kelly, O. (1984) *Community, Art and the State – Storming the Citadels*, London: Comedia.

Klau, T. (2002) What does France want?, *Prospect*, March, pp. 36–40.

Kleberg, C.-J. (1998) *Promoting Cultural Research for Human Development – Report from Three Seminars*, Stockholm: Bank of Sweden Tercentenary Foundation.

Kleberg, C.-J. (2000) The concept of culture in the Stockholm action plan and its consequences for policy making, *International Journal of Cultural Policy*, 7.1: 49–69.

Klein, N. (2000a) *No Logo – Taking Aim at the Brand Bullies*, London: HarperCollins.

Klein, N. (2000b) The tyranny of the brands, *New Statesman*, 24 January, pp. 25–8.

Klein, N. (2000c) Does protest need a vision?, *New Statesman*, 3 July, pp. 23–5.

Knutsson, K. (1998) *Culture and Human Development – Report of the Conference on Culture, Cultural Research and Cultural Policy held in Stockholm, August 1997*, Stockholm: Royal Academy of Letters, History and Antiquity.

Kuhn, T. (1970) Logic of discovery or psychology of research?, in I. Lakatos and A. Musgrave (eds), *Criticism and the Growth of Knowledge*, Cambridge and New York: Cambridge University Press, pp. 1–23.

Lainsbury, A. (2000) *Once Upon a Time an American Dream – The Story of Euro Disneyland*, Lawrence: University of Kansas Press.

Lang, J. (1983) Culture and the economy, in J. Ahearne (ed), *French Cultural Policy Debates*, London: Routledge, pp. 111–20.

Lasn, K. (1999) *Culture Jam: The Uncooling of America*, New York: Eagle Brook.

Lazarsfeld, P. (1941) Remarks on administrative and critical communication research, *Studies in Philosophy and Social Science* 9, pp. 2–16.

Leadbeater, C. and Oakley, K. (1999) *The Independents – Britain's New Cultural Entrepreneurs*, London: Demos.

Leavis, F.R. (1979 [1930]) *Mass Civilization and Minority Culture*, in F.R. Leavis, *Education and the University*, Cambridge: Cambridge University Press.

Leavis, F.R. and Thompson D. (1933) *Culture and Environment – The Training of Critical Awareness*, London: Chatto and Windus.

Leonard, M. (1997) *Britain TM – Renewing Our Identity*, London: Demos.

Lewis, B. (1999) *Looking for Mandy's Place – An Epic Millennium Poem*, Loughborough University School of Art and Design.

Lewis, J. and Miller, T. (eds) (2003) *Critical Cultural Policy Studies – A Reader*, Malden, MA and Oxford: Blackwell.

Lewis, P., Richardson V. and Woudhuysen J. (1998) *In Defence of the Dome*, London: Adam Smith Institute.

Lipset, S.M. and Marks, G. (2000) Social democracy lives on, *New Statesman*, 26 June, pp. 25–7.

Livingstone, S. and Lunt, P. (1991) *Talk on Television – Audience Participation and Public Debate*, London and New York: Routledge.

Looseley, D. (1995) *The Politics of Fun – Cultural Policy and Debate in Contemporary France*, Oxford and New York: Berg.

Looseley, D. (2000) Facing the music – French cultural policy from a British perspective, *International Journal of Cultural Policy* 7.1: 115–29.

Lovell, T. (1980) *Pictures of Reality – Aesthetics, Politics and Pleasure*, London: British Film Institute.

Lukes, S. (1974) *Power – A Radical View*, London: Macmillan.

Lyotard, J.-F. (1984 [1979]) *The Postmodern Condition – A Report on Knowledge*, Manchester: Manchester University Press.

Lyotard, J.-F. (1991 [1988]) *The Inhuman – Reflections on Time*, Cambridge: Polity Press.

Maguire, J. (1999) *Global Sport – Identities, Societies, Civilizations*, Cambridge: Polity.

Marshall, T.H. (1992 [1950]) *Citizenship and Social Class*, London: Pluto.

Martin, P. (2000) Dome and gloom, *Sunday Times Magazine*, 9 July, pp. 40–6.

Matarasso, F. (1997) *Use or Ornament? The Social Impact of Participation in the Arts*, Stroud: Comedia.

McCannell, D. (1989 [1975]) *The Tourist – A New Theory of the Leisure Class*, New York: Schocken Books.

McCannell, D. (1992) *Empty Meeting Grounds – The Tourist Papers*, London and New York: Routledge.

McCannell, D. (2001) Tourist agency, *Tourist Studies* 1.1: 23–37.

McChesney, R.W., Wood, E.M. and Foster, J.B. (eds) (1998) *Capitalism and the Information Age – The Political Economy of the Global Communication Revolution*, New York: Monthly Review.

McGrath, J. (1981) *A Good Night Out – Popular Theatre, Audience, Class and Form*, London: Methuen.

McGuigan, J. (1981) *Writers and the Arts Council*, London: Arts Council of Great Britain.

McGuigan, J. (1992) *Cultural Populism*, London and New York: Routledge.

McGuigan, J. (1993) Reaching for control – Raymond Williams on mass communication and popular culture, in W.J. Morgan and P. Preston (eds), *Raymond Williams – Politics, Education, Letters*, London: Macmillan, pp. 163–88.

McGuigan, J. (1995) 'A slow reach again for control' – Raymond Williams and the vicissitudes of cultural policy, *European Journal of Cultural Policy*, 2.1: 105–15. Reprinted in Wallace, J., Jones, R. and Nield, S. (eds) (1997) *Raymond Williams Now – Knowledge, Limits and the Future*, London: Macmillan, pp. 56–70.

McGuigan, J. (1996) *Culture and the Public Sphere*, London and New York: Routledge.

McGuigan, J. (1997a) Cultural populism revisited, in M. Ferguson and P. Golding (eds), *Cultural Studies in Question*, London, Thousand Oaks and New Delhi: Sage, pp. 138–54.

McGuigan, J. (1997b) Boiling the frog, *International Journal of Cultural Policy*, 4.2: 225–31.

McGuigan, J. (1998a) What price the public sphere?, in D.K. Thussu (ed.), *Electronic Empires – Global Media and Local Resistance*, London: Arnold, pp. 91–107.

McGuigan, J. (1998b) National government and the cultural public sphere, *Media International Australia incorporatiing Culture and Policy*, 81, May, pp. 68–83.

McGuigan, J. (1999) *Modernity and Postmodern Culture*, Buckingham and Philadelphia: Open University Press.

McGuigan, J. (2000) British identity and 'the people's princess', *The Sociological Review* 48.1, pp. 1–18.

McGuigan, J. (2002) The public sphere, in P. Hamilton and K. Thompson (eds), *The Uses of Sociology*, Oxford: Basil Blackwell, pp. 81–128.

McGuigan, J. (2003a) Cultural change, in J. Hollowell (ed.), *Britain Since 1945*, Oxford: Basil Blackwell, pp. 279–95.

McGuigan, J. (2003b) The social construction of a cultural disaster – new labour's millennium experience, *Cultural Studies*, 17.6, Winter.

McGuigan, J. (2004a) A shell for neo-liberalism – New Labour Britain and the millennium dome, in S. Burnett, S. Caunes, E. Mazierska and J. Walton (eds), *Relocating Britishness*, Manchester, Manchester University Press.

McGuigan, J. (2004b) A community of communities, in J. Littler and R. Nadoo (eds), *The Politics of Heritage*, London and New York: Routledge.

McGuigan. J. (2004c) The cultural public sphere, in A. Benchimol and W. Maley (eds), *Spheres of Influence – From Shakespeare to Habermas*, Frankfurt: Peter Lang.

McGuigan, J. and Gilmore, A. (2001), Figuring out the dome, *Cultural Trends*, 39, pp. 39–83.

McGuigan, J. and Gilmore, A. (2002), The millennium dome – sponsoring, meaning and visiting, *International Journal of Cultural Policy*, 8.1: 1–20.

McLachlan, S. and Golding, P. (2000) Tabloidization in the British press – a quantitative investigation into changes in British newspapers, 1952–1997, in C. Sparks and J. Tulloch (eds), *Tabloid Tales – Global Debates Over Media Standards*, Oxford: Roman and Littlefield, pp. 75–89.

McLaren, D. (1998) *Rethinking Tourism and Ecotravel – The Paving of Paradise and What You Can Do to Stop It*, West Hartford: Kumarian Press.

McLuhan, M. (1964) *Understanding Media*, London: Routledge and Kegan Paul.

McRobbie, A. (1998) *British Fashion Design – Rag Trade or Image Industry?*, London and New York: Routledge.

McRobbie, A. (1999) *In the Culture Society – Art, Fashion and Popular Music*, London and New York: Routledge.

Medved, M. (1992) *Hollywood vs. America – Popular Culture and the War on Traditional Values*, New York: HarperCollins.

Mercer, C. (2002) *Towards Cultural Citizenship – Tools for Cultural Policy and Development*, Stockholm: Bank of Sweden Tercentenary Foundation and Gidlungs Forlag.

Meredyth, D. and Minson, J. (eds) (2001) *Citizenship and Cultural Policy*, London, Thousand Oaks and New Delhi: Sage.

Merli, P. (2002) Evaluating the social impact of participation in arts activities, *International Journal of Cultural Policy* 8.1, May: 107–18.

Miege, B. (1989) *The Capitalization of Cultural Production*, New York: International General.

Miller, D. and Philo G. (1996) Against orthodoxy – the media do influence us, *Sight and Sound*, December: 18–20.

Miller, T., Govil, N., McMurria, J. and Maxwell, R. (2001) *Global Hollywood*, London: British Film Institute.

Miller, T. and Yudice, G. (2002) *Cultural Policy*, London, Thousand Oaks and New Delhi: Sage.

Morley, D. and Worpole, K. (eds) (1982) *The Republic of Letters – Working Class Writing and Local Publishing*, London: Comedia.

Morrison, B. (2000) That was the dome that was, *The Independent on Sunday, Sunday Review*, 3 December, pp. 14–16.

Mosley, I. (ed.) (2000) *Dumbing Down – Culture, Politics and the Mass Media*, Thorverton: Academic Imprint.

Mulgan, G. and Worpole, K. (1986) *Saturday Night or Sunday Morning? – From Arts to Industry, New Forms of Cultural Policy*, London: Comedia.

Mulgan, G. and Perri 6 (1996) The new enterprise culture, *Demos Quarterly*, 8: 2–4.

Mulhern, F. (2000) *Culture/Metaculture*, London and New York: Routledge.

Myerscough, J. (1988) *The Economic Importance of the Arts in Britain*, London: Policy Studies Institute.

Myerscough, J. (1994) *Cultural Policy in the Netherlands – Report of a European Group of Experts*, Strasbourg: Council of Europe.

Nederveen Pieterse, J. (2001) *Development Theory – Deconstructions/Reconstructions*, London, Thousand Oaks and New Delhi: Sage.

Negroponte, N. (1995) *Being Digital*, London: Hodder and Stoughton.

New Statesman (2000), special supplement, Generation e – the internet and what it means to you, 10 July.

Nicholson-Lord, D. (2002) Against the Western invaders, *New Statesman*, 9 December, pp. 22, 24.

Nicolson, A. (1999) *Regeneration – The Story of the Millennium Dome*, London: HarperCollins.

NMEC (2000) *Millennium Experience – The Guide*, London: New Millennium Experience Company.

O'Reagan, T. (1992) (Mis)taking policy – notes on the cultural policy debate, *Cultural Studies* 6.3, October, pp. 409–23.

O'Reagan, T. (2002) Too much culture, too little culture – trends and issues for cultural policy-making, *Media International Australia, incorporating Culture and Policy* 102, February, pp. 9–24.

Osborne, D. and Gaebler, T. (1992) *Reinventing Government – How the Entrepreneurial Spirit is Transforming the Public Sector*, Reading, MA: Addison-Wesley.

Page, T. (2000) The millennium dome, *RSA Journal* 3–4: 1–8.

Palast, G. (2001) Ask no questions . . ., *The Observer, Business*, 25 March, p. 6.

Paine, T. (1985 [1791, 1792]) *Rights of Man*, London: Penguin.

Painter, C. (1994) Public service reform – reinventing or abandoning government?, *The Political Quarterly*, 26.3: 242–62.

Paretsky, S. (2003) The new censorship, *New Statesman*, 2 June, pp. 18–20.

Parton, J. (1999) My doomsday at the dome, *The Mail on Sunday Review*, 5 September, pp. 58–9.

Patriat, C. (1998) *La Culture, Un Besoin d'Etat*, Paris: Hachette.

Pearson, G. (1983) *Hooligan – A History of Respectable Fears*, London: Macmillan.

Pecheux, M. (1982) *Language, Semantics and Ideology*, London: Macmillan.

Perez de Cueller (1996 [1995]) President's forward, World Commission on Culture and Development, *Our Creative Diversity*, Paris: UNESCO, pp. 7–13.

Perri 6 (1995) Governing by cultures, *Demos Quarterly*, 7: 2–8.

Perin, C. (1992) The communicative circle – museums as communities, in I. Karp, C. M. Kreamer & S. D. Lavine, eds., Museums and Communities – The Politics of Public Culture, Washington: Smithsonian Institution

Petley, J. (2003) Consumers or citizens? Re-regulating communications, *Radical Philosophy* 120, July–August: 7–10.

Petropoulis, J. (2000) *The Faustian Bargain – The Art World in Nazi Germany*, London: Allen Lane, Penguin Press.

Philo, G. and Miller, D. (eds) (2001) *Marketing Killing – What the Free Market Does and What Social Scientists Can Do About It*, Harlow: Pearson.

Potter, D. (1986) *The Singing Detective*, London: Faber and Faber.

Potter, D. (1994) *Seeing the Blossom*, London: Faber and Faber.

Prelinger, R. (2002) Yes, information wants to be free, but how's that going to happen? Strategies for freeing intellectual property, in J. Schalit (ed.), *The Anti-Capitalism Reader – Imagining a Geography of Opposition*, New York: Akashic Books, pp. 263–78.

Quart, A. (2003) *Branded – The Buying and Selling of Teenagers*, London: Arrow.

Rees-Mogg, W. (1985) *The Political Economy of Art*, London: ACGB.

Renard, J. (1987) A cultural elan, in J. Ahearne (ed.), *French Cultural Policy Debates*, London: Routledge, pp. 127–34.

Renard, J. (1994) *Cultural Policy in Finland – Report of a European Group of Experts*, Strasbourg: Council of Europe.

Rheingold, H. (1995) *The Virtual Community – Surfing the Net*, London: Minerva.

Richards, I.A. (1965 [1936]) *The Philosophy of Rhetoric*, New York: Oxford University Press.

Richards, S. (1997) Interview: Peter Mandelson – I used to be a sceptic, but now I'm a true believer, says Millennium dollar man. The alternative would be spam, spam and more spam, *New Statesman*, 4 July, pp. 16–17.

Richards, T. (1991) *The Commodity Culture of Victorian England – Advertising and Spectacle, 1851–1914*, London and New York: Verso.

Ridderstrale, J. and Nordstrom, K. (2000) *Funky Business – Talent Makes Capital Dance*, Harlow: Pearson.

Rifkin, J. (2000) *The Age of Access – How the Shift from Ownership to Access is Transforming Capitalism*, London: Penguin.

Rifkin, J. (2001a) The age of access – the new politics of culture vs. commerce, *Renewal* 9.2/3, Winter, pp. 33–48.

Rifkin, J. (2001b) Worlds apart, *The Guardian*, 3 July, p. 15.

Rifkind, C. (1997) America's fantasy urbanism – the waxing of the mall and the waning of civility, in K. Washburn and J. Thornton (eds), *Dumbing Down – Essays on the Strip-Mining of American Culture*, New York: Norton, pp. 261–9.

Ritzer, G. (1998) *The McDonaldization Thesis*, London, Thousand Oaks and New Delhi: Sage.

Robertson, R. (1992) *Globalization – Social Theory and Global Culture*, London, Thousand Oaks and New Delhi: Sage.

Rocco, F. (1995) The great millennium lottery, *The Independent on Sunday, Sunday Review*, pp. 8–12.

Roche, M. (2000) *Mega-Events and Modernity – Olympics and Expos in the Growth of Global Culture*, London and New York: Routledge.

Rodgers, P. (1989) *The Work of Art*, London: Policy Studies Institute.

Rose, H. and Rose, S. (eds) (2000), *Alas, Poor Darwin – Arguments Against Evolutionary Psychology*, London: Jonathan Cape.

Roy, A. (2002 [2001]) *The Algebra of Infinite Justice*, London: Flamingo.

Runnymede Trust (2000) *The Future of Multi-Ethnic Britain*, London: Profile Books.

Ryan, M. (2000) Turning on the audience, in I. Mosley (ed.), *Dumbing Down – Culture, Politics and the Mass Media*, Thorverton: Academic Imprint, pp. 159–65.

Sassoon, D. (1997 [1996]) *One Hundred Years of Socialism – The West European Left in the Twentieth Century*, London: Fontana.

Saunders, F.S. (1999) *Who Paid the Piper? The CIA and the Cultural Cold War*, London: Granta Books.

Schech, S. and Haggis, J. (2000) *Culture and Development – A Critical Introduction*, Oxford and Malden, MA: Basil Blackwell.

Schech, S. and Haggis, J. (eds) (2002) *Development – A Cultural Studies Reader*, Oxford and Malden, MA: Basil Blackwell.

Schiller, H. (1989) *Culture Inc. – The Corporate Takeover of Public Expression*, New York: Oxford University Press.

Schwengell, H. (1991) British enterprise culture and German *Kulturgesellschaft*, in R. Keat and N. Abecrombie (eds), *Enterprise Culture*, London and New York: Routledge, pp. 136–50.

Scruton, R. (1998) *An Intelligent Person's Guide to Modern Culture*, London: Duckworth.

Seabrook, J. (1990) *The Myth of the Market – Promises and Illusions*, Bideford: Green Books.

Seltzer, K. and Bentley, T. (1999) *The Creative Age – Knowledge and Skills for the New Economy*, London: Demos.

Selwood, S. (2001) *The UK Cultural Sector – Profile and Policy Issues*, London: Policy Studies Institute.

Sewall, G. (1997) The postmodern schoolhouse, in K. Washburn and J. Thornton (eds), *Dumbing Down – The Strip-Mining of American Culture*, New York: Norton, pp. 57–67.

Shaw, R. (ed.) (1993) *The Spread of Sponsorship – In the Arts, Sport, Education, the Health Service and Broadcasting*, Newcastle: Bloodaxe Books.

Shklovsky, V. (1974) *Mayakovsky and His Circle*, London: Pluto.

Shils, E. and Young, M. (1953) The meaning of the coronation, *The Sociological Review* 1.2, pp. 63–81.

Sim, S. (2001) *Lyotard and the Inhuman*, Cambridge: Icon Books.

Simon, J. (1997) Introduction, in K. Washburn, and J. Thornton (eds), *Dumbing Down – The Strip-Mining of American Culture*, New York: Norton, pp. 43–54.

Sinclair, S. (1999) *Sorry Meniscus – Excursions to the Millennium Dome*, London: Profile Books.

Sklair, L. (2001) *The Transnational Capitalist Class*, Oxford and Malden, MA: Blackwell.

Sklair, L. (2002) *Globalization – Capitalism and its Alternatives*, Oxford and Malden, MA: Blackwell.

Slevin, J. (2000) *The Internet and Society*, Cambridge: Polity.

Smith, C. (1998) *Creative Britain*, London: Faber and Faber.

Stallabrass, J. (1999) *High Art Lite – British Art in the 1990s*, London and New York: Verso.

St Clair, J. (1999) Seattle diary – it's a gas, gas, gas, *New Left Review*, 238: 81–96.

Steinert, H. (2003 [1998]) *Culture Industry*, Cambridge: Polity.

Sterne, J. (2002) Cultural policy studies and the problem of representation, *The Communication Review* 5.1: 59–89.

Stevenson, N. (ed.) (2001) *Culture and Citizenship*, London, Thousand Oaks and New Delhi: Sage.

Stiglitz, J. (2002) *Globalization and its Discontents*, London: Allen Lane, Penguin Books.

Tallis, R. (1997) *The Enemies of Hope – A Critique of Contemporary Pessimism*, New York: St Martin's Press.

Tawney, R.H. (1931) *Equality*, London: Unwin Books.

Thompson, J.B. (1990) *Ideology and Modern Culture – Critical Social Theory in the Era of Mass Communication*, Cambridge: Polity Press.

Thompson, K. (1997) Regulation, de-regulation and re-regulation, in K. Thompson (ed.), *Media and Cultural Regulation*, London, Thousand Oaks and New Delhi: Sage, pp. 1–68.

Throsby, D. (2001) *Economics and Culture*, Cambridge: Cambridge University Press.

Tudor, A. (1999) *Decoding Culture – Theory and Method in Cultural Studies*, London, Thousand Oaks and New Delhi: Sage.

Tusa, J. (1999) *Art Matters – Reflecting on Culture*, London: Methuen.

Urry, J. (2002 [1990]) *The Tourist Gaze*, London, Thousand Oaks and New Delhi: Sage.

Urry, J. (2001) Transports of delight, *Leisure Studies* 20: 237–45.

Vestheim, G. (1994) Instrumental cultural policy in Scandinavian countries – a critical historical perspective, *European Journal of Cultural Policy* 1.1: 57–71.

Vidal, J. (1997) *McLibel – Burger Culture on Trial*, London: Macmillan.

Volkerling, M. (2000) From cool Britannia to hot nation – creative industries policies in Europe, Canada and New Zealand, *International Journal of Cultural Policy* 7.3: 437–55.

Voltaire (1947 [1758]) *Candide*, London: Penguin.

Wachtel, D. (1987) *Cultural Policy and Socialist France*, New York and London: Greenwood.

Walden, G. (2000) *The New Elites – Making a Career in the Masses*, London: Allen Lane.

Wallinger, M. and Warnock, M. (2000) *Art for All? Their Policies and Our Culture*, London: Peer.

Washburn, K. and Thornton, J. (1997) (eds), *Dumbing Down – Essays on the Strip-Mining of American Culture*, New York: Thornton.

Webster, F. (1999) Information and communications technologies – Luddism revisited, in J. Downey and J. McGuigan (eds), *Technocities*, London, Thousand Oaks and New Delhi: Sage, pp. 60–89.

Wernick, A. (1991) *Promotional Culture*, London, Newbury Park and New Delhi: Sage.

Wheen, F. (1999) *Karl Marx*, London: Fourth Estate.

White, A. (1990) *De-Stalinization and the House of Culture – Declining State Control Over Leisure in the USSR; Poland and Hungary 1953–89*, London: Routledge.

Wilhide, E. (1999) *The Millennium Dome*, London: HarperCollins.

Williams, R. (1971 [1958]) *Culture and Society*, London: Penguin.

Williams, R. (1961) *The Long Revolution*, London: Chatto and Windus.

Williams, R. (1974) *Television – Technology and Cultural Form*, London: Fontana.

Williams, R. (1979) The Arts Council, *Political Quarterly*, 50.2: 157–71.

Williams, R. (1981a) *Culture*, London: Fontana.

Williams, R. (1981b) Marxism, structuralism and literary analysis, *New Left Review*, 129: 51–66. Reprinted as Crisis in English Studies in Williams's (1984) *Writing in Society*, London: Verso, pp. 192–211.

Williams, R. (1984) State culture and beyond, in L. Apignanesi (ed.), *Culture and the State*, London: Institute of Contemporary Arts, pp. 3–5.

Williams, R. (1985 [1983]) *Towards 2000*, London: Penguin.

Wilson, E. (2001) *The Contradictions of Culture – Cities, Culture, Women*, London, Thousand Oaks and New Delhi: Sage.

Winston, B. (1995 [1990]) How are media born and developed?, in J. Downing, A. Mohammadi and A. Sreberny-Mohammadi (eds), *Questioning the Media*, 2nd edn, London, Thousand Oaks and New Delhi: Sage, pp. 54–74.

Winston, B. (1996) *Technologies of Seeing – Photography, Cinema and Television*, London: British Film Institute.

World Commission on Culture and Development (1996 [1995]) *Our Creative Diversity*, Paris: UNESCO.

Wright, S. (1998) Encaging the wind, *International Journal of Cultural Policy* 5.1: 173–82.

Wu, C-t. (1998) Embracing the enterprise culture – art institutions since the 1980s, *New Left Review*, 230, July/August, pp. 28–57.

Wu, C-t. (2002) *Privatising Culture – Corporate Art Intervention Since the 1980s*, London and New York: Verso.

Young, R. (ed.) (1981) *Untying the Text*, London: Routledge.

Yuval Davis, N. (1999) What is 'transversal politics'?, *Soundings* 12, Summer: 94–9.

INDEX

g indicates a glossary definition

CRITICAL READINGS: MEDIA AND GENDER

Cynthia Carter and Linda Steiner (Eds)

- How is gender constructed in the media?
- To what extent do media portrayals of gender influence our everyday perceptions of ourselves and our actions?
- In what ways do the media reinforce and sometimes challenge gender inequalities?

The Media and Gender Reader provides a lively and engaging introduction to the field of critical media and gender research, drawing from a wide menu of exciting and important international scholarship in the field. Featured here is the work of authors studying a wide array of entertainment, news, grassroots and new media texts, institutions and audiences from a diverse range of conceptual and methodological approaches. The topics featured include, among others, gender identity and television talk shows, the commercialization of masculinity, historical portrayals of women in advertising, representing lesbians on television, the cult of femininity in women's magazines, gender and media violence, the sexualization of the popular press, racist sexual stereotyping in Hollywood cinema, women in popular music, media production and the empowerment of women, soap opera audiences, girl gamers, the impact of media monitoring, pornography and masculine power, and women's historical relationship to the Internet. It will have international appeal to readers in the Humanities and Social Sciences, especially in Mass Communication, Communication Studies, Media Studies, Cultural Studies, Women's Studies, Gender Studies, Journalism Studies and Sociology.

Contents

Series editor's foreword – Acknowledgements – The contested terrain of media and gender: editors' introduction – Part one: Gendered texts in context – Readings 1–5 – Part two: (Re)Producing gender – Readings 6–10 – Part three: Gendered audiences and identities – Readings 11–15 – Index.

288pp   0 335 21097 X (Paperback)

CRITICAL READINGS: SPORT, CULTURE AND THE MEDIA

David Rowe (Ed)

This is a carefully selected anthology of important and contemporary work dedicated to understanding the relationships between sport, culture and the media. It is both a stand-alone work and a useful accompaniment to the editor's highly praised book *Sport, Culture and the Media: The Unruly Trinity*.

The book covers both how media sport is produced and the ways in which it can be interpreted. It is divided into two related sections:

'Media Sport Construction: History, Labour, Culture and Economics' addresses such important topics as globalization, media convergence, the corporate contest for broadcast rights, the making of sports pages and broadcasts, and the staging of mega-media sports events like the Olympic Games.

'Media Sport Deconstruction: Readings, Forms, Ideologies and Futures' is concerned with issues including nationalism, gender, sexuality, ethnicity and race in sports television, the press, fiction and new media.

Readers will, therefore, gain a comprehensive grasp of the cultural significance of media sport.

Contents

c374pp   0 335 21150 X (Paperback)   0 335 21151 8 (Hardback)

CRITICAL READINGS: MEDIA AND AUDIENCES

Virginia Nightingale and Karen Ross (eds)

- How have media researchers changed the ways in which the audience is perceived over time?
- How have audiences become fragmented in the search for ratings?
- What next for audience research in the 21st century?

The study of 'audience' is a central concept in both media and cultural studies. Although it has become an academic fashion to turn away from imagining that groups of people can share common purpose or interests, there are still reasons enough for wanting to explore the way in which audiences behave, understand and interact with media texts in all their various forms, not least because of the vast sums of money which are persistently expended by advertisers and broadcasters trying to give 'the audience' what 'it' wants and therefore maintaining or preferably increasing market share.

This collection of readings brings together some of the important developments in the history of audience and media studies and the significant research trajectories which have shaped the field until now. It is sometimes difficult to locate specific examples of audience research or discussions of research practice, as opposed to description, conjecture or critical reflection about audiences, which are in abundant supply: the Reader allows students and lecturers to source original research commentaries and better understand the rationale, findings and forms of analysis undertaken at different points in the field's research-based career.

Contents

Series editor's foreword – Introduction – The passive-active continuum: competing theories of agency and affect – The segmented audience: niche consumers and the ratings agenda – Interactive audiences: fans, cultural production and new media – Glossary – Index.

288pp   0 335 21150 X (Paperback)   0 335 21151 8 (Hardback)